Britten,
Voice & Piano
Lectures on the Vocal Music of Benjamin Britten

Preface

In publishing this very individual series of lectures by a renowned performer, writer, scholar and teacher under the series title of Research Studies we are aware that we could be raising expectations in our readers of a rather different collection of writings. What Graham Johnson has given us in these lectures, which accompanied a series of eight concerts, is a highly personal and perceptive commentary on works that he has had the privilege of experiencing not only with Britten and Pears but through many performances in which he was sitting where Britten would have sat, at the piano. In a collection of lectures as opposed to a book, there is an enhanced opportunity for the reader to experience more closely the 'voice' of the writer and to connect even more strongly with the spirit of his time. The author is Senior Professor of Accompaniment at the Guildhall School of Music & Drama, and he devised and presented this series of concerts to celebrate Britten's life and music and to give the accompanists in his charge the opportunity to study the music of this consummate composer, pianist and accompanist.

Britten himself wrote next to nothing about his own music, neither did Pears, so to have a performer's insight into the music, its context and meaning, by one who was a close friend and colleague of both men is extraordinarily valuable. Graham Johnson has his own vision of this music as a performer, which stems from his personal link with the composer. He writes not only as a scholar and an artist, but also as a member of the gay community, and is able to speak for the composer and to convey information and attitudes about the genesis and performance of Britten's music as a privileged friend.

When the series of concerts *Let the Florid Music Praise* was first planned, there was no intention of making this the basis for a publication. I asked

Britten,
Voice & Piano
Lectures on the Vocal Music
of Benjamin Britten

by

Graham Johnson

ASHGATE   GUILDHALL
School of Music & Drama

Co-published in 2003 by:
The Guildhall School of Music & Drama
Barbican
Silk Street
LONDON
EC2Y 8DT
Tel: 0044 (0)20 7628 2571
Fax: 0044 (0)20 7382 7212
www.gsmd.ac.uk
and
Ashgate Publishing Limited
Gower House
Croft Road
Aldershot
Hampshire
GU11 3HR
England
Tel: 0044 (0)1252 331551
Fax: 0044 (0)1252 344405
www.ashgate.com

Ashgate Publishing Company
Suite 420
101 Cherry Street
Burlington, VT 05401-4405 USA

British Library Cataloguing in Publication data
Johnson, Graham 1950-
Britten, voice and piano: lectures on the vocal music of Benjamin Britten – (Guildhall research studies)

        1. Britten, Benjamin, 1913-1976 – Criticism and interpretation
        I. Title II. Odam, George III. Guildhall School of Music & Drama
        780.9'2
ISBN: 0 7546 3872 3

Library of Congress Control Number: 2003104862

We gratefully acknowledge the support of the Britten Estate Limited.

Printed and bound in Great Britain by Antony Rowe Ltd, Chippenham, Wiltshire permission to record whatever he said during the concerts and had intended to publish transcripts in a slim volume in celebration of the event. However, when Graham Johnson received the transcripts of the pre-performance talks, he immediately added to them and worked them up into the format you see here.

The festival spanned the whole of Britten's chamber vocal output but not the major works with orchestra such as *Serenade* and *Les Illuminations*. It was not a comprehensive survey of every vocal piece; instead, each programme was based around a theme. Significant pieces such as *Songs from the Chinese* and *A Charm of Lullabies* are absent. The complete catalogue of Britten's published music is issued by the Britten–Pears Library, compiled and edited by Paul Banks (1999). The programmes also covered a selection of other relevant chamber works, chosen to illuminate or reinforce thematic strands in the lectures. Like the text, the CD selection from the Festival includes some of these other works. We hope that the inclusion of some of them on the accompanying CDs will be equally illuminating and that they will lead readers towards further exploration and performance of this exceptional repertoire, nearly all of which is available in a selection of commercial recordings.

Part of our work in the Research Centre at the Guildhall School of Music & Drama is to capture and make concrete a few of the many high-quality lessons, workshops, lectures, festivals and masterclasses that take place here every day of the academic year. Research Studies 1 was a volume of lectures and papers on the work of Schnittke given at the Guildhall and the Barbican in 2000, also as part of a festival. We consider it important, where we can, to capture and preserve some of this unique information that otherwise would disappear into memory.

George Odam
Editor & Research Fellow, Guildhall School of Music & Drama

Acknowledgements

This book would not have been possible without Graham Johnson's encouragement, assistance and generosity throughout the project. Neither would it have been possible to reproduce these lectures in book and CD form without the invaluable musical and literary skills and administrative expertise of Pamela Lidiard of the Guildhall School of Music & Drama and the technical skills of David Foister. We are most grateful for the help given us by Judith LeGrove for checking the text and Dr Nicholas Clark for access to and use of the photographic archives at the Britten–Pears Library, Aldeburgh. We are in the debt of all members of staff and students of the Guildhall School who willingly gave their permission for recordings of their live performances to be reproduced on the CDs. Also to those members of staff who have worked on the editorial team and advised on contractual matters, many thanks.

Sources

The quotations from the diaries, letters and writings of Benjamin Britten are © copyright the Trustees of the Britten–Pears Foundation and may not be further reproduced without the written permission of the Trustees.

The quotations from the letters and writings of Peter Pears are © copyright the Executors of the late Sir Peter Pears and may not be further reproduced without written permission.

Music:

Boosey and Hawkes: [*Michelangelo Sonnet* musical example]
Faber and Faber: [*Death in Venice* musical example]

Poetry:

The excerpt from 'Song: Lift-Boy' by Robert Graves is from *Selected Poems*, ed. Paul O'Prey (Penguin, 1986), and is reproduced with permission from Carcanet Press Limited.

The excerpt from 'Still Falls the Rain' by Edith Sitwell is from *Collected Poems* (Sinclair-Stevenson, 1986), and is reproduced with permission from David Higham Associates.

De la Mare, 'Silver', 'A Song of Enchantment' and 'Tit for Tat' are reproduced thanks to the Literary Trustees of Walter de la Mare and the Society of Authors as their representative.

A.E. Housman, excerpt from *A Shropshire Lad* is reproduced thanks to the Society of Authors as the Literary Representative of the Estate of A.E. Housman.

Edited by George Odam

Editorial Team GSMD Research Centre
Pamela Lidiard
George Odam
Peter Shellard
Adrian Yardley

Copy-editor: Sara Peacock
Index made by Judith Wardman
Designed and typeset by John Peacock

List of illustrations

Introduction

This book has grown out of the Britten festival at the Guildhall School of Music & Drama in London – a sequence of eight concerts given in November 2001 under the overall title *Let the Florid Music Praise.* Each of these essays reflects the shape of a concert programme, and each of them is an expansion of a shorter commentary spoken from the platform during a live performance where programme length was a primary consideration. The aim of this monograph is to discuss the music in greater detail than was possible during those concerts, at the same time as preserving a record of what was actually performed during the festival by a wide range of Guildhall students and staff.

The series began on 22 November, which would have been the composer's 88th birthday; 4 December 2001 marked the twenty-fifth anniversary of his death at the age of 63. This was indeed an appropriate time for a survey. It is a cheering fact that those of us who knew Britten and loved his work in his lifetime have not seen his reputation go into the steep decline that was confidently predicted for it in the 1970s; there were a number of commentators who were convinced that the audiences of the new century would be too busy whistling Boulez and humming Stockhausen to remember a note of Britten.

This has not proved to be the case. Indeed, doors have continued to open for Britten's music when it is the received wisdom that they almost always slam shut after a composer's death: it was only fairly recently that the *Wiener Staatsoper* capitulated to *Peter Grimes.* More than fifty years after that work's première the Viennese public was enraptured with this music, the 'discovery' of which

Opposite: Britten on the beach at Aldeburgh, 1959

Graham Johnson

seemed to them a triumph of their own adventurous perspicacity. The composer had believed that, come what may, this house would never stage his operas. In Britten's student years the director of the Royal College of Music had vetoed a plan for the young composer to study with Alban Berg, and since then Vienna had been a city where he had registered more as a song accompanist than as an opera composer. He never lived to see these barriers fall, but tumbled they now have, and this is as good an indication as any that his posthumous reputation is in good shape.

Home-grown Britten enthusiasts of my generation were often scorned by their *avant garde* contemporaries for their admiration for this music which was so accessible that it *had* to be worthless; but when compared with the new and sometimes extravagant romanticism of many of today's young composers Britten's music can seem ascetic and reserved. Far from being yesterday's dated sentimentalist he remains a classic with a lean and economical style that has held the stage and stood the test of time: there is never a note too many, and each note is the result of almost Mozartian calculation. This ultra-professional probity is a sign of the craftsman, but Britten is much more than that of course, he is a magician: Auden described St Cecilia's ability to 'startle composing mortals with immortal fire' and times without number Britten's music is illuminated with the flames of his prodigiously inspired creativity. When St Cecilia is as radiant as this she induces in us, from time to time, that inner frisson which is reserved for the recognition of great art.

This is especially apparent in Britten's setting of poetry. This he does with an *aptness* (a small word for a vast musical challenge) that seems almost eerily prescient. When we have heard how Britten responds to a text the dormant composer in each of us imagines that we too would have set these words in the same way. But we are wrong of course. The idea of weaving Wilfred Owen's English poems in and out of the Latin Mass (as in the *War Requiem*) seems obvious now, as does Schubert's fancy that he should use Wilhelm Müller's bleak *Winterreise* poems for an extended cycle. No one else had imagined doing these things but, once thought of, the ideas seem always to have been 'in the air'. And this is before a note of music has been written! The planning and the composing are part of the same impulse: a directness and simplicity that goes to the heart of the matter, regardless of how sophisticated the resources used to make that journey. This has led to Britten's music being dismissed as 'musical journalism', the sort of underestimation from which Schubert suffered in his time. The two composers share what has been allowed to only a handful of musical creators: the unfailing ability vividly to translate words into musical terms that seem inevitable.

This aspect of their genius goes beyond mere illustration, it invades the poetry from within and cleaves to it until it is impossible to separate word and tone into their constituent parts. It is exciting enough when we are aware of this happening in the German lied, but when it comes to the setting of one's own language the reaction to such alchemy is even more immediate. Putting Purcell to one side, the worthiness and the undeniable and various beauties of English song are seldom a match for Britten's ability to become the poet's alter ego, each musical gesture a match for verbal imagery that encourages us to experience the poem afresh, as if for the first time. It is this which makes him Purcell's successor, and the composer whose destiny it was to take British music 'back into Europe' after a long and insular exile.

It is because of Britten's links with literature and with the human voice that the Guildhall festival was centred on the vocal department and the accompaniment course. After discussions with Damian Cranmer I devised the programmes in broad outline; Pamela Lidiard and Robin Bowman completed the complicated task of 'casting' that had begun with auditions. Every one of the school's student accompanists was involved, as well as a cross-section of singers from the BMus, Postgraduate Diploma in Vocal Training and Opera courses. Six members of staff (Adrian Thompson, Ronan O'Hora, Eugene Asti, Pamela Lidiard, Timothy Boulton and myself) also took part. It is important that a festival such as this should also include a certain amount of instrumental music, and our thanks go to Ronan O'Hora, David Takeno, Peter Gane, Manon Morris and Robert Brightmore for arranging the inclusion of pianists, cellists, a horn player, two harpists and a guitarist in the line-up. Two former students, counter-tenor David Clegg and pianist Catherine Milledge, completed the cast list. A representative sample of performances from the festival is given in the accompanying compact discs.

With a composer as prolific as Britten eight concerts were far too few to promise a complete survey of any kind. I hope that this selective homage offers readers the chance to consider music that is both well-known and 'Rich and rare' (the title of one of the composer's Irish folksong settings; incidentally, this is one area – the folksongs – where there is an almost complete coverage of the output). The progress of the series was not chronological, although the first lecture *The Young Britten* begins with the earliest songs and encompasses the composer's literary preoccupations before his engagement with the poetry of W.H. Auden. In *Britten Abroad: Italy, Poland, France and Germany* we concentrate on Britten the European stylist – pastiche is an inadequate word for this type of musical role-play, both vocal and instrumental.

At the heart of the festival there was a folksong marathon of a kind. Apart from the chance to hear these wonderful arrangements more or less in their entirety, these concerts were planned as a showcase of Guildhall vocal talent, a mixture of advanced and younger students. It is a notable part of a festival such as this in an international school that Britten's songs in his native language were sung (and played!) by a number of artists who are not English. How Britten would have approved of this! In teaching throughout the world I have found the appetite for singing this music knows no national boundaries.

Stylisation of a different kind – the time-honoured musical art of time-travel – is dealt with in *Britten the Elizabethan, Britten the Baroque*. Here was a chance to hear the great Donne settings that Britten wrote after a shocking visit to Belsen in 1945. *Beginnings (Auden) and ends (Eliot)* examines the literary influences at the poles of Britten's life: the early cycles and Auden settings (including cabaret songs) alternating with the two canticles to poems of T.S. Eliot written towards the end of the composer's life.

The penultimate lecture is *Britten and Russia*, which is almost inevitably centred on two great Russian artists who did much to inspire the music of Britten in the 1960s and 1970s – the cellist Mstislav Rostropovich and his wife, the soprano Galina Vishnevskaya. The closing lecture brings the composer home to where he finally belongs; despite everything that made him a more cosmopolitan figure than his predecessors he was through and through an English composer. This programme marks Britten's often ambivalent attitude to the City of London, the 'Great Wen', scene of William Blake's nineteenth-century poetry, as well as Edith Sitwell's from the Second World War. The festival ended with two of the composer's masterpieces: the great Hardy cycle *Winter Words* (in his songs Britten never gave the musical immortality to Suffolk that he here lavishes on Hardy's Wessex) and then *Canticle II*, which is Britten's inspired setting of the Chester miracle play.

I have spent my entire career in the study of Schubert, and Britten is the one English composer whom I would place at Schubert's side – because Britten was not only an accompanist *sans pareil*, but a setter of words where the entire musical character of the piece in hand springs from the poem. The two composers also shared a phenomenal fecundity that has led to waves of posthumous publication. The fact that there were still new Schubert songs appearing in print nearly seventy years after his death drew amused comment; the appearance of new Britten works from the attic of his youth shows little sign of abating. Both composers seem to have been in touch with a magic source of music from which they drank as easily as others painfully thirsted in search of the oasis of inspiration. Both composers silently stored their efforts without comment, knowing that their gift would always provide them with newer and better ideas.

Such a gift comes with its costs. 'Whom the Gods love dies young' said Menander, and by the standards of his time Britten died far too young. There have been attempts to stir up biographical scandals after his death but there is not much mileage in these. In any case, anything we ever wanted to know about this composer is already in his music. (Without labouring the point, I believe this is also true of Schubert.) Britten writes *himself* into the music, and he never writes about what he does not know at first hand. There was a risk in this, but it also ensures truthfulness, and that seems to me to be a primary requirement for the making of great art. Considering his sometimes isolated status as a homosexual pacifist who chose to return from America to England in the middle of the war in the company of the great singer who was to be his lifelong companion, there is an almost incredible openness and honesty about the man and his dealings with the world. Some go to their psychiatrists to talk through their preoccupations and problems; Britten seems to work them out in his music for all to hear.

Britten and Pears at Dartington Summer School, 1959

This surrendering of himself to the public gaze (as well as the snide ridicule that in the 1950s and 1960s was a constant consequence of his self-outing through music) was always counterpointed by the utmost need for privacy and a reticence. This led some people to underestimate, to their cost, the enormous will-power which animated that slender, deferential-seeming figure. A list of his operas, and how he saw them through to performance year after year, will show that this was a man who got things done. But who can doubt his energy and determination when one hears even the opening notes (the first bars of the *Michelangelo Sonnets*, of *On This Island*, of *Winter Words*) of so much his music? In almost any of his mature works both listener and performer feel themselves in the presence of a master. In those four days we at the Guildhall did our best to honour a composer who some of our younger artists had come to love only in working on this music in the course of the previous few months. But love him they now do, and it was wonderful to see the birth of the astonishment, followed by reverence, which is the familiar sign of this composer casting his spell. In the midst of such a multi-cultural school as the Guildhall where the Norwegian students are rightly proud of their Grieg, and the Australians of their Percy Grainger, those who are English should permit themselves a moment of pride in a fellow countryman, even if Britten, like Shakespeare, now belongs to the world.

Benjamin Britten, letter to
Graham Johnson,
September 1971

(2)

THE RED HOUSE, ALDEBURGH-ON-SEA, SUFFOLK. IP15 5PZ

The libretto of the new oper is getting on fine. We go to Venice to work with Myfanwy Piper on the rest of it in October — back to England to start the music in November — & then ready for you in January, & you can really face getting involved with it ??!

Much love, & from P., & lots of thanks
Yours ever
Ben.

Memories of Ben – a personal note

Benjamin Britten died on 4 December 1976. I well remember my alarm on seeing and speaking with him for the last time in the summer of 1975. He was in a wheelchair and already very weak; the wiry vitality that had characterised him for so many years had been replaced by a vulnerable fragility. He seemed half the size. During an operation for a long-standing heart condition he had suffered a stroke – he was no longer able to play the piano. One of the indignities he suffered through his illness was to have all his teeth extracted before that operation (the doctors were concerned about any possible source of secondary infection) and this had changed the shape of his face. Above all, it was shocking to think that he was only in his early sixties; his appearance and speech suggested someone much older. There was no pretence that my short time alone with him was anything other than a farewell, one of many that he took of his friends and colleagues during that period. Fighting back tears I thanked him for everything that his music had meant to me. He said something to the effect that his music would soon be all forgotten, and that other composers would appear who would 'do it all better'. This was almost whispered but it was without bitterness or rancour; it was just as if he was very tired, as if he were at last paying a terrible price for the non-stop activity of the preceding decades. In fact his confidence in the talent of the future, at the expense of his own reputation, has proved unfounded. A number of fine younger British composers have emerged since 1976, but not even the prodigiously gifted Thomas Adès, now a director of the Aldeburgh Festival, can rival Britten in terms of productivity and fame at a similar age.

A sufficient period of time has elapsed since Britten's death to assess his achievements while discounting the vicissitudes that usually assail a composer's standing immediately after his death. His presence is still a vivid memory for those of us lucky enough to have known him personally. Twenty-five years after the death of Mozart or Beethoven it would still have been possible to find many people who were these composers' close friends and associates. If students and scholars at the time had asked the right questions of these 'survivors',[1] how much more we should know about various aspects of these composers' music! At the Guildhall School of Music & Drama a number of people on the staff still have vivid memories of the composer as a conductor or pianist, either in his own work or as an accompanist. A few staff members played in orchestras under his baton. Penelope MacKay was a member of the English Opera Group and sang in the first performances of *Death in Venice*. George Odam, Research Fellow at the Guildhall, had personal contact with Britten as a young composer (they

1. This is not to say that a number of these composers' contemporaries did not take the trouble to assemble their recollections. Anton Schindler's memoirs of Beethoven are notoriously unreliable while Ferdinand Luib's gathering together of Schubertian documentation in the late 1850s, thirty years after the composer's death, is a mixed bag of treasure and dross.

were linked by their shared Suffolk heritage) and some of Odam's own photographs illustrate this book. The tenor Adrian Thompson, now a Guildhall singing professor, was a boy soprano with the Wandsworth Boys' Choir; he experienced Britten at work not only in the composer's larger choral music but also in such special pieces as *The Golden Vanity* and *Children's Crusade*. It seemed that the time was ripe for the Guildhall to maximise opportunities for the passing of first-hand experience about Britten from one generation to another while that knowledge was still based on personal memories of the man himself.

It was in the winter of 1967–68, in London, that I came to know much of Britten's music through gramophone recordings. I was a newly arrived music student from Rhodesia where there had been no such thing as a live performance of Britten's music – not at least since the performances of *Gloriana* for the Rhodes Centenary Exhibition in 1953 in my home town of Bulawayo. At the time I was too young to appreciate their significance. I wrote a fan-letter to the composer in 1968 and received a hand-written reply by return of post. I was lucky enough to meet Britten the following year, during the Aldeburgh Festival. The Maltings had just burnt down and for this, my first visit to the festival, I heard some of the finest music-making of my life in improvised performing conditions in Blythburgh church. Despite all the pressures of that period, Britten granted me an interview at Red House. A year later I organised a concert at the Royal Academy of Music to celebrate the seventieth birthday of the composer Alan Bush; at my invitation Peter Pears took part in this tribute to his old friend, and my composition teacher. I was then invited to help the great tenor learn the demanding role of Gustav von Aschenbach in *Death in Venice* a long time ahead of the projected first performance. That Britten was writing a new opera based on this novella was top secret for some time. Part of the reason for this was because there was a conflict with the film-maker Luchino Visconti regarding the use of a story that had so recently been turned into a film starring Dirk Bogarde. I was a weekend guest at the Red House during the recording of the St John Passion in Pears's own English translation. The composer somehow found time to give me some highly revealing composition lessons (the main revelation for me was that I should shelve my ambitions to be a composer) and took me through some of his own vocal music with piano. The latter was a more successful experience; at first I helped Pears with recital repertoire that Britten was too busy to rehearse, and then I became the official pianist for the first Pears master classes at Snape in 1972 (the great singer's debut as a teacher in public). I remember that Murray Perahia was in the audience, fresh from his triumphant win at the Leeds Piano Competition. This made me less nervous than the presence of Britten himself in the back row. Just before I went on stage to accompany the *Winter Words* I noticed, to my relief, that there was no one in his seat. It was only afterwards, when he seemed to materialise from nowhere and began to comment on my playing of one of the songs, that he confessed to slipping behind a screen at the back *in order to make me less nervous*. He had listened to the whole class from this hidden position. For me this was a powerful indication of his sympathy for the trials and tribulations of young people, born no doubt of his surprising reticence and touchy insecurity concerning his own sovereign performing talents.

The success of these classes eventually led to the foundation of the Britten–Pears School (now the Britten–Pears Young Artist Programme); in its early years I worked at Snape regularly as a staff pianist, a tradition continued by, among others, our own Pamela Lidiard, Deputy Head of Keyboard Studies at the Guildhall. In November 2002 I gave a week of Schubert masterclasses at the Britten–Pears School and devised a celebratory concert at the Wigmore Hall on 22 November for the composer's birthday. I sensed that Pears (highly critical as always) was keeping an eye on me, and that Britten was around the corner hiding from my panic-stricken gaze, or (as in Aldeburgh's Jubilee Hall when I accompanied Pears in the first performance of the *Cabaret Songs* since the thirties) watching from a wheelchair in the shadows of the back row.

Letter to Graham Johnson from Peter Pears, June 1973

THE RED HOUSE, ALDEBURGH-ON-SEA, SUFFOLK. IP15 5PZ

Dearest Graham

I am so grateful for your dear letter — as well as for all those hours we spent together creating Aschenbach.

my love Peter

The programme at the 2001 Britten festival was comprised of: 'Beware!' (Longfellow); 'The Birds' (Belloc); 'A Poison Tree' (first version) (Blake); **from Tit for Tat (de la Mare)**: 'A Song of Enchantment', 'Silver', 'Tit for Tat'; **from Holiday Diary Op. 5**: Sailing, Funfair; 'Lift-Boy' (Graves); **from Friday Afternoons Op. 7**: 'Begone, Dull Care!' (Anon.), 'A Tragic Story' (Thackeray), 'Cuckoo!' (Taylor), 'A New Year Carol' (Anon.), 'I Mun Be Married on Sunday' (Udall), 'Fishing Song' (Walton), 'Old Abram Brown' (Anon.)

Lecture 1

The young Britten
1913–35

Benjamin Britten was born in November 1913, the fourth of four children, and six years younger than his brother Robert – a Benjamin in a Biblical sense. He was protected and indulged by his mother (aged 40 at his birth), who believed from very early on that he would become one of the 'great Bs' of music. (This is rather comical considering the composer's later dislike of the music of both Beethoven and Brahms.) Edith Britten (née Hockey) was a very strong character and almost unreasonably ambitious for her son. She was also a fine amateur singer with a voice that had a timbre very similar to that of Peter Pears.[1] (Pears himself told me that Edith Britten's rendition of Liza Lehmann's enchanting song *The Swing* especially delighted her son.) It is nothing new for highly gifted musicians both to benefit and suffer from an over-protective parent. Mrs Britten's early death in 1937 (his father died in 1934) left Britten an orphan at the age of 23. It is significant that the flowering of the composer's friendship with Peter Pears took place only after both of his parents were dead; it seems noteworthy that Pears took on a protective role in Britten's life as his public voice and exponent and often shielded him from criticism and worry.

The first sound that the composer of the *War Requiem* remembered was the sound of an exploding Zeppelin, very near to his house in Lowestoft, the coastal town in Suffolk where his father had a dental practice. This reminds us that Britten was a young child during the First World War, and that talk of the bereavement experienced by almost every family in Britain at the time must have been among his earliest memories of adult conversation. (Whether the sound of this Zeppelin played a part in his lifelong horror of war we shall never know.) Britten's first attempts at composition date from 1919 when he was six – incidental music for a play he had written himself entitled *The Royal Falily* (he was unable to spell 'family', just as he was to

1. This was noted by Basil Reeve, who mentioned it to Beth Britten. See Benjamin Britten *Letters from a Life*, Volume 1, eds Donald Mitchell and Philip Reed (Faber and Faber, 1998), p.14.

Opposite: Edith, Benjamin, Robert (junior) and Robert (senior), c.1930

11

mis-spell 'waltzes' as 'walztes' on another early manuscript). The fact that the six-year-old Britten wrote a fanfare (decorative notes on paper rather than precisely imagined music), and that he stage-managed the whole enterprise, is a prophecy of the highly controlling opera composer of the future. This piece was inspired by the death of Prince John, the youngest son of King George V.[2] It is interesting that even as a child Britten already had one foot in the fantasy of fairy-tale and the other in the realities of what was happening in the outside world. In those days royal tragedies were discussed with heartfelt

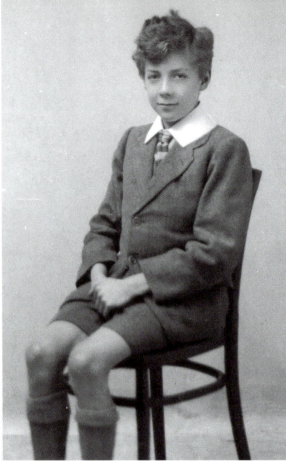

Benjamin Britten, aged ten, 1923

2. Prince John was the subject of a BBC television play by Steven Poliakov in January 2003.

loyalty at the dinner tables of faithful subjects across the land. 'The Child is father of the Man' as Wordsworth put it: this is the same composer who would later work for the GPO Film Unit when he was able to produce music for films on contemporary subjects at very short notice.

Britten began piano lessons at about the age of eight but, no doubt thanks to his mother, he was already way ahead in his musical development. The early 1920s saw the composition of a 'Symphony' in F major/minor for violin, cello and piano as well as an incomplete 'Symphony' in C for piano. Right from the beginning Britten's attraction to the voice is also apparent. There were many early songs dating from this period but only two were selected for posthumous publication in 1985. Is it sheer chance (or can one detect a humorous intent on the part of the publisher) that the texts of both songs (Burns's 'O that I'd ne'er been married' and Longfellow's 'Beware!') are almost comically appropriate to Britten's status as a lifelong bachelor? The Longfellow poem with which our festival began has a note of wary misogyny:

12

Beware! (Henry Wadsworth Longfellow)
I know a maiden fair to see,
    Take care!
She can both false and friendly be,
    Beware! Beware!

Trust her not,
She's fooling thee! Beware!
She has two eyes, so soft and brown,
    Take care!

She gives a side-glance and looks down,
    Beware! Beware!
    Trust her not,
She's fooling thee! Beware!

For someone of eight or nine to write music that is this direct, this aware of the vocal line and potential of the human voice, is almost a Mozartian feat. The trap that most young composers fall into is running before they can walk; here this is avoided. The musical calligraphy of this piece (the manuscript is reproduced in the Mitchell/Evans *Pictures from a Life*) is extraordinarily neat for so young a composer (the proud creator 'E.B. Britten'). His attention to spacing, lay-out and the painstaking addition of a decorative scroll for the title shows the meticulous nature of someone who was to remain fussy and demanding with his publishers, and always insistent on their close attention to his wishes.

This commentary now continues as a chronology, year by year, which forms an overview of Britten's vocal output in these early years; if full details of the piano pieces, orchestral works and chamber music were also to be listed this would of course be a much longer catalogue. Works preceded by an asterisk are still to be published and are usually still relatively unknown to the public and most scholars:[3]

1923 (aged 10–11)
*'Here we go in a Flung Festoon' (Kipling) voice and piano
*Recitative: 'And Seeing the Multitudes' and aria: 'Blessed are they that Mourn' (incomplete) for voice and piano

1924 (aged 11–12)
This year seems to have been given over to works for piano and strings. In

3. Much work has been done on Britten's juvenilia recently, and several of these unpublished early works were broadcast on BBC Radio 3 in 'Britten's Apprenticeship': four programmes (November to December 1995) with Philip Reed and Paul Hindmarsh (presenters). Other early works have received concert performances.

October 1924 Britten saw Frank Bridge, his future teacher and mentor, conduct his orchestral suite *The Sea* at the Norwich Triennial Festival.

1925 (aged 12–13)

The achievements of 1925 include larger-scale orchestral music, not forgetting piano music: ten waltzes, six *scherzos, seven *fantasias and four *sonatas. It is little wonder that Britten composed so little for solo piano in later life; he seems to have exhausted his curiosity for this medium early on. The most unusual piece so far was *Variations on Dyke's 'How Bright these Glorious Spirits Shine' for chorus, string orchestra, organ and piano. A *Mass in E minor was begun in March.

1926 (aged 13–14)

Britten passed his finals (Associated Board Grade VIII) with honours. The fascination with piano writing continued unabated: an example is *Sonata (Grand) No. 8 in C minor, but titles like Mazurka, Rondo, *Suite fantastique*, *Poème* all make an appearance. The onset of puberty seems to have caused a veritable flood of music. Britten also begins to write for his beloved viola (a piece entitled *'First Loss') – an instrument which he had begun to study in 1923. *'The Brook' for voice and violin strikes a Schubertian note, at least in its title. In terms of precocity Britten was somewhere between a Mozart and a Schubert – indeed, the twelve- or thirteen-year-old Britten struggling to become himself makes a fascinating comparison with Schubert at the same age in 1811. Between 12 November and 5 December 1926 Britten composed a set of six songs for voice and piano; these have not since seen the light of day.

1927 (aged 14–15)

Four Nursery Rhymes for voice and piano were composed in January of this year; these were perhaps inspired by a contemporary vogue for humorous settings of this kind by Victor Hely-Hutchinson and Herbert Hughes. In February he composed a *Kyrie in B-flat minor for chorus and orchestra. *Eight Rounds* (Sacred) for voices shows a continuing interest in choral music. A *Cavatina for String Quartet shows that Beethoven was still a revered model (see, for example, the Cavatina from that composer's String Quartet Op. 130). The most ambitious choice of text so far was a scene from Shelley's *Prometheus Unbound* in B flat for chorus, strings and piano. The young composer's *Piano Sonata No. 10 (September) happens to be in the same key. In October Britten once again attended the Norwich Triennial Festival; here he heard Frank Bridge conduct the première of his

Britten with Ethel and Frank Bridge, c. 1930

Enter Spring. After the performance Britten's viola teacher, Audrey Alston, introduced the young composer to the visiting celebrity. This meeting, a month before Britten's 14th birthday, was arguably the most important of his life. The next day (28 October) Bridge looked at some of the younger composer's more recent compositions and agreed to take him on as a pupil. From then on Britten visited Bridge's homes in London and Friston (near Eastbourne in Sussex) on a regular basis; his progress to technical mastery was now amazingly quick and sure-footed.

To the end of his days a framed photograph of Frank and Ethel Bridge had pride of place in Britten's bedroom. Bridge was a mentor and parental figure for the young Britten and there is nothing else in the history of British music quite like this relationship between the generations. Mammoth lessons lasted for hours; Mrs Bridge would come into the room saying 'Frank, the boy has had enough!' Bridge's teaching was characterised by lots of contrapuntal exercises, constructive criticism that pulled no punches, and detailed discussion of harmony, form, orchestration and so on. The older composer taught the boy to be technically ambitious and how to be nothing more, nor less, than himself. 'You should try to find yourself and be true to what you found', was how Britten later summed up what Bridge taught him.[4] Although shy by nature Britten was already precociously outspoken about what he thought was good music or bad. The sparring sessions with Bridge reinforced a natural tendency to judge music in terms of either adoration or active dislike. In these respects Britten was usually a man for black and white judgements rather than grey.

4. 'Britten Looking Back', *Sunday Telegraph*, 17 November 1963.

15

1928 (aged 15–16)

A major feature of this year is the appearance of a French influence on Britten's musical landscape. We shall talk more of this early dalliance with French poetry in a later lecture. The English songs of 1928 include *'The Waning Moon' (Shelley) as well as another nocturnal picture, 'Silver' (Walter de la Mare).

Silver (Walter de la Mare)
Slowly, silently, now the moon
Walks the night in her silver shoon;
This way, and that, she peers, and sees
Silver fruit upon silver trees;
One by one the casements catch
Her beams beneath the silvery thatch;
Couched in his kennel, like a log,
With paws of silver sleeps the dog;
…
A harvest mouse goes scampering by,
With silvery claws, and silver eye;
And moveless fish in the water gleam,
By silver reeds in a silver stream.

This is one of the very first of Britten's many nocturnes. The poem was already famous in musical terms: Cecil Armstrong Gibbs (1889–1960) had made a setting in 1920, which had been sung in countless festivals throughout the land. Gibbs's accompanimental motif binds the song together with amazing economy (in this case chords in minims rocking gently between different registers of the keyboard). Britten was to use this same technique, typical also of Schubert, in his maturity (in the *Winter Words* for example) but here his style owes much to the looser, discursive chromaticism of the later Bridge songs. There was also another de la Mare setting composed at the same time:

A Song of Enchantment (Walter de la Mare)
A song of enchantment I sang me there,
In a green-green wood, by waters fair,
Just as the words came up to me
I sang it under the wildwood tree.
Widdershins turn'd I, singing it low,
Watching the wild birds come and go;

16

No cloud in the deep dark blue to be seen
Under the thick-thatched branches green.
Twilight came; silence came;
The planet of evening's silver flame;
By darkening paths I wander'd through
Thickets trembling with drops of dew.
But the music is lost and the words are gone
Of the song I sang as I sat alone,
Ages and ages have fallen on me –
On the wood and the pool and the elder tree.

Even more than the episodic 'Silver', this song seems to have been designed to suggest the ease of speech, a type of arioso where an undemonstrative melody seems to be invented on the spot. This is far nearer to the 'wandering' chromatic style of Warlock and Delius than anything else in Britten's song output.[5] This song was actually written at the beginning of 1929; like 'Silver' it was published in 1968 as part of the de la Mare cycle *Tit for Tat*. This was a Brittenian equivalent of Alban Berg's *Sieben frühe Lieder* – old songs re-worked (or at least retouched) at a later stage by the same, if by now older and more experienced, hand. Another song of 1928, 'Of a' the airts', has a text by Robert Burns. Britten had begun this song in 1926 and now returned to it; this revisiting of a poem was a new sign of a conscientiousness born of Bridge's teaching, which encouraged stringent self-criticism. The composer was to return to the poetry of Burns at the other end of his life in *A Birthday Hansel* for voice and harp (1975).

Britten had entered South Lodge Preparatory School (as a day boy) in 1923. He was Head Boy from 1927 and by the summer of 1928 he was also captain of cricket and victor ludorum (sports champion). So far his schooling had been relatively happy. For someone whose health was never very good he was an enthusiastic sportsman; throughout his life he played cricket and tennis whenever he was able. I found him a merciless croquet player who very much resented my inexperience in the game when I was his partner on one occasion in the early seventies. In this and other respects Britten was highly competitive and remained something of the schoolboy at heart. These settings of the poems of Walter de la Mare represent a side of Britten's Englishness that is both outdated and movingly nostalgic. It occurred to me recently that both ⊙ 'A Song of Enchantment' and 'Silver' were composed by a precocious schoolboy with 'magical' abilities, a boy who seems to have been selected for a great destiny by a higher power. In the recent phenomenon of J.K. Rowling's Harry Potter we have seen a vast

5. At a concert of songs by Schubert and Britten at the Wigmore Hall (22 November 2002) given by students from the Britten–Pears School, this song was performed before Schubert's 'An den Mond' (Hölty). The juxtaposition worked perfectly – even at this early age, Britten was composing songs that had an unconscious affinity with those of Schubert.

⊙ **CD 1, track 2**

17

contemporary audience drawn to the mystique of old England (as exemplified by public-school ritual) with the added elements of whimsy and magic. What a wonderful 'Harry Potter' opera Britten might have written; the marriage of his music and film technology might have created something unique in children's music. To the end of his life the composer used words like 'ripping', 'cor!' and 'beastly' – a curiously 'safe' schoolboy vocabulary from the 1920s and 1930s, which somehow chimes with the theme of lost innocence that runs throughout this composer's music. He seems to have been nostalgically attached to these early school days as if they represented a distant Nirvana. The description in the Harry Potter stories of the steam train departing from Platform 9¾ for a new term at Hogwarts could have its parallel in 'The Journeying Boy' from *Winter Words* (see Lecture 8). The destination and the means of getting there represent a mix of enchantment and whimsy that is also to be found in these de la Mare settings, which are both arcane and naïve. The poetry, once famous and now almost completely neglected, contains images for the nursery which can also encompass the supernatural, nightmare and danger (see also 'Vigil' and 'Autumn' from *Tit for Tat*). Both those songs feature ghosts in a disturbed emotional milieu which is not all that far from that of Miles in *The Turn of the Screw*.

The dream of a perfectly happy school life where the victor ludorum is the favourite son of the establishment now came to an abrupt end. Britten left South Lodge under a cloud in July 1928 as a result of an end-of-term essay on 'Animals'; this was an impassioned diatribe against cruelty in which he challenged the great British tradition of hunting. Even worse, he spoke up on behalf of pacifism, which, in the wake of the First World War, was considered cowardice by those stiff upper-lips. The end-of-term paper was not even marked. In this fall from grace Britten suddenly seems to have realised that he was not like the other boys. The expulsion from Eden had even darker overtones: an awareness, however distant, of an emerging and guilt-inducing sexuality must have added to feelings of alienation and 'otherness'. If he now had to change schools, Mrs Britten must have done everything to ensure that the new establishment favoured artistic sensibilities. In September 1928 Britten entered Gresham's, at Holt in Norfolk; it was clear from the start that he had nothing in common with the music master but it was nevertheless a liberal school for its time (one can imagine how unhappy the composer might have been at Rugby or Marlborough). The lessons with Bridge continued. On New Year's Eve 1928 Britten began the composition of 'Tit for Tat'; its title served as a collective motto for the group of Walter de la Mare settings published forty years later.

Tit for Tat (**Walter de la Mare**)

Have you been catching of fish, Tom Noddy?
   Have you snar'd a weeping hare?
Have you whistled, 'No Nunny,' and gunned a poor bunny,
   Or blinded a bird of the air?

Have you trod like a murderer through the green woods,
   Through the dewy deep dingles and glooms,
While ev'ry small creature cries shrill to Dame Nature,
   'He comes – and he comes!'?

Wonder I very much do, Tom Noddy,
   If ever, when you are a-roam,
An Ogre from space will stoop a lean face
   And lug you home:

Lug you home over his fence, Tom Noddy,
   Of thorn-stocks nine yards high,
With your bent knees strung round his old iron gun
   And your head dan-dangling by:

And hang you up stiff on a hook, Tom Noddy,
   From a stone-cold pantry shelf,
Whence your eyes will glare in an empty stare,
   Till you are cooked yourself!

In Walter de la Mare Britten now found a collaborator of another kind; dreams are replaced by the harsh realities of life and death in the country-side. The gentleman poet and anthologist of *Come Hither*, a singer of English Arcadia, is here revealed as an enemy of brutality and cruelty. He is disgusted by the philistine yokel Tom Noddy who takes an unseemly delight in the shooting of rabbits. For the first time we hear anger in Britten's music and the awakening of the powerful voice that would reprove and warn in works ranging from the anti-establishment *Our Hunting Fathers* to the *War Requiem*, a work of national mourning and catharsis.

1929 (aged 16–17)

Britten was extraordinarily productive in the Gresham years. In the summer of 1930 he sat his School Certificate public examination; it is astonishing that he had the time to compose as much as he did as well as taking part in sports. The following list discounts the many works (some of them substantial) for piano, violin, viola and string quartet:

*'Oh, why did e'er my thoughts aspire' (Charles Sackville) for voice and piano
Two Tennyson settings: *'Lilian' and *'The Owl' for voice and piano
*'Witches' Song' (Jonson) for voice and piano
Various works for SATB including *'The Quartette' (de la Mare), two settings of Fletcher, and *'Children of Love' (Munro) for SSA.

Inspired no doubt by the orchestral song cycles of Mahler (heard on the radio) there is another de la Mare setting entitled *'Wild Time' – this time for soprano and string orchestra. The much-set poem 'Diaphenia' (Constable) is composed for tenor and piano. Perhaps Britten knew the famous 78 rpm recording of this lyric (set by William Whittaker) sung by the British tenor John Coates (1865–1941). The young Peter Pears was to be hailed as Coates's successor some fifteen years later.

1930 (aged 17–18)

The Britten enthusiast experiences something of a frisson in reading of a song from this period that is specifically designated for 'tenor and piano'. This voice is called for again in a work from February 1930 – *'Everyone Sang' for tenor and small orchestra. If Britten has not yet discovered the poetry of Wilfred Owen it is clear that he had been attracted to the work of Siegfried Sassoon, another poet of the Great War. In 'Everyone Sang' (the implication in the poem is that this singing takes place in the trenches) we have distant intimations of both the *Serenade* and *War Requiem*. There is also a taste for duets in this period, as if the dramaturgy of song were stretching slowly into operatic dimensions: *'May in the Green Wood' (Anon.) is for two voices and piano, as is *'O Fly Not, Pleasure, Pleasant-hearted Pleasure' by yet another poet from the First World War, Wilfred Blunt. *'The Nurse's Song' (Blake) is assigned to soprano, contralto and piano. The same poet and the same forces were to be employed for the 'Cradle Song' (1938), which was published only in 1994 and which was an earlier (completely different) setting of the 'Cradle Song' that opens the cycle *A Charm of Lullabies* (1947). It is clear that Blake was one of those poets for whom Britten believed it was worth taking a lot of trouble.

1930 also includes Britten's only James Joyce setting. This is entitled *'Chamber Music (V)' (the poem begins 'Lean out of the window, Goldenhair'). The deliberate obscurity of the title suggests that Britten felt rather awkward in tackling the same poem that Frank Bridge had set so eloquently in 1925 with the simple title of 'Goldenhair'. Are these the first signs of the competitive rivalry that always begins to exist in father–son relationships? Other songs are *'A Widow Bird Sate Mourning' (Shelley), a poem that had been set by Liza Lehmann (a favourite of Edith Britten's) and

Herbert Howells. Britten's only solo setting of Robert Herrick, was *'To Electra, (I dare not ask a kiss)', which is a rare instance in Britten's output of a conventional love song in praise of female beauty.

'The Wealden Trio: The Song of the Women' (Ford Madox Ford) for women's voices is one of the few vocal works from this period that the composer himself selected for re-publication in 1967. The work is dedicated to Rosamund Strode, who was Britten's formidably accomplished music assistant during the period that I knew him. 'I Saw Three Ships' (revised and issued as 'The Sycamore Tree') was published in the same year. 'The Birds' (Hilaire Belloc) was originally conceived for soprano and strings, but is much better known as a song for voice and piano. Here is a song which Britten allowed to be published by Boosey and Hawkes as early as 1934. The lyric itself is a very famous one (Peter Warlock and others also made settings of the poem).

This has long been considered Britten's 'first' song. In a similar way Schubert's 'Gretchen am Spinnrade' Op. 1 was erroneously thought of for a long time as that composer's first foray into the lied. With the unavailability of the majority of the early Britten songs it is easy to see why 'The Birds' has occupied this favoured position, apart from the fact that the composer himself chose to issue it as such: it has the advantage of suggesting the emotional directness of childhood albeit expressed in deceptively sophisticated terms. This childlike aspect fits the theme of the poem uncommonly well; the accompaniment evokes small hands carefully negotiating the keyboard with a sudden rush of magical virtuosity for the words '*Tu creasti Domine*'. There is a *naïveté* to this music, which is perhaps not quite as naïve as it seems – Britten's craftsmanship was employed in full force. 'I had a terrible struggle with this before finding what has been called "the right ending in the wrong key"', he said, 'worrying out what hadn't come right, until I spotted that the cycle of changing keys for each verse needed such an ending'.[6] The sense of release as the newly created birds soar into the sky is beautifully balanced by the closing prayer with the supplicant's suitability for paradise remaining more of a fervent wish than a granted prayer.

Britten had become an accomplished composer years before most other young musicians would think of systematically acquiring a technique. His audition at the Royal College of Music (RCM) rang certain alarm bells concerning his future reception by older colleagues in the British musical establishment. One of the examining panel wondered 'What is an English public schoolboy doing writing music of this kind?'[7] Britten went into the room with a bundle of compositions under his arm. 'Is that all?' Vaughan Williams asked, with a twinkle in his eye. Britten blinked, and replied, 'Oh

6. 'Britten Looking Back'.

7. Humphrey Carpenter, *Benjamin Britten: A Biography* (Faber and Faber, 1992), p.37.

21

8. Paraphrased from Michael Kennedy, *Britten* (JM Dent, 1983), p.10.

no, I've got two suitcases full outside.'[8] Many of these still unknown early songs would have been in those suitcases.

From late September there was a change of teachers: Britten's new composition professor was John Ireland, who was astonished, and also somewhat intimidated, by his new charge; his piano professor was Arthur Benjamin, later the dedicatee of *Holiday Diary*. Britten was never happy working with Ireland; the older composer, unhappy with his own closeted sexuality, was unable to take over the position in *loco parentis* that had been occupied by Bridge. In terms of vocal music, the young composer continued on the same tracks he had already established for himself.

1931 (aged 18–19)

Now that Britten was devoting himself entirely to composition, the slew of works of every kind (for piano, string quartet, even a ballet) seems almost alarmingly prolific. We must attempt to concentrate here on our chosen field of vocal music, but it is enough to note that the String Quartet in D major (published in 1974) and Twelve Variations for piano (published in 1985) date from 1931. There were many more de la Mare settings including the duet *'I Saw Three Witches'; the songs 'Vigil' and 'Autumn' were both later re-worked and incorporated into *Tit for Tat*. *'The Moth' (a song for bass) was also a de la Mare setting, and there was also a W.H. Davies song (also for bass) entitled *'Sport'. *Three Small Songs* for soprano and small orchestra have texts by Samuel Daniel and John Fletcher. Such literary names are memorably linked with other composers of English song (Davies with, among others, Michael Head; Daniel with W. Denis Browne; Fletcher with Warlock) and it is fascinating to see Britten exploring poetry of this kind to which he was never to return. The same applies of course to his slightly earlier settings of Herrick, Shelley, Blunt and Joyce.

He was now setting his sights on grander projects than mere songs with piano, but these often contained important vocal elements: 'Sweet was the Song' for women's voices; a *Mass for four voices; *'Love Me Not for Comely Grace' (for SSAT) and *'To the Willow-tree' for SATB; *'O Lord, forsake me not' for double chorus; 'Variations on a French Carol' for women's voices, violin, viola and piano; Psalm 150 'Praise ye the Lord' for chorus and orchestra (a setting of Psalm 130 was begun at the same time for the same forces). *The King's Birthday* (Southwell and the Bible), a Christmas suite for soprano, contralto and mixed chorus, was performed at the Aldeburgh Festival in 1991 and published as *Christ's Nativity* in 1994. This seems to have been a trial run for the later Christmas cycle *A Boy was Born* – a work that was to help to make Britten world-famous.

22

It may not be a surprise that the composer was awarded the Ernest Farrar prize for composition by the RCM in July 1931. As yet his music had not received any public performances; this was soon to change.

1932 (aged 19–20)

The output of 1932 is less prolific than that of 1931, but at last we move into a period of composition where the titles are more familiar. Here are the beginnings of the works to which Britten assigned opus numbers and allowed to see the light of day: the Phantasy in F minor for string quintet (published in 1985), the Sinfonietta Op. 1 for chamber orchestra, and the Phantasy Op. 2 for oboe, violin, viola and cello. The Phantasy was awarded the Cobbett Prize in July.

The *Three Two-part Songs* (de la Mare) for high voices and piano were performed by the Carlyle Singers conducted by Iris Lemare at the Mercury Theatre in London. The titles were 'The Ride-by-nights' (yet another nocturne with Harry-Potter-like witches and dragons), 'The Rainbow' and 'The Ship of Rio'. The third of these songs has stayed in the repertoire, one of the few Britten songs to be published by the Oxford University Press. From the same period are the *Two Part-Songs*. These are 'A Love Sonnet' (George Wither – the 13-strophe poem is anything but a sonnet) and 'Lift-Boy'. The set was performed by the same Lemare forces in 1933.

⊙ CD1, track 5

⊙ Lift-boy (Robert Graves)

Let me tell you the story of how I began:
I began as the knife-boy and ended as the boot-man,
With nothing in my pockets but a jack-knife and a button,
With nothing in my pockets but a jack-knife and a button,
With nothing in my pockets.

Let me tell you the story of how I went on:
I began as the lift-boy and ended as the lift-man
With nothing in my pockets but a jack-knife and a button,
With nothing in my pockets but a jack-knife and a button,
With nothing in my pockets.

I found it very easy to whistle and play,
With nothing in my head or my pockets all day,
With nothing in my pockets.

But along came Old Eagle, like Moses or David.

He stopp'd at the fourth floor and preached me Damnation:
'Not a soul shall be savèd, not one shall be savèd.
The whole First Creation shall forfeit salvation:
From knife-boy to lift-boy, from ragged to regal,
Not one shall be savèd, not you, nor Old Eagle,
No soul on earth escapeth, even if all repent.'
So I cut the chords of the lift and down we went,
With nothing in our pockets.

Can a phonograph lie? Can a phonograph lie?
Can a, can a phonograph?
A song very neatly
Contriv'd to make you and me
Laugh.

This zany four-part setting is prophetic of a new type of Britten: a young man aware of modern culture (and poetry), London life and American jazz. There are signs that the serious and devoted music student is beginning to 'lighten up' at last. From Graves (a poet never revisited) it is a short step to W.H. Auden and another, new phase in the composer's career. The choice of poem also has a certain significance; cheeky lift-boys in smart uniforms were a common feature of large department stores. They also came from a class which was often under-paid and exploited. The suicidal and anarchic lift-boy is a distant relation of Tom in *Let's Make an Opera* and Blake's *The Chimney-Sweeper*. As always, Britten writes himself into his music and into his choice of text. The powerful wave of feelings, romantic and idealistic as well as sexual, that set him apart from the majority of his peers was something he was not yet able to cope with (in this respect he was young for his age) but this choice of poem seems eloquent testimony of a developing sexual awareness.

1933 (aged 20–21)

In writing his first songs for schoolchildren Britten began a life-long commitment to writing music for the community, music which was actually needed for practical purposes. The *Friday Afternoon* songs Op. 7 were probably begun in November 1933 and were completed in 1935. The composer had an uneasy relationship with his elder brother Robert (this was a source of grief to him to the end of his life) but it was thanks to the fact that Robert Britten was headmaster of Clive House School, Prestatyn, that the composer assembled a suite of children's songs for school performance, called *Friday Afternoons* – so called because choral singing took place at Clive House on that day of the week.

These songs were written for performance by unison choir, but they are also rewarding for the solo performer; they are a showcase for Britten's multifarious talents expressed in miniature form. There are so many delicious musical details to enjoy: the robust melodic singability (and melodic memorability) of 'Begone, Dull Care!' and ⊙'I Mun Be Married on ⊙ **CD1 Track 4** Sunday' – both songs for spirited little bruisers and cheeky tykes; the sheer wit of 'A Tragic Story' (set by Hans Pfitzner in German translation in a comparatively leaden manner); the irresistible charm of the minimalist duet 'Cuckoo!'; the unforced melodic beauty of ⊙'A New Year Carol' as if ⊙ **CD1, track 3** Britten were capable of writing his own folksongs; the cleverly disguised contrapuntal mastery of 'Old Abram Brown', which always makes an effect more massively eloquent than one would ever imagine. In the 'Fishing Song' Britten shows his hand as a great writer of modified strophic song. The first two verses are enchanting enough, but a slower tempo and the addition of new harmonies in the third instantly transfer a pleasant day for fishing into exhausting sweltering heat with its resulting hedonistic lassitude. This is a transformation achieved with simple means but with positively Schubertian felicity, surely the sign of a great composer at work with effortless ease and economy.

The big work for voices of this year is the composer's Op. 3 – the choral variations *A Boy Was Born*, the single work in Britten's output that might be said to have been influenced by the tuition of John Ireland at the RCM. The head of that institution, Sir Hugh Allen, effectively scuppered a proposal (with a curiously English reasoning that equated the practice of atonality with immorality) that Britten should be allowed to go to Vienna to study with Alban Berg. Here was a rare instance where, following Sir Hugh's advice, Britten's father put his foot down, and mother was of the same opinion. A second Ernest Farrar prize for composition from the RCM seemed little consolation. On 13 December he successfully obtained his ARCM (he told me with some pride that he played the Chopin Sonata in B-flat minor). This, however, was the end of his time at the RCM. He had spent three years and one term at Prince Consort Road and never returned as a student.

1934 (aged 21–22)

In this year Britten moved in more ways than one into the outside world. He came to an understanding with Boosey and Hawkes whereby some of his works were to be published. The BBC Wireless Singers conducted by Leslie Woodgate gave the first performance of the choral variations *A Boy Was Born* in February. The poems are all fifteenth- and sixteenth-century poetry with the exception of 'Mid-Winter', which is Britten's only setting of Christina Rossetti, perhaps the most important female poet in the English song repertoire. In March the Norwich String Orchestra, conducted by the composer, gave the first performance of the Simple Symphony. The movements that make up this enchanting work are a kind of string-music equivalent of the *Friday Afternoons* songs – one can only wonder that such a very clever young man is capable of putting on a hat of effortless simplicity. One goes back to the theory that Britten had the ability – for the deepest emotional reasons – of being able to think himself back into a childhood state. But real childhood was quickly coming to an end. During a visit to Florence in April for the International Society for Contemporary Music (ISCM) Festival he received news of his father's death. At the other end of the year he visited Vienna with his mother, the town where he might have been a music student had things turned out differently.

Once again the year is not rich in songs with piano – the single example is 'May' for unison voices with piano – the text is the famous anonymous text from Elizabethan times 'Now Is the Month of Maying'. There was also a Te Deum in C major for choir and organ, and a Jubilate Deo in E flat for the same forces (this was published posthumously in 1984).

The suite for solo piano *Holiday Diary* (originally entitled *Holiday Tales*) was composed in October and premièred at the Wigmore Hall at the end of November by Betty Humby, later Lady Beecham. It was dedicated to Arthur Benjamin, Britten's piano teacher at the RCM. The water-borne 'Sailing' is a highly atmospheric mood piece from a composer who had a special relationship with the sea as a Suffolk man, a relationship that was to achieve its most potent expression in *Peter Grimes* eleven years later. 'Funfare' shows that at this stage Britten still found the bustling energy of the neo-classical Stravinsky exciting, as well as the noisy virtuosity of the Bartók piano pieces.

This set of four pieces has never really caught on with pianists; perhaps this is because it includes some music typical of Britten's genius, and some that seems dependent on sources of inspiration not yet quite his own. The work (together with the Piano Concerto) is a portrait of the composer's pianism at the time – he comes across, accurately I think, as nervy and virtuosic, as brilliant as a Chinese firework, and something of a speed-merchant. There was a dash in his playing that betokened someone with a natural command of the keyboard (he never seemed to practise). The absence of a piano sonata in Britten's output is puzzling (he told me he wanted to write one for Sviatoslav Richter) until one realises that the piano is the composer's own instrument and he prefers to make his self-revelatory statements at one remove, i.e. through the voice. For this reason the solo piano writing seems less personal than almost any other aspect of his output; he is inclined to construct technical smoke-screens rather than allow himself to give himself away in that vulnerable position, alone on the stage. Accompanying, and the accompaniments themselves, were quite another matter of course. Via the voice, and other people's talents – above all that of Peter Pears – he was able to commit himself to the emotional revelations that eluded him when he was alone at the keyboard and under public scrutiny. It is perhaps for that reason that one has the impression in the Piano Concerto that the composer is attempting to create piano writing that accompanies rather than dominates the orchestra.

1935 (aged 22–23)
Early March marks the composition of the last song of Britten's long youthful apprenticeship: a setting of William Blake's 'A Poison Tree'

⊙ **A Poison Tree (William Blake)**　　　　　　　　　⊙ **CD1, track 1**

　I was angry with my friend:
　I told my wrath, my wrath did end.
　I was angry with my foe:
　I told it not, my wrath did grow.
　And I water'd it in fears,
　Night & morning with my tears;
　And I sunned it with smiles,
　And with soft deceitful wiles.
　And it grew both day and night,
　Till it bore an apple bright.
　And my foe beheld it shine,
　And he knew that it was mine.
　And into my garden stole
　When the night had veil'd the pole,
　In the morning glad I see
　My foe outstretch'd beneath the tree.

As with 'Cradle Song', this great text was to inspire a second setting much later in the composer's career, part of the enormous cycle of Blake's *Songs and Proverbs*, which was composed for Dietrich Fischer-Dieskau in 1965 (see p. 216). In the meantime we find here a young composer in transition.

By now he was working for the GPO Film Unit as well as being the official composer for the Group Theatre and the Left Theatre companies. For the GPO in this year he provided the music for some fifteen different films of one kind or another (mainly what were termed 'shorts') as well as incidental music for the theatre. Here was a young man who was earning his living, which was just as well – he had to! Unlike the majority of earlier English 'gentlemen' composers, he had no independent means. This surely contributed to his no-nonsense professionalism, which in turn gave the music a vitality that had absolutely nothing to do with the leisurely ruminations of the famous cows of English music looking over gates.

He was alive to the influences of composers such as William Walton and Arthur Bliss, Arnold Schoenberg, Darius Milhaud, Francis Poulenc and Maurice Ravel. He accompanied the Swiss soprano Sophie Wyss in Mahler songs for the BBC in March 1935 ('The Birds' was also on the programme). He said much later that he felt figures such as Walton were like prefects of a school in which he was a new boy. For knowledge of the European composers he relied on careful listening to radio broadcasts. Hundreds of works were heard during these almost nightly wireless vigils; in fact one might almost say that the BBC educated Britten to a very large degree and brought him into contact with music from the Continent, particularly French music. That, however, is the subject of another part of these lectures. In the meantime 'A Poison Tree' is full of spiky and characterised rhythms that suggest more posture than feeling. We are astonished rather than moved by this music (it has the panache of the Violin Suite Op. 6 and parts of the Frank Bridge Variations); we detect a young man with an array of new and clever friends who has become recently aware that a certain uncompromising modernity is expected of him.

Britten's first meeting with W.H. Auden took place on 5 July 1935 at Colwall in Herefordshire, where the great poet was a schoolmaster (see photograph on p. 141). This was another red-letter day in his career. Britten would need every ounce of his technical independence and hard-won confidence to keep his individuality in the next decade. For years he had been his mother's little genius, but there were other geniuses in England and he was now mixing with a number of them on a daily basis. Fortunately for him he was up to the challenge; and it was his good fortune that friendship and love were there to help him find his way.

The programme at the 2001
Britten festival was comprised of:
Six Metamorphoses after Ovid
Op. 49: Pan, Phaeton, Niobe,
Bacchus, Narcissus, Arethusa;
Seven Sonnets of Michelangelo
Op. 22: XVI, XXXI, XXX, LV, XXXVIII,
XXXII, XXIV; ***Introduction and***
***Rondo alla burlesca* Op. 23, No. 1**
***Mazurka Elegiaca* Op. 23, No. 2**;
Eight French Folksongs: 'La Noël
passée', 'Voici le printemps', 'Fileuse',
'Le Roi s'en va-t-en chasse', 'La Belle
est au jardin d'amour', 'Il est
quelqu'un sur terre', 'Eho! Eho!',
'Quand j'étais chez mon père'

Lecture 2

Britten abroad:
Italy, Poland, France and Germany

The first lecture was firmly rooted in East Anglia with a glimpse of London towards the end. Now we must explore Britten further afield; he was a supremely confident stylist who, time after time throughout his career, went outside his own country, even if only as an armchair traveller, in search of inspiration.

Six Metamorphoses after Ovid Op. 49 (1951)

The starting point in this chapter is a rare instance of Britten turning to a literary source in order to provide the idea for a set of purely instrumental pieces. In this instance his gaze is directed toward Italy or, more particularly, ancient Rome; the result is a spectacular piece of modern music that manages also to be antique in its effect – a genuine piece of time travel. This oboe somehow suggests the classical, yet sybaritic, sound of Pan's pipes, and of an epoch in the distant past that is all but lost to us in musical terms.

This set of miniatures could only have been written by a master of a larger medium such as opera. It seems that the smaller the musical form, the more potently a composer is capable of exploiting it, provided he has had experience in writing for bigger forces. By 1951, when the *Six Metamorphoses* were written, Britten had already composed *Peter Grimes*, *The Rape of Lucretia* (another work inspired by ancient Rome) and *Albert Herring*; he was working towards *Billy Budd*, and *Gloriana* would soon follow. The *Metamorphoses after Ovid* are character pieces that translate six of Ovid's stories into musical terms. There was an unforgettable first performance of this work by the oboist Joy Boughton, daughter of the composer Rutland Boughton, seated in a punt on Thorpeness Mere; she played from Britten's manuscript, which fell into the water and had to be rescued. The term 'metamorphosis' implies the change of each of the gods into another form, but it also sums up the com-

Opposite: Britten in Copenhagen, late 1940s

31

positional process of variation and elaboration that is especially evident in Britten's handling of this unaccompanied melodic line. The short descriptions following the titles are printed before each piece in the score.

(i) *Pan* ('who played upon the reed pipe which was Syrinx, his beloved')

Pan is the god of shepherds and huntsmen. There are numerous visual and musical allusions to this god. There is a wonderful song ('Pan') by the Swedish composer Ture Rangström to a text of Bo Bergman; the teenage Bilitis is seduced by the player of the *La Flûte de Pan* in the first of Debussy's three *Chansons de Bilitis*. Britten's setting is marked 'senza misura'. It immediately sets the tone of an ancient and timeless music, and the decorative roulades suggest the pagan energy of the seductive Pan.

(ii) *Phaeton* ('who rode upon the chariot of the sun for one day and was hurled into the river Padus by a thunderbolt')

Son of the sun, vain and beautiful, Phaeton was responsible for the chariot crash of Helios, which turned Africa into a burnt desert. See also the orchestral piece entitled *Phaeton* by Saint-Saëns (1873), as well as Alan Ridout's radio opera of this title (1975). Goethe worked on this theme, and the poem was translated from Ovid by Friedrich Hölderlin; Britten was later to set both these great German poets (see pp. 57–8). Britten's music is a wonderful evocation of a bumpy ride. Phaeton's lack of skill in mastering the chariot is evident in the way flowing triplets are interrupted by stuttering duplets, and there is a spectacular musical description of the crash as the oboe is made to plunge to the bottom of its register. Phaeton drives a rickety version of Diana's silver-chaired chariot in the 'Hymn' from Britten's *Serenade*.

(iii) *Niobe* ('who, lamenting the death of her fourteen children, was turned into a mountain')

In Shakespeare's *Hamlet* the eponymous hero compares his mother's grief to Niobe's; the nymph is a favourite theme of painters such as Tintoretto and Veronese. The latter completed *Eight Scenes from Ovid's Metamorphoses*. Britten's lament is in D-flat major/B-flat minor. The weeping Niobe is the embodiment of 'Lachrymosa'. Perhaps it should be no surprise that in a hauntingly beautiful B-flat minor section of the War Requiem, this word is set to a remarkably similar phrase beginning on F, falling to D flat and then plunging further down the stave. It is clear that Britten has responded to the musical imagery of mourning with a tonal analogue that has remained in his mind.

(iv) *Bacchus* ('at whose feasts is heard the noise of gaggling women's tattling tongues and shouting out of boys')

Bacchus was the god of wine, who married Ariadne. See also *Ariadne auf Naxos* by Richard Strauss. Britten would give musical voice – a counter-tenor – to this god (under his Greek name of Dionysus) in *Death in Venice*. Bacchus allows Britten a great deal of raucous fun. A heavy peasants' dance ('Allegro pesante') in 4/4 begins to totter and weave with 3, 5 and 2 beats in the bar. This is music for a drunken spree with the burps built in. The part really gets going at the con moto section. In a slew of teeming semiquavers, Britten somehow depicts a Bacchanalian mêlée. The coda suggests the adipose and inebriated god struggling to get up, and then falling heavily to the ground.

(v) *Narcissus* ('who fell in love with his own image and became a flower')

See also 'A Grecian Lad' ('Look not in my eyes …') by Butterworth and Ireland, and other settings of A.E. Housman's poem from *A Shropshire Lad*. Szymanowski's *Narcisse* is for violin and piano (another movement of this set is *The Fountain of Arethusa* – see below). Of all these Britten pieces, this is perhaps the most ingenious in that it suggests imitative writing in two parts – Narcissus and his reflection, of course. Delicate demi-semiquaver figurations suggest the rippling reflections. Otherwise, the music is languidly seductive and self-regarding.

(vi) *Arethusa* ('who, flying from the love of Alpheus the river god, was turned into a fountain')

See also Shelley's poem *Arethusa*, and Coleridge's River Alph. Britten here sets the oboist a task that requires the greatest virtuosity. This is water music, with never a moment for the instrumentalist to breathe. The cascades of semiquavers both reflect Arethusa's flight from Alpheus and her metamorphosis into a torrential fountain. Those who know the Szymanowski piece for violin and piano on this subject can only marvel how Britten is equally expressive, using one instrument and more economical means.

It is clear from these few random examples that Britten takes his place in a long line of European artists who have turned to Greek and Roman mythology for enlightenment. One of these was his beloved Franz Schubert, a composer whose lieder were performed by Pears and Britten with sovereign insight. Among their favourites were such songs of classical inspiration as 'Ganymed' (Goethe) and the Schiller setting 'Die Götter Griechenlands' ('The gods of Greece'). Both singer and composer were touched by the poems of Schubert's friend and mentor Johann Mayrhofer,

1. Decca SXL 6722

who was almost certainly homosexual. On the last recording of Schubert songs the couple made together in November 1972[1] there is a performance of Mayrhofer's 'Atys' D585; the song, relatively unknown, is one of those magical pieces in A minor/major on which Schubert lavishes all of his love and compassion. The poem concerns the myth of the shepherd boy who is castrated in the service of the goddess Cybele; he longs to return home but as an outcast he is unable to do so. He jumps from a precipice to his death (the same way in which Mayrhofer was to jump to his death from the balcony of his office in Vienna in 1836). The postlude is the longest of any in Schubert's songs and, especially in Britten's hands, one of the loveliest.

Classical literature makes an occasional appearance in Britten's own work, never more poignantly than in the monologue towards the end of *Death in Venice* where the dying poet Aschenbach paraphrases the Platonic dialogue *Phaedrus* ('Does beauty lead to wisdom, Phaedrus?'). This work by Plato (its theme is the nature of love, as is the same philosopher's *Symposium*) was an important feature of two books by the novelist Mary Renault (a great favourite of both Britten and Pears). These were *The Charioteer* and *The Last of the Wine*, two of the first post-war British novels that dealt openly, if over-idealistically, with the subject of homosexuality – the first is set in Britain during the Second World War, the second in the Athens of Socrates. The latter work was the beginning of a long and distinguished series of classical novels by Renault, who lived in Cape Town. I became a friend of the author by correspondence in the late 1960s and I treasure the gift of a Greek ring from the 5th century BC, given to me recently by her lifelong companion Julie Mullard. At the same time as he was preparing the role of Aschenbach, Pears was reading *The Persian Boy* (its eponymous hero Bagoas, a eunuch slave – shades of 'Atys' – is in the service of Alexander the Great) and Renault's work figured sometimes in our conversations. In 1984 Michael Tippett set a passage from Renault's *The Mask of Apollo* in his choral symphony *The Mask of Time*.

Of course, on many occasions Britten's travels were real rather than imaginary: during his three-year sojourn in the United States, and during his extended trip to the Far East in 1955–56, he was acutely aware of what he could learn by careful listening and assimilation. Britten was a world citizen, certainly in comparison to many of those artists who were active in the aftermath of the First World War. Some of these composers suffered from the insularity that was the result of Britain's withdrawal from Europe (in every sense) after this catastrophe. This betokened both the arrogance of the victor and the horror of re-engagement with ill-fated excursions abroad which had brought untold grief. From Britten's beginning his musical interests radiated outwards in all directions, and Europe was very much in his sights.

Between the wars, practitioners of that noble form known as 'English song' had more or less officially turned away from European models (Schoenberg, Berg, Webern, Stravinsky and so on); this was a period when English music seemed set on self-sufficiency, and it drew most of its nourishment from home-grown folk culture including Celtic as a means towards that end. Names such as John Ireland, Herbert Howells, Peter Warlock and Arnold Bax come to mind, although it would be wrong to argue that European influences are never to be found in their songs; on the contrary, there is considerable borrowing that seems covert and disguised rather than admiring and celebratory. The difference in language is the heart of the matter. During the time they were writing their songs there was an unspoken rule that, as in folk song, there should only be one note per syllable in word-setting. They allowed themselves a chromatic richness of harmony that sometimes seemed to border on Viennese atonality by another name, but this self-imposed discipline regarding words now seems a musical expression of British *sang froid* – unfussy, non-showy, thrifty, terse, a type of manliness where florid vocal melisma would be considered so affected and insincere as to be unthinkable. The musical extravagance and daring of Henry Purcell must have seemed as foreign to these composers as the idea of men wearing wigs and perfume in the reign of Charles II. The point is that the extravagance of Purcell's style derives in part from that composer having had a similar openness to Europe as Britten possessed – in Purcell's case a knowledge of music by French and Italian composers at the court of Louis XIV. Purcell wore a wonderful wig, the pictures tell us this much, and probably perfume too when it was available. In Britten's youth, long before after-shave of any kind was permissible for English men, foreign film stars such as the German actor Conrad Veidt (1893–1943), a famous ladies' man, wore Guerlain's *Jicky* on the Ealing set. My friend Jill Balcon remembers sitting on Veidt's lap as a little girl (her father ran the studios) and being almost overpowered by this pleasurable aroma.

For the English youngster born early in the first quarter of the twentieth century, 'the continent' had long seemed the source of such heady and forbidden delights. In actual fact the attraction goes back for centuries. For the rich and powerful, two successive Princes of Wales for example, Paris was always a playground of licentiousness (the British middle classes' view) or an unparalleled centre of painting, music, cuisine and amusement (the view of liberals, and most artists). But one cannot help wondering if Britten would have been so interested in Europe as a source of texts and cultural inspiration if, side by side with his developing sensibility as an Englishman, and an English composer, he had not been learning how to cope with being a gay man in a hostile environment. There was little about him that was intrinsically epicurean or hedonistic, and he was completely loyal to most things English. To the end of his life he looked askance on fancy French cooking, preferring what might be termed 'nursery' food (the greatest dish to be enjoyed at the Red House was Miss Hudson's dover sole); the composer loved cricket and croquet and he had a penchant for cold baths first thing in the morning, a habit acquired in his public-school days; he owned English cars and had a passion for the English countryside – no other country moved him by its beauties in remotely the same way. He was not a particularly gifted linguist and for fine French wine he did not care a jot; Peter Pears was much more of a connoisseur in the sybaritic aspects of life. One is left wondering if Britten had possessed the same emotional make-up as, say, Gerald Finzi, we would have had any *Sonnets of Michelangelo* or *Illuminations*, much less a *Death in Venice.*

The answer is probably no, particularly when we consider that both Michelangelo and Rimbaud were both famous for, and troubled by, their homosexuality, and that Thomas Mann grappled for years with an alternative side to his nature. Britten did not find these texts by chance; they were in the literary pantheons of friends like Edward Sackville-West, W.H. Auden and E.M. Forster, and for a very good reason. It was well known that Europe (and by extension European literature) was more sympathetic to gay people; homophobia was a peculiarly British obsession and English homosexuals had long had a way of looking (and travelling) abroad to find a more humane attitude to their way of life. As soon as Oscar Wilde was let out of Reading gaol he fled to Paris; that literary martinet A.E. Housman had an unlikely relationship with a Venetian gondolier; the young W.H. Auden and Christopher Isherwood rampantly explored Berlin during the last years of the decaying Weimar Republic; Britten and Pears were drawn to the wide open spaces of America where homosexuality, though officially illegal, seemed more accepted by the artistic community. As a gay man one is, like it or not, a citizen of a larger constituency, a fellowship to which Britten was introduced almost as soon as he met W.H. Auden in 1935. I believe it could be argued that much of the tension in Britten's life was this struggle between a part of him that was devotedly (and almost parochially) English, and the other which was drawn to a larger world view where the unspoken Esperanto was a shared sexual sympathy, a brotherhood of a kind. It could not have made things easier that, when he emerged from the RCM into the musical world in 1934, the eminent composers were such people as Vaughan Williams, Howells and Bliss, and the great white hope of English music was the 31-year-old William Walton. On this evidence English music was a very heterosexual constituency indeed.

In Britten's case his loyal identification with England eventually triumphed against the odds. This overwhelming feeling precipitated the return of both composer and singer through dangerous waters to Britain in 1942. Britten always knew that queer freemasonry ('queer' was the word used then, and now is a term of the new political correctness) encompassed people with whom he felt little in common, as well as a bohemian way of life that temporarily threatened his sense of order and routine in his New York period. But this secret international passport, where one had friends and contacts all over the world (from the past as well as the present), continued to represent an escape route; the setting of foreign languages and the assumption of foreign styles constituted a smokescreen, a disguise, for a man who, like many others, was made to feel like a foreign agent in his own country, a law-abiding patriot who was breaking the law (up to 1967 at least) simply in being himself.

We have little evidence in words of any guilt feelings on the composer's part, but the music is a rich field for study; in certain works one can discern the sort of defiant defence of his feelings that only comes about in reaction to emotional discomfort. Growing up in the milieu that he did it would be astonishing if self-reproach were not part of his make-up, no matter how strong the intellectual or human argument in favour of sexual freedom. For this reason Britten was a composer who was English with every fibre of his being with an inner nature which, like Schubert's 'Der Wanderer', was at home in every land without, perhaps, being completely at home in any. One thinks of the actor or clown who finds it easier to amuse and divert his audiences lest they see his tears. The saving grace for Britten's art was an uncanny ability to remain himself no matter how florid the temporary disguise; the reader is referred back to the previous chapter and Britten's own summing-up of how Frank Bridge had taught him to remain true to himself.

It is interesting to see that other more or less contemporary homosexual composers coped with the conflict between their national or cultural background and their sexual orientation. Aaron Copland came to fame with music that encapsulated the great American outdoors; one would never have thought that the ultra-manly traditions behind *Billy the Kid* or *Rodeo* would have been so enthusiastically taken up by the shy and bespectacled son of Russian Jewish emigrants. Samuel Barber's *Dover Beach* for string quartet and baritone is an example of an American wearing an impeccably English guise, as if a musical version of Patricia Highsmith's talented Mr Ripley. These seem to me no less 'foreign' stylisations than Britten writing in Italianate melismas, and these may also be seen as the disguises of men trying on new identities because they were uncomfortable (or dissatisfied) with various aspects of their own inheritance. In any case, being an outcast has a way of sharpening the imagination; dreams of travel are a way of removing oneself from conflict or unhappiness. Copland's champion as a conductor, Leonard Bernstein, had a different way of coping with the conflicts of his Jewish background and his sexuality. He had a wife and children but, determined to have his cake and eat it, enjoyed a Bacchanalian existence in an ambience of New York hype no matter where in the world he found himself. (We glimpse Britten's revulsion to the Dionysiac way of life in the orgiastic and frightening music for Aschenbach's nightmare in *Death in Venice*.) Bernstein, in turn, would have found Britten's rural isolation boring beyond belief; but the composer of the *Chichester Psalms* must have envied the composer of the *War Requiem* for an immortality based on serious music which was outside his own grasp.

Michael Tippett was a nearer contemporary; after his own travails of self-discovery he spoke more openly about his sexuality than Britten, and he flirted with a slightly 'hip' means of expressing himself (which can be heard in his libretti for his later operas). He was astonishingly young at heart until late in life. He was Britten's friend but also a life-long rival, although this aspect of their friendship was underplayed on both sides. I remember a lunchtime conversation at the Red House after Britten's death when Peter Pears (admittedly still in a mood of mourning) was enraged by Michael Tippett's insistence at the table that he himself felt completely un-English – that he, Tippett, belonged to the world as a whole and was no longer beholden to any single country. When Britain's greatest living composer (as he was then) had left the room, Peter Pears remarked acidly that 'Michael has always had the capacity to talk a lot of balls'. Perhaps Tippett was simply teasing us with balls thrown in the air, but I knew what he had meant with his protest against English insularity. I also understood Pears's point: that, whatever he said in this flip and provocative manner, Tippett remained as rooted in the English tradition as Britten was. No matter where their travel agenda had taken them, both Britten and Tippett were English composers in the same way that Jonson and Shakespeare were English poets. I felt proud to be of British stock because they were too, and I must admit to another sense of identification that linked me to these admired icons: youngsters beginning to find their own way in life need inspiring role models, and in the 1970s this is exactly what these composers were to me and many others. It did not strike me at the time that Britten too, as a young man, needed a similar pantheon of comrades to help him make sense of his emotional world. That some of these people were European poets of the past (Verlaine, Rimbaud, Michelangelo) is hardly surprising.

Britten's first signs of interest in Europe are to be found in February of 1928 with the composition of a work entitled *Dans les bois* for orchestra. The title seems to have come from a poem of the same name by Gérard de Nerval, which the fifteen-year-old composer set in June for voice and piano. In the same year there were *Quatre chansons françaises* for soprano and orchestra, which were published posthumously in 1982. These were two settings of Victor Hugo ('Nuits de juin' and 'L'Enfance') and two of Paul Verlaine. The Verlaine poems were already famous in other settings. 'Sagesse' ('Le ciel est, par-dessus le toit/Si bleu, si calme!') shared a text with Fauré's 'Prison' and Hahn's 'D'une prison'; it had also been set in English translation by Vaughan Williams in 1908 as 'The Sky above the Roof'. The fourth poem set by Britten in this set, 'Chanson d'automne', was the first of Reynaldo Hahn's *Chansons grises*, and was to be a Charles Trenet hit with the title 'Verlaine'. This set was Britten's most ambitious vocal work to date, and he dedicated it to his parents for their 27th wedding anniversary.

The inspiration for this French phase does not seem to have been literary (his French lessons never left him enraptured) but simply aural. Perhaps encouraged by Frank Bridge to widen his listening, Britten seems to have been entranced by the *sound* of French music over the radio; we know that in 1928 he invested in a set of records of Ravel's wordless *Introduction and Allegro*. The sheer sensuality of a sound-world that combined the timbres of harp, flute, clarinet and string quartet with such originality had beguiled a young man with an ear brilliantly attuned to imitation. *Quatre chansons françaises* is the first of his many stylisations, and an astonishing achievement in one so young. When the work came to be published by Faber in 1982 (there is a piano score of the work), the composer Colin Matthews, charged with editing it, had almost nothing to change in the orchestration. But he did alter the prosody of the vocal line where the composer had wrongly accented certain words.

Britten's radio listening, and his debt to the BBC of the time, could never be over-estimated. He heard Schoenberg conduct on the wireless and was so entranced with *Pierrot Lunaire* that he requested the RCM to buy a copy of the piece for its library; a request that was turned down. He was able to hear Ravel conduct the first performance in England of his Piano Concerto, with Marguerite Long, and thought the second movement was piffle. His diaries contain the most precocious reactions – sometimes wise, often surprisingly childlike, but always honest and businesslike. He was much more tuned into detecting and unmasking the pretentious, overblown and badly scored than bemoaning differences in harmonic language. From the start he seemed able to appreciate a piece for the sincerity and depth of feeling behind it – in other words, on its own terms. This is why he had no difficulty at all with *Pierrot Lunaire* and did not even comment on its *Sprechgesang* or atonality. It was enough for him that the orchestration and musical ideas *worked*.

In the decade between 1928 and 1938 the vocal enthusiast will find that this composer made few excursions into foreign lands, but vocal music was not the only means of reaching out to influences beyond our shores. The *Soirées musicales* Op. 9 after Rossini (1936) is for orchestra; this suite shows a delight with the bubbling and melodic style of an Italian opera composer without having to come to grips with the Italian language. But it was surely the *Variations on a Theme of Frank Bridge* Op. 10 (1937) that first revealed the composer's genius as an international parodist. Each of the variations wears a different mask of course, but at least three of the movements display strongly nationalist affinities: the Aria Italiana and Bourrée Classique evoke the Italy of Rossini and Vivaldi, and Wiener Walzer the Vienna of Mahler. At the end of 1937 Britten, together with Lennox Berkeley, completed *Mont Juic* Op. 12, an orchestral work based on Catalan folk music and a tribute to the struggles of the Republican struggle against Franco's fascism in Barcelona. There was more music inspired by the Spanish Civil War in the incidental music to *Spain* (1938), a piece performed by the Binyon Puppets in the Mercury Theatre.

In 1939 the composer began work on his second song-cycle in French, *Les Illuminations*, to the poems of Arthur Rimbaud who had had a relationship with Verlaine – indeed, Verlaine had written the poem of Britten's 'Sagesse' during the time he was imprisoned in Belgium for having shot Rimbaud during a lover's quarrel. Britten must have read the remarkable introduction by Edith Sitwell to the English translations of these poems, which was published in 1933 and republished in 1936 (the date of the extant copy in his library). Sitwell explains the whole story of the Verlaine–Rimbaud friendship with vivid sympathy. But Rimbaud, that trouble-making genius, was already one of Auden's (rather few) French heroes, and his poetry was both important in itself and important to other gay intellectuals in the composer's circle who were aware of their literary heritage.

In this remarkable work Britten's unfamiliarity with the exactitudes of French prosody is unfortunately considered a problem by the natives; the work seems to have been taken up by few French-speaking musicians, although its first performer and dedicatee was the Swiss soprano Sophie

Wyss. Rimbaud occupies almost a sacred place in French literature, and it is significant that on the whole French composers have left him unset. For the rest of the world, however, Britten's understanding of Rimbaud's various moods seems extraordinarily vivid; he does indeed seem to possess 'la clef de cette parade sauvage' ('the key to this savage parade') – the words with which the cycle begins. The work has a flair and elegance, a sumptuous sensuality notwithstanding an economy of means, which encapsulates the English-speaking view of the 'luxe, calme et volupté' which is French song. The 'calme' of Baudelaire's phrase is quite rightly not all-pervasive, however, and the work has more than a touch of the sinister and disturbing, reflecting the poet's complex and highly strung nature, and no less the composer's.

Les Illuminations had been begun before Britten and Pears's departure to the United States in May 1939. A piece with mythical and classical over-tones, *Young Apollo* for piano and strings (the title is actually taken from the closing lines of Keats's *Hyperion*) was among the first to be composed on American soil. It was published as Op. 16, withdrawn, and re-issued posthumously in 1982. The over-ture *Canadian Carnival* (*Kermesse canadienne*) is the first work with a truly North American dimension, but the most important was the operetta *Paul Bunyan* to a libretto of W.H. Auden. Here was an opportunity to develop an American style based partly on the composer's long-stand-ing awareness of the idioms of popular music (Gershwin, Porter) and partly on a ballad style that recalls the rough-hewn simplicities of American folk music. At the same time as he was contemplating this work (where his involvement with an American myth was intended as a symbolic sign of his commitment to becoming an American citizen at some time in the future), Britten was composing the first work that he was to write specifically for the voice of Peter Pears. This was to the Italian texts of the painter and sculptor Michelangelo Buonarroti, who was also a passionate poet. His sonnets were concerned mainly with the subjects of love and death. Wolf had also set three of these for bass voice in 1897. Shostakovich was to use the same voice for his *Suite* of fourteen Michelangelo songs Op. 145 (1974). These works emphasise the pessimism of Michelangelo's words, but Britten chose poems to suit the enraptured radiance of the tenor voice, that instrument which, from now on, was to be his main ambassador and mouthpiece.

Britten and Pears in Italy, late 1940s

Britten was susceptible to Italy throughout his life. He visited Florence when he was still a teenager, to hear his *Phantasy Quartet*, an occasion that was burned into his memory because it was in Florence that he received the news of his father's death. Although Britten's operas were far from Italian in their inspiration (indeed, he mercilessly parodies the clichés of Italian *bel canto* opera in the 'Pyramus and Thisbe' section of *A Midsummer Night's Dream*), there was always a side of him that admired the melodic spontaneity of the Italian composers. There is a wonderfully contented photograph – one of the happiest I know in the published iconography of his life – where he sits smiling happily at the foot of a statue of Giuseppe Verdi. He was also delighted to go to Venice to work on the opera *Death in Venice*, which is incidentally remarkable for an accurate notation of gondoliers' calls across the lagoons, cunning evocations of the sound of the *vaporetto* and the bells of San Marco, and a magical and ominous parody of Italian popular song with piano accordion accompaniment. This immersion in Italian atmosphere was infinitely more to Britten's musical tastes than a visit to Berlin would have been: the heavier German repertoire of Beethoven and Brahms (the former hardly a favourite, the latter a great bugbear) represented for him a muddle-headed confusion of stodgy sounds. He was after light and clarity, and the Italian sunlight was a metaphor for these musical qualities. I remember that even Peter Pears had a sneaking fascination for the bigger tenor roles of the Italian repertoire; he confessed to a glowing admiration of Placido Domingo in *Otello* and was very proud to take part in a recording of Puccini's *Turandot* (as the old emperor of China) at the end of his career.

Seven Sonnets of Michelangelo Op. 22 (1940)

The *Seven Sonnets of Michelangelo* were conceived in America but given their first performance in September 1942 in the Wigmore Hall. They marked the return of the composer from America. It was amazingly audacious of Britten to return with Pears in the middle of the war and give a first performance of songs based on the great painter's love poems to a handsome and much younger man, the gifted and gracious Tommaso Cavalieri (c. 1509–87). What is more the significance of these poems for that event was not theoretical: there, before the very eyes of the audience were the two lovers, already controversial figures for having left England in 1939 (albeit before war was declared). Just in case there is any doubt that these poems were addressed to a man there is the reference (couched in heroically masculine music), that the singer is 'captive of a cavalier at arms'; this is of course Michelangelo's pun on Tommaso's surname, at the end of Sonnet XXXI. The writing and the designation of the score thoroughly preclude the performance of the work by a soprano. Britten includes his own pun by giving the words 'Spirto *ben* nato' to Pears to sing – words which he meant Pears to sing *to him*, Ben Britten. In a way these words, a paean of private love, were also meant for the whole world to hear.

In retrospect the openness of this declaration seems almost foolishly indiscreet for the times, but it is somehow typical of this composer throughout his life. These pieces were performed at an early evening concert at the Wigmore Hall (23 September 1942) organised by Boosey and Hawkes. They were 'concealed' between the first performance in England of Bartók's *Contrasts* and a new quintet by Bliss. Presented in this way the content of the work may have worried the publishers somewhat less than if it had formed part of a complete recital. Britten was retiring and reticent about his private life but in another sense he was almost brazen about displaying his sympathies in his

Britten and Pears on holiday in the Alps, Austria, mid-1950s

choice of texts (including libretti later in his career) and performers. Anyone at that concert with half an ounce of sophistication would be able to discern the sub-text of the occasion, but it seems that the majority of the audience allowed the Italian poems to skate over the surface of their imaginations without being aware that they were in any way 'queer'. (How many people have allowed lieder texts to float over them without ever coming to grips with their real meaning! Was Britten relying on this?) One is reminded of a similar feat of legerdemain when A.E. Housman issued *A Shropshire Lad* in 1896 in the wake of Oscar Wilde's trial (secretly and anonymously he sent a copy to Wilde in Reading gaol). This was as homosexually inspired a book of poems as has ever been printed; but this aspect of it seems only to have struck those who were 'in the know' – Butterworth among composers for example, but seemingly not Vaughan Williams. Famously the book became the favourite reading of such establishment figures as homophobic generals who were strangely blind to what the texts were actually saying.

Housman was secretly filled with rage about the treatment of his own kind (he refused all honours from his own country, including the Order of Merit). That he was offered this decoration in the first place is an indication of how poorly the establishment had comprehended his private life. At times one thinks that if he had been younger he would have been an ideal recruit to the Guy Burgess or Anthony Blunt spy rings, and for some of the same reasons of disaffection. It was Britten's librettist E.M. Forster who said that he hoped he would have the courage to betray his country before his friend. Housman, Forster and Britten shared a certain genius in educating the British public about forbidden and unfamiliar emotions, doing so gradually and subversively. That Britten had been taught by Bridge was an important factor in 'being himself at all costs'; writing conventional love music and operas with heroines was never an option for him. But just as Housman smuggled *A Shropshire Lad* into the English consciousness, many of Britten's works, beginning with these *Sonnets*, are passionate declarations of an emotional difference, simultaneously bold and reticent. His friend Forster was never able to publish his gay novel *Maurice* during his lifetime; but Britten was able to sing of his own deepest feelings from the start because words, sometimes conveniently in foreign languages, were clothed in music. Britten was anything but a gay activist and his way of fighting for his rights represents nothing more or less than the triumph of subversion. One remembers that Auden's text for *Our Hunting Fathers* was against hunting, but disguised with a modernism that made its intent a little obscure. Again subversion! The closing bars of the *War Requiem* seem to ask a gigantic question whereby a great occasion of Establishment mourning was turned into a haunting reproach from a conscientious objector (some of Shostakovich's works cleverly attacked Stalinism from within in a similar way). So it is that some of Britten's works often eschew bellicose confrontation in favour of subtly undermining such things as the horsey hunting set, the jingoism of the smug patriot and, above all, Puritan morality that failed to recognise his right to love in the manner of his choosing.

⊙ CD1, track 6   ### ⊙ Sonetto XVI

From the beginning we can hear that Michelangelo is a sculptor, work that requires tremendous physical energy. In the piano's introduction the hammered music of the three-quaver upbeat to the first bar seems remarkably concentrated and earnest. These quavers are written out separately with individual tails, each with a tenuto marking to emphasise the careful placement of each chiselled attack on the marble. These white notes in the bass clef are followed by a leap upwards to clusters of black keys in the treble. Both hands, simultaneously reckless and precise, land on dotted crotchet chords in a manner that suggests a leap into new uncharted regions, the prerogative of those with innovative genius. The marble bends to Michelangelo's will in the same way that the vocal line here seems forced to follow the contours of the accompaniment. This is a marvellous musical metaphor for artistic control; the sculptor draws images out of stone through his sheer will-power and imagination. Everything about this music suggests masculinity, professionalism and suppression of self-indulgence.

This rigorous opening recalls the music that closes Schubert's 'Prometheus' D674, where the rebellious son of Zeus, a potter rather than a sculptor, creates the human race with blasphemous abandon. One can hear the clay being thrown at the wheel in defiance. In the case of Britten's sonnet this mood of fierce physical engagement prevails for one and a half pages, and then there is a complete contrast. At the words 'Così, signor mie car' Britten permits a ravishing tenderness to enter the music. The sharp edges of F-sharp minor are made to melt into a C major that is memorably tinged with an F sharp – the Lydian fourth, which will play such an important role in the third song. The vocal line is transfixed on a single note as if spell-bound by Cavalieri's appearance, but it also tells us something about his beauty: no flirtatious siren this, but someone noble, dignified and very much his own man. From these ingredients the composer fashions a discourse that follows the poem's drift: the young man's beauty has unsettled Michelangelo's intense, self-absorbed creativity. Those chiselled upbeats now sound more tentative, even woebegone (the old sculptor has lost his edge) and the vocal line is inflected with sadness at words such as 'sospir' and 'gran duolo'. The repetition of the words 'Signior, mie car' at the end is the composer's, not the poet's.

Britten's achievement here is manifold: the music of the opening seems to throw down the gauntlet both to conventional English song and to conventional English morality; it is also a veritable launching-pad for a new vocal career, that of Peter Pears. Whoever first sang the notes of this song's opening page demanded to be taken seriously. One can sense, in his composer–accompanist's role of lifting and supporting the voice to new heights, that Britten was determined that this should be so.

Sonetto XXXI

The overall impression made by this slew of notes, both sung and played, is of an almost over-the-top emotional commitment that seems typically Italian. And yet the piece, like everything in this cycle, is something of a hybrid. This song has always reminded me, funnily enough, of the Schumann of *Dichterliebe* – a combination of 'Die Rose, die Lilie' in terms of its swiftness of tempo, and 'Im Rhein, im heiligen Strome' in terms of the dotted rhythms. (It was at this time of course that Britten and Pears were reading through all the great cycles at the beginning of their work as a lieder duo.)

The dialogue between the voice and the pianist's left hand reinforces a feeling of vehemence – it is as if the feelings are pouring out of the singer. The harmonic subtleties (on the word 'morir', for example, there is a marvellously telling C natural in the middle of an A-flat minor chord) suggest that these distraught emotions are changing constantly, and liable to move into new regions at any moment. This music is unanchored and unsettled, although behind the hysteria the composer exercises an iron control with never a note too many. On the passage beginning 'Però se'l colpo' the composer requires the voice to stay on the same note – it is a D on the fourth line of the stave – for no less than nine bars. It is as if the singer were lashed to the mast of a ship in the vortex of a storm generated by the accompaniment. This signifies the steadfastness of love, even when it borders on masochism. Indeed the ecstasy of a situation where the sculptor is the 'prisoner of a cavalier in arms' is emphasised by an almost radiant modulation into C major for the song's final page. The words 'Resto prigion d'un Cavalier armato' are set twice. The first time we hear a climax in a shining A major tonality, with the tenor blazoning his captive status with a pair of high As. What a glorious thing it is to yield to another with such abandon! – this is perhaps the 'voluntary love' of which Auden speaks in the song 'Fish in the Unruffled Lakes' (see Lecture 6). The second time we hear this phrase set to music, pride has been replaced by a more tremulous emotional diffidence. The halting, somewhat breathless repetitions of the postlude figurations remind us of the huge responsibility borne by Tommaso Cavalieri in being the gaoler of Michelangelo's emotions. A note of yearning, as if a plea for mercy, concludes this roller-coaster of a song. In the space of a few minutes we have moved from restless grief to reckless happiness and back again.

⊙ CD1, track 7   ## ⊙ Sonetto XXX

Over the last sixty years, many of those who have fallen in love with Britten's music – that defining moment in the capturing of a listener's affection which can hold him or her a prisoner for a lifetime – have capitulated to this particular song before any other. So far the cycle has been strong and vivid, music to convince the Sadler's Wells management that, yes, Peter Pears had the verve and spirit to sing Rodolfo in *La Bohème* and the Duke in *Rigoletto* – roles he did indeed undertake, among others, a year or so after the première of this cycle. But with the third number we suddenly come across an oasis of calm, a song to fall in love with because love is precisely its subject. In the first two songs we have heard amative passion in its less settled guises; here we find music to mirror the inter-dependence of lovers, if only because the poet sees himself as half of a whole where his beloved enables him to function as a complete human being. Michelangelo must have known Plato's *Symposium* where Aristophanes maintains that men were first created in pairs, then split in half by Zeus. The result is that

46

'each of us when separated, having one side only … is but the indenture of a man, and he is always looking for his other half'.[2] Michelangelo's beautiful poem is well worth quoting in full. These words are as touching a description of devotion as one could find in any literature; sung by the dedicatee of their musical incarnation with the composer at the piano, they become as clear a portrait of mutual commitment as has ever been penned:

2. Plato, *The Dialogues of Plato*, trans. B. Jowett (Oxford University Press, 1924).

Sonnet XXX (Michelangelo Buonarroti)

Veggio co' bei vostri occhi un dolce lume
che co' mie ciechi già veder non posso;
porto co' vostri piedi un pondo adosso,
che de' mie' zoppi non è già costume.

Volo con le vostr'ale senza piume;
col vostr'ingegno al ciel sempre son mosso;
dal vostr'arbitrio son pallido e rosso,
freddo al sol, caldo alle più fredde brume.

Nel voler vostro è sol la voglia mia,
i mié pensier nel vostro cor si fanno,
nel vostro fiato son le mie parole.

Come luna da sè sol par ch'io sia,
chè gli occhi nostri in ciel veder non sanno
se non quel tanto che n'accende il sole.

With your lovely eyes I see a sweet light that yet with my blind ones I cannot see; with your feet I carry a weight on my back which with my lame ones I cannot; with your wings I, wingless, fly; with your spirit I move forever heavenward; at your wish I blush or turn pale, cold in the sunshine, or hot in the coldest midwinter.

My will is your will alone, my thoughts are born in your heart, my words are on your breath.

Alone, I am like the moon in the sky which our eyes cannot see save that part which the sun illumines.

Translation Elizabeth Mayer and Peter Pears

The key is G major enriched with the C sharp of the Lydian fourth. The song is cast as a seraphic dialogue between two twinned souls: singer and pianist. For thirteen and a half bars the bass is a repeated G major triad. The vocal line is a gloriously sinuous melody, a bel canto creation that constantly seeks to reinvent itself in a series of melodic metamorphoses. Each of the singer's utterances is mirrored by arpeggio-like figurations that yearningly seek to climb up to the tenor's tessitura – or so it seems on the printed page. In the ascent and descent of these limpid pianistic patterns we can hear both the self-abasement of a humble suitor, and the magnetic attraction which pulls him, harnessed to those rising arpeggios, to the regions of higher aspiration and accomplishment represented by the voice. The ebb and flow of this music seems positively tidal, sidereal perhaps, and similarly inevitable. The range of colouring encompasses the gentlest of moonlight to the hottest sunlight (both images are to be found in the poem) – and, after having made us wait for it, Britten changes the left-hand harmony time and again to miraculous effect.

Setting a mood as Britten does with this opening shows an ability to create a calm spacious atmosphere which is one of the marks of a fine song composer (I think, for example, of how effective 'Silver' by Armstrong Gibbs is in this regard). But it is in the *development* of the material that we can hear the truly great composer at work, and many minor figures are found wanting in this regard. Britten now sets about showing his mastery: the exchanged promises and declarations become more impassioned, dialogue between voice and piano warms into the passionate entwining of the two instruments, and this in turn is set up to introduce one of those modulatory moments that once heard always remains something to anticipate with swooning pleasure: in three languid bars the piano line falls, suspended as translucently as a spider's web, from the very top of the keyboard to the bottom; a lingering juxtaposition of D major in the right hand and E-flat major in the left resolves into the most hushed B major chords. Here, as if balancing on a high trapeze (this was a part of Pears's voice which Britten always knew could be used to magical effect) the vocal line breathes a tenderness, and a kind of starlit remoteness, that reminds us that this sonnet inhabits a region above and beyond the physical – it is about the Platonic ideal, friendship, the marriage of two minds. (Is it fanciful to imagine that the Lydian harmony has somehow contributed to the mood of Attic purity that pervades the song?) The music aches with devotion; here surely the composer strikes a note that is as holy as an intoned prayer. After this, the music becomes passionate enough to encompass the cycle's highest note, a resolutely sung high B – something Pears never found very easy, nor any tenor after him. The final *mezza voce* phrase ('il sole', a leap of a ninth in pianissimo) is accompanied by one of those moonstruck bi-tonal arpeggios which make the whole of this piece seem to come from another planet. Certainly it is music that is out of this world.

⊙ CD1, track 8   ⊙ **Sonetto LV**

The preceding song has been a nocturne in all but name. Those who know the 'Nocturne' from *On This Island* ('Now through night's caressing grip') will recognise that the two pieces are closely related in manner. Now the composer needs to enliven the atmosphere, and this he does in a scherzo-like song marked 'Poco presto ed agitato'. It is perhaps at this point that one should acknowledge that the poetry of Michelangelo did not really mirror the happy emotional circumstances of Britten and Pears. Three years separated the ages of composer and singer; the sequence of Cavalieri poems, created mainly between 1532 and 1538, was written by a great master of 58 for a young man of 24. It is not that Tommaso was unworthy of the attention: in 1547 the humanist Benedetto Varchi referred to Cavalieri's 'incomparable physical beauty … grace in demeanour … excellence of intelligence … refinement of manners'. It is clear that Michelangelo had fallen in love with someone infinitely worthy of admiration, and by all accounts someone who turned out to be a true and noble friend to Michelangelo in the long term. Addressing the older man, Cavalieri wrote: 'I promise you truly that the love I bear you in exchange is equal or perhaps greater than I ever bore any man'. Tommaso was later to marry, and the whole question of sexual attraction, clearly on Michelangelo's side only (and he found it almost impossible to acknowledge), brought pain and tension to the relationship. Michelangelo at this stage was a gruff and prickly semi-recluse who was thoroughly unaccustomed to being emotionally dependent on others. Because the artist was on tenterhooks about Cavalieri (and we can hear this in the poetry – 'Sonetto LV' for example, and Britten's music for it) there were no doubt moments of misunderstanding that led to quarrels. The rage that Britten has allowed to enter this song, for example, seems entirely appropriate; but it must be understood that the poet's anger is mainly with himself for being so susceptible. In this instance it seems that Tommaso has withdrawn somewhat, no doubt on account of Michelangelo's moods – a clear sign of the poet's struggle to live with unrequited passion, or at least passion where there is no question of physical release, no matter how much the younger man may have admired, revered and even loved the old master.

The accented offbeats of this music have much about them that represents a nervous tic. The vocal line seems breathless and even unreasonably volatile (the high G sharps and As of 'Rompasi il mur frall'uno e l'altro messo'). All this was a good vehicle for Pears in rhetorical or dramatic mode. In a marvellous piano interlude Britten allows this tension to evaporate: the idea is simple – an ascending right-hand scale in diminuendo and ritardando, with the ghost of the pervasive offbeat rhythms in the left – but the effect is magical. It is as if a storm has cleared and a ray of sunlight is at last discernible. This leads to the song's final page, which is in the manner of a tender recitative with sequences of heart-stopping beauty. And then suddenly the touchy awkwardness is reignited by a sudden return to Tempo I with a high A flat, and an ominously voiced reference to death.

⊙ Sonetto XXXVIII

⊙ CD1, track 9

This is the only song in the set where Britten has allowed himself a Renaissance colouring suitable for the historical provenance of these sixteenth-century words. The plucked lute, or strummed guitar, is cleverly suggested by piano writing where use of the sustaining pedal is proscribed, but the *una corda* is a requirement. How graciously this accompaniment falls under the hands as they alternate lightly and deftly at the keyboard! While the voice is transfixed on a single note the ghost of a little melody is outlined in the piano part; this requires the right hand to stretch out, as if attempting to reach for something that has been lost – the plea 'Rendete' translated into both music and movement. The composer who rather strangely comes to mind here is Debussy: how similar this writing is to 'Serenade for the Doll' from the *Children's Corner*, as well as the pizzicato-like piano texture in the same composer's Cello Sonata (a work which Britten was later to play masterfully with Rostropovich).

The composer invents a vocal line in 6/8 rhythm which is conjured out of repeated notes – as if the singer were murmuring his pleas under his breath. Time after time these gently pulsating As rise to the E a fifth above, and affectionately linger there before falling a seventh and completing the cadence. This is one of the very rare Britten pieces where the marking actually calls for rubato (the composer reacted badly to the application of rubato in his own music when not required, and where it seemed the result of a singer's self-indulgent 'artistry'). Once these ideas are established Britten's working out of the material is, as usual, sovereign. The emotional heat rises in the middle of the song where hemiolas in 3/4 (2 + 2 + 2 quavers instead of 3 + 3) impose a peremptory drama and majesty on the otherwise gently lilting textures. The song ends with a vocal portamento after which the piano teases the listener's ear with rumblings right at the bottom of the bass stave. With this piece we have the impression of an elegant stylisation, rather than any attempt to depict Michelangelo's misery.

Sonetto XXXII

The vehemence of this moto perpetuo scherzo makes the Italian (already very difficult in its ornate style) all but incomprehensible to native speakers. Little wonder: the poem is made up of no fewer than ten conditional 'ifs' ('se' in Italian); thirteen lines of the poem make up a single sentence, the main clause of which is delayed to the twelfth and the thirteenth lines. This must have been one of the reasons that Britten chose a tempo which hurried to its conclusion like a river impatient to join with the sea. Nevertheless, it is also here that the composer's prosody is at its weakest – it would take a composer formidably experienced in Renaissance Italian to ensure the correct accentuation of every vowel. Britten rushes in where *angeli* would fear to tread. The result is helter-skelter, exciting, and a marvellous contrast to the big, serious song that will follow it. All in all this is what the composer meant it to be, and we are swept away by his enthusiasm. The accompaniment rattles along, relying on the strength of the

50

pianist's wrists, an ardent, pulsating background that helps turn up the heat in the interests of creating an Italianate atmosphere.

At 'Se mille e mille non sarien centesmo' there is a unique bow of homage (whether deliberate or no) to Puccini – this is a quasi-pentatonic vocal line that might have come directly from *Turandot*. It stretches the voice and encourages a heroic timbre that seems indisputably *verismo*. The final question set in the last dying throbbings of the piano writing is almost flirtatious – a sign, surely, of a lovers' quarrel mended. One is strongly reminded of another Italian stylisation: 'Nun lass uns Frieden schliessen' from Hugo Wolf's *Italienisches Liederbuch*.

⊙ **Sonetto XXIV**   ⊙ **CD1, track 10**

This is surely the cycle's crowning glory. The poem dates from 1528 or later; strictly speaking it is not now thought to belong to Tommaso Cavalieri's sequence of poems. On the other hand the sentiments seem exactly to fit Michelangelo's feeling for his young friend. From Britten's point of view that 'Spirto *ben* nato' must have been too much to resist. The composer creates a grandiose baroque musical effect by alternating pianistic ritornelli with passages of unaccompanied arioso. Some singers make the mistake of interpreting this as recitative and, in so doing, ignore the note values. This was not Britten's intention: nothing in this music should be hurried or thrown away, as there is nothing casual about these emotions, which should be counted for every semiquaver of their true worth. Everything in this music is of the grandest emotional import.

The heavy-footed introduction begins deep in the bass; gradually the left hand climbs the stave getting higher and higher until the voice enters as if it were a spark ignited by the tinder of the piano writing – we can almost hear this vocal explosion generated by the intensity of the increasingly adventurous harmonic clashes between the accompanist's hands. These left-hand octaves in dotted rhythm make one think of Ravel's song of the peacock, 'Le Paon' from *Histoires naturelles*. That song is about a wedding ceremony and, in a way, the Britten is too. (The peacock's wedding is postponed but the ceremony remains.) The vocal line of this sonnet is nothing less than a proclamation; one can almost imagine the words being read from an unfurled parchment. Michelangelo is in the mood to announce to the world the virtuous glories of his well-born friend.

The second piano ritornello moves from the celebratory D major of the opening to the more introspective key of D minor. In this second verse – in reality the fifth to the eighth lines of the sonnet – tiny but telling interjections from the piano (arpeggio fragments which are light as a bee's wing brushing harp strings) colour and emphasise the meanings of words. Three great qualities 'amor, pietà, mercè' (love, compassion, kindness) are left unaccompanied. But the harmonic change of direction on 'Cose sì rare' (things so rare) is tinged with a poignancy that tells us more than one thing: yes, certainly Tommaso has those chivalric qualities in plenty, but the full possessing of them by the poet is another matter. Michelangelo must remain outside the magic circle of the deepest intimacy and regard these beauties from without. As an older man he must also be prepared to die earlier than his friend.

In this way the music is tinged with farewells of a kind that Britten and Pears would have to take of each other in 1976, but not in 1942 with their whole working lives still ahead of them. But Britten is too great a composer not to react to Michelangelo's predicament, and it is here, as elsewhere in the cycle, that the two very different love stories, from two different centuries, diverge. 'Love takes me' says Michelangelo ('L'amor mi prende') and Britten's C minor tonality implies panic rather than acquiescent joy. There is a bitter pain in an older man's obsession with a much younger man, an obsession that could never achieve anything like a satisfying closure. After the words 'par che ne doni' the pianist's two hands converge on a plangent arpeggiated chord, marked fortissimo, that is snatched away as soon as it is played. When

Ex. 1: Death in Venice
Ex. 2: Sonetto XXIV

I talked to Britten about this cycle in 1972 my ears were full of the new music he had just written for *Death in Venice*, and which I had been asked to help Peter Pears memorise. I was also learning the *Michelangelo Sonnets* for the first time as a performer. When I came across this very chord on the cycle's last page (mentioned above) I was immediately struck by the fact that it prophesied the harmonic world of Tadzio, the boy who enslaves Aschenbach in *Death in Venice*.

Ex. 1

Ex. 2

52

The same total commitment to hopeless love that is expressed in this final sonnet is reflected in the music for the Polish boy who is the cause of Aschenbach's pain and downfall in the last of Britten's operas. It was as if Britten's music had come full circle, an arc traced between 1940 and 1971. This chord encompasses the Tadzio theme on which much of his music in his last opera is based. Britten was fully aware of that chord when I pointed it out, and then he said 'Look what's written on the second-to-last line of the piece'. I scanned the passage. The final page of the song reverts to that beautiful arioso accompanied by other-worldly fragments of arpeggios. And then the postlude brings a huge and calm peace to the cycle – to me it has always seemed to illustrate an ascension to heaven, as in Schubert's 'Ganymed'. For those last seven bars the marking is '*sempre pianissimo*' written out as '*sempre pp*' – or, in another reading (more double-takes and subversion), 'Always Peter Pears'. At the time I was very moved by Ben's revelation: I knew that after that promise made in 1940, another of his secret communications, Britten had kept his faith in what by 1972 had already become a lifelong partnership.

It so happened that after composing the Michelangelo set (which contained the seeds of Tadzio's music of thirty years later) Britten's next work had a Polish theme. Instead of commemorating a beautiful Polish boy, the second of these pieces for two pianos pays a tribute to an old man on his death – the former Polish prime minister, the composer Ignaz Paderewski (1860–1941). On a Polish note, one should also record here that Britten and particularly Pears were admirers of the work of Witold Lutosławski (1913–94) later in their lives. That fine Polish composer, an exact contemporary of Britten, wrote the cycle *Paroles tissées* (in the French language) for the English tenor in 1965.

⊙ *Introduction and Rondo alla burlesca* Op. 23 No. 1 (1940) ⊙ CD1, track 11
Mazurka Elegiaca Op. 23 No. 2 (1941)

The words 'alla burlesca' promise an Italian character to this music which is partially fulfilled. Britten's next opus, the *Matinées musicales* Op. 24 has another Italian connection, being more Rossini arrangements, and was conceived as a ballet for Lincoln Kirstein in New York. The Introduction and Rondo is one of Britten's most superbly crafted pieces for piano, the introduction in particular making a dramatic impression. The haunting lilt of the *Mazurka Elegiaca* (memorably recorded by Britten with Clifford Curzon) is a testament to Britten's affection for Chopin (Britten had made an arrangement of *Les Sylphides* in 1940, also for a New York ballet company). In terms of music for piano Britten never wrote music finer than this, and it is further proof of his ability to assume any national style he chose. The next work that

53

he completed for the two-piano team of Ethel Bartlett and Rae Robertson (this time with orchestra) was yet another stylisation, this time deriving from the British Isles. This is one of the composer's least known works, the *Scottish Ballad* Op. 26.

Folksong arrangements, Volume II (France) (1942)

Britten and Pears returned to England in 1942. From this year, somewhere between America and Britain, the composer's second book of folksongs was arranged.

The famous arranger of French folksongs is Joseph Canteloube, whose luxuriously indulgent settings are meant for sopranos with wall-to-wall voice. Chabrier's arrangements, as well as those of Déodat de Séverac, are finer because more simple, but little known. With one exception Ravel's arrangements of folk songs are not from his own country. Britten made a volume of French folksong settings in December 1942. These include, among others, the delightfully playful 'Voici le printemps', a melting setting of 'La Belle est au jardin d'amour', and a potent and hypnotic 'Il est quelqu'un sur terre', a French 'Gretchen am Spinnrade' with its obsessively grinding spinning wheel. The rollicking 'Quand j'étais chez mon père' seems to have been conceived alongside *Peter Grimes*; there is a vivid resemblance between the folksong and the dance music (also marked *alla Ländler*) for off-stage band, as Mrs Sedley in that opera makes her meddling accusations in the opera's last act. This was not Britten's real domain, however, and the British folksongs (as well as the Irish) bring out a richer vein of invention, perhaps because in sheerly harmonic terms they are more interesting. There is little doubt that these arrangements were made in loyalty to the singer Sophie Wyss, who was from French-speaking Switzerland.

Despite the sensual evidence of *Les Illuminations* France was never Britten's natural habitat. Perhaps he had a hand in the officers' anti-French remarks in *Billy Budd*: 'Don't like the French, don't like their Frenchified ways'. There is an unintentionally hilarious passage in Britten's diary that describes a disastrous visit to Paris in January 1937: an excursion to the *Folies Bergères* backfired badly as the group of English visitors was diverted by a wily pimp to another show, which turned out to be a brothel. Britten's own puritanism at the age of 24 is never more evident than in his remarks concerning this episode.[3] Even if a certain 'uptight' quality was to unwind somewhat later in the year with the initiation of his relationship with Peter Pears, the whole episode shows Britten singularly unable (or unwilling) to embrace 'la belle France' in the spirit of a natural Francophile. In later years, in reaction to the unfavourable opinions about his music that streamed

3. Donald Mitchell and Philip Reed (eds) *Letters from a Life: Selected Letters and Diaries of Benjamin Britten*, Volume 1 (Faber and Faber, 1991), pp.467–8.

from the French avant-garde, he took against the Nadia Boulanger cult (which had Stravinsky as its main icon). He had found Boulanger intimidating and pretentious since an occasion in the 1930s when he had inadvertently spilt ice-cream over her velvet dress at a dinner preceding a Queen's Hall concert. She never forgave him, it seems, and the feeling was mutual. He told me that he thought she had 'ruined Lennox [Berkeley]'. 'Imo', he said (meaning Imogen Holst), 'knows just as much about music as Nadia without all the chi-chi'.

The one exception to Britten's distaste for France was Francis Poulenc, who was an admired friend. Here is further evidence of the freemasonry of sexual sympathy overruling national and stylistic boundaries. Britten performed Poulenc's *Tel jour telle nuit* with Pears (otherwise the French *mélodie* was rather lacking in the duo's repertoire) and Poulenc's Apollinaire opera *Les Mamelles de Tirésias* was featured at the 1958 Aldeburgh Festival. In return, Poulenc was a real admirer of the English composer; their friendship dated back to 1945 when the two composers had performed Poulenc's Concerto for two pianos together at a so-called Saturday Book concert at the Albert Hall in January 1945. To commemorate this occasion Britten inscribed a copy of his newly published *Ceremony of Carols* for the French composer (pictured right). There is also charming photograph of Poulenc arm in arm with Britten and Pears in Cannes in 1960.

Ceremony of Carols inscribed to Poulenc

A CEREMONY *of* CAROLS

For Treble Voices and Harp

By

BENJAMIN BRITTEN

Op. 28

PRICE 3/6 NET

WINTHROP ROGERS EDITION

Boosey & Hawkes Ltd., 295 Regent Street, London, W.1.   Boosey, Hawkes, Belwin, Inc. 43-47 West 23rd Street, New York City.   Boosey & Hawkes (Aust.) Pty. Ltd., National Building, 250 Pitt Street, Sydney.   Boosey & Hawkes (Canada) Ltd. 10a Shuter Street, Toronto.

Britten returned to the world of French literature only once, and then only obliquely. The words of his cantata *Phaedra* for mezzo-soprano and small orchestra (1975) are drawn from Racine's *Phèdre*, but the composer, whose life was drawing to a close, decided to set the work in English to the free translation of the American poet Robert Lowell. His last vocal work thus unites two of the countries to which his earlier vocal stylisations are beholden.

Britten and the German language

In 1934, at the age of 21, Britten went on a long European trip with his mother, taking in Munich, Basel and Salzburg. The Vienna part of the trip was partly a consolation prize: he had been awarded a scholarship at the RCM for foreign study and had hoped to go to Vienna to study there with Alban Berg. He never discovered what happened at the time, but pieced together the story of Sir Hugh Allen's unenlightened intervention some years later. This was surely a hugely important factor in Britten's development, and one is not certain whether Sir Hugh is to be condemned or thanked. I am certain that if he had gone to Vienna as Berg's apprentice Britten would have emerged as a different composer; he would certainly have made different friends and been open to different influences. Nevertheless, German song, and its utterly memorable performance, became part of his life, and that of Peter Pears. It was hearing their performance of *Winterreise* at the Maltings in 1971 that set my life as an accompanist on course, and in particular inspired my devotion to Schubert. There are immortal recorded performances of the Schubert cycles, of Schumann's *Dichterliebe*, of miscellaneous Schubert songs and, right at the end of Britten's life, a group of Wolf songs recorded at Snape and issued under the auspices of the Maltings.

Now that I know something more about the tradition of German and Austrian lied performance it is clear to me that Britten's accompanying of Schubert songs would also have been different if he had studied in Vienna and heard artists like Julius Patzak in their prime. Pears and the composer evolved their own Schubert style, which was developed not according to established traditions (particularly regarding tempo) but following their own formidable instincts. In the post-war years the influence of émigré musicians from Vienna (Erwin Stein, Hans Keller and so on) must have played its part in refining the duo's interpretations, as well as yearly visits to the music festivals at Schloss Elmau (near the Richard Strauss stronghold of Garmisch-Partenkirchen) in Bavaria, where they had enthusiastic German audiences. If the absence of the remonstrances of a Viennese 'Herr

Professor' is evident in certain of their lieder readings, the freshness and daring of their performances successfully challenge the conventional wisdoms of an art form that was always in danger of being set in its ways.

It was inevitable that Britten should set the German language in a cycle. He spoke it more happily than French, albeit in an English word-order, which became known as 'Aldeburgh Deutsch' during the visits of Mstislav Rostropovich. The *Sechs Hölderlin-Fragmente* Op. 61 date from late 1958. Their dedicatee was Prince Ludwig of Hesse, an enthusiast of the poetry of Friedrich Hölderlin. He was the sensitive and poetic husband of Margaret ('Peg') Princess of Hesse who played a large part in the composer's life as a patron of the Aldeburgh Festival. This couple had been the companions of Britten and Pears on their Far Eastern holiday in 1955–56, and there is a wonderful photograph of the four of them in Balinese costume. After the death of Prince Ludwig, Peg Hesse (as she was known) was Britten's affectionate and considerate hostess; he wrote much of *Death in Venice* at her castle, Schloss Wolfsgarten near Darmstadt. It was on one of his earlier visits to Wolfsgarten that Britten had astonished a whole room of German dignitaries by banging the table, yelling 'Du Depp!' ('You imbecile!') to the high-ranking woman next to him, and storming upstairs. It turns out that she had made the huge mistake of saying she was sorry that the recital just heard by the guests should not have been *entirely* of Britten's own music; why was it necessary to have songs by that rather inferior composer, Schubert? She had intended to flatter him of course, but anyone who knew Britten even slightly would know that this was a recipe for disaster. There were some composers of whom absolutely nothing critical could be said in his presence, and Schubert was one of them. Any comparisons between himself and these geniuses, however well meant, and particularly if favourable, was met with fury.

The choice of Hölderlin as a poet for this cycle was typically astute. Britten did not relish the idea of going where other great German composers had been before him. The Hölderlin songs of Max Reger (1912) and Paul Hindemith (1933) were not in the general repertoire, and neither were those of Hanns Eisler (1943) at the time (the reputation of this composer, and of his Hölderlin settings, has since grown considerably). All in all, Hölderlin is a poet, rather like Rimbaud, whose literary significance has not really been matched by a correspondingly important catalogue of musical settings. As a result Britten felt free to write lieder for the only time in his life. Hölderlin was another outsider who suffered much in his life, though not for sexual reasons; he was more or less insane for his last thirty-six years and thus joins hands with another of Britten's wonderful 'mad' poets, Christopher Smart of *Rejoice in the Lamb*. The word 'Fragmente' (fragments) is an important key to the terse epigrammatic style of this perfect little set. There is never a note wasted, and never a detail of counterpoint which is not effective and telling. This is the only song cycle for voice and piano between the *Winter Words* (1953) and the *Songs and Proverbs of William Blake* (1965), and the piano writing here represents a transition between two very different Britten styles. The flowering of sensuous melody occurs here and there, but it is always controlled. It is as if each jewel-like word, engineered by the poet with a fastidious precision, had to be matched by similar music. As one plays this cycle one feels that voice and piano are interlocking levers in a perfect, watch-like mechanism. It is significant that the third song, 'Sokrates und Alcibiades', is a return to the probity of the classical philosophers. It takes as its subject the chaste passion of the older sage for the beautiful young man as described in Plato's *Symposium*. The aggressive questioning of the sceptics in the first strophe is answered by Socrates in the second with music of rare serenity and beauty.

4. This is the only surviving song from a projected Goethe cycle (the idea was suggested by Prince Ludwig of Hesse).

There is only one more German setting, and that is a poem of Goethe, 'Um Mitternacht', which was written in 1960 but published only in 1994.[4] The poem is a great one from the poet's maturity, but neither Schubert nor Wolf attempted it, possibly because it is both strange and modern for its time – it has an almost Proustian resonance in its conception of time past and present. The only other setting of significance is by Carl Friedrich Zelter (1758–1832), a beautiful song, but probably unknown to Britten at the time. In determining a lack of competition he feels he has *carte blanche* to set a poet who is forever linked with so many great composers. The poem is a nocturne (one of Britten's least known, but surely one of the most compelling) in which we can hear the beginnings of the composer's late style with its layers of unbarred sound designed to resonate as if in a church acoustic. This is powerful music, one of Britten's greatest songs I think, where semibreve chords, deep in the bass, underpin wandering dream-like right-hand crotchets. In this midnight song it is no surprise to discover that there are no less, and no more, than twelve of these bell-like chords. The aptness of Britten's music never fails to astonish, as well as the aptness of his choice of words. The poem represents three phases of understanding in life: first the little boy frightened of walking past the church (and grave-yard) and enchanted by the stars; then the lover whose nocturnal journeys have a romantic purpose; then, finally, the older man who sees past, present and future as an entity where the beginning and end of life connect in a circle. And still the stars shine. The wonderful thing is that, at the age of 47, the composer at the very height of his powers had chosen to set these words at exactly the right time of his life.

The programme at the 2001 Britten festival was comprised of: **Volume I**: 'The Salley Gardens' (Yeats); 'Little Sir William' (Trad.); 'The Bonny Earl o'Moray' (Trad.); 'O Can ye Sew Cushions?' (Trad.); 'The Trees they Grow so High' (Trad.); 'The Ash Grove' (Trad.); 'Oliver Cromwell' (Trad.); **Volume III**: 'The Plough Boy' (Trad.); 'There's None to Soothe' (Anon.); 'Sweet Polly Oliver' (Trad.); 'The Miller of Dee' (Trad.); 'The Foggy, Foggy Dew' (Trad.); 'O Waly, Waly (Trad.); 'Come you not from Newcastle?' (Trad.); **Volume V**: 'The Brisk Young Widow' (Carey); 'Early One Morning' (Trad.), 'Sally in our Alley' (Trad.); 'Ca' the Yowes' (Burns); 'The Lincolnshire Poacher' (Trad.)

Lecture 3

The British folksong settings

For many centuries composers have delighted in embedding strains of popular music, both sacred and secular, within their own original creations. Josquin and Palestrina, among others, produced mass settings on a bawdy crusading song, *L'Homme armé*; instrumental arrangements and elaborations of folk melodies by such sixteenth-century composers as Thomas Morley and William Byrd were not uncommon; Purcell used the bass line of *Lilliburlero* for a stage jig; Bach wove well-known Lutheran chorales into his grander structures. It seems that the manipulation of familiar tunes is a test of a composer's humour; it also shows whether or not he is able to descend from the ivory tower and engage with the music whistled by his less sophisticated listeners on their way to work. When I was a student pianist at school in Southern Rhodesia I could curry favour with my sports-obsessed contemporaries by improvising Mozartian variations on the latest Beatles tunes. The identification of these pop melodies in a pseudo-classical context made them feel more informed in my own field, and I felt they were less likely to mock my own preoccupations with real Mozart. 'Dumbing-down' is a new way of describing an age-old marketing ploy.

The arranged folksong, given new life by composers of contemporary repute and marketed as such, is one of the few branches of music that seem to have originated in Britain. During the 1780s George Thomson of Edinburgh (1757–1851) initiated an ambitious project that would occupy him until the 1840s: this was the publication of folksong arrangements by the greatest living European composers. By the turn of the century – the turn of the eighteenth into the nineteenth century that is – there was something of a nation-wide vogue for clothing popular melody in a more 'civilised' garb. This interest in folksong had been partially fuelled by the

Opposite: Britten on the Thorpeness Road, Suffolk, c. 1959

61

Ossianic craze (the Gaelic poetry of James Macpherson – alias Ossian – which had supposed links with ancient times), which brought many foreign tourists to Scotland, including Mendelssohn. Britain, which was regarded as artistically backward by most Europeans, became famous as the home of the erstwhile noble savage. Our country's misty rusticity suddenly became appealing.

Over a period folk songs came to represent a curious sort of British chic. They were to be heard in the grand salons of London and Edinburgh, Bath and Brighton, but also in the homes of the middle classes where the piano in the parlour, and rising musical skills, both vocal and instrumental, created a demand for suitable material. This was many decades before German or French composers became interested in their own folk music. The British music-buying public had a seemingly endless appetite for arrangements of Scots, Irish, Welsh and English songs, which had hitherto only existed in dusty collections as unaccompanied melodic lines. Thomas Moore's *Irish Melodies*, arranged by Sir John Stevenson, are a focal point of Lecture 4; in riposte (and hoping to have the same financial success) Byron wrote *Hebrew Melodies* in 1815 specifically for the Jewish composer Isaac Nathan (1790–1864) to set to tunes that Nathan claimed were originally sung in Solomon's temple before its destruction by the Romans.

Stevenson and Nathan both claimed a type of authenticity for their work. The latter was bogus of course (in order to escape his creditors he fled to Australia where he was later fêted as that country's first composer – there is a statue of Nathan in Sydney) but Moore's *The Last Rose of Summer* in Stevenson's simple arrangement survives until this day. As an arranger Stevenson takes a back seat in favour of the vocal melody, and frankly he did not have skill enough to take up any other position. George Thomson's ambitions were different from the start: simple folk melodies, such as he must have heard unaccompanied in his childhood, did not appeal to him. He envisioned a grand collaboration between British tunes and the arranging talents of the best foreign composers that money could buy. Not too much money, mind: he was a typically thrifty Scot and shrewd businessman.

Thomson first recruited Ignaz Pleyel to his cause (between 1791 and 1797); then Leopold Kozeluch (1797 to 1809) and then no less a luminary than Josef Haydn (between 1799 and 1804). Haydn's arrangements are described as being for voice and piano trio, but the music for violin and cello derives from the two staves of the very simple piano part. The ageing composer seems to have done the minimum of work and he contributed far more to the song repertoire with his English Canzonets, which were composed earlier during his two London visits. The high point of Thomson's edition was his collaboration with Ludwig van Beethoven between about 1803 and 1820 (after this there were brief dealings with J.N. Hummel and Carl Maria von Weber). The resonance in music-loving Britain of the names of Haydn and Beethoven was enormous; this seemed to be a way of making money out of their reputations without requiring the public to sit through interminable piano sonatas or symphonies. Thomson was a man with a mission, but he was also a businessman. Promoting Beethoven as a setter of folksongs with *comprehensible English texts* (an important point this in a musical world where Italian arias held sway) must have felt like stumbling on the idea of using Pavarotti as a musical mascot for the World Cup. In actual fact Thomson spent a lot of his own money on this project, and never managed to recoup his outlay. Indeed, it is touching to see how his love of this musical project gradually overtook financial considerations.

For the enlisted composers this eccentric idea was purely a commercial proposition; it is well known that Beethoven treated these tasks as hack work and grumbled a good deal about his dealings with Thomson. Nevertheless he was a great composer whose *amour propre* prevented him from delivering music below a certain standard. 'So neat a professional job … that they summon admiration like a well-baked apple' is how another Thomson, the American Virgil of that name, described these arrangements in 1970.[1] It is Beethoven's work in this field, rather than that of the other composers, that has survived and is occasionally to be heard on the concert platform of today. Thomson sent Beethoven the melodies as single vocal lines, requesting arrangements of the music mainly for piano trio, with introductions and postludes. Thomson was rewarded by music of much greater richness and invention than Haydn's arrangements; Beethoven's pieces were fully worked-out and made a charming effect. An added advantage was that the variety of Beethoven's vocal requirements (the settings are cast as vocal duets and trios as well as solos) allowed for music-making in which all the family could participate. The chief source of friction between Thomson and Beethoven was that the commissioned arrangements should be of only moderate difficulty; this was important for Thomson's market, but the Scotsman's notion of what was difficult constricted Beethoven's creativity and annoyed him greatly. These were two very stubborn men.

Beethoven also needed more information than he was given in order to do his best. He begged Thomson to send him the texts of the poems with their many strophes of varied mood and meaning; Beethoven was an experienced lieder composer and knew the importance of the words. These requests fell on deaf ears; Thomson was seemingly unaware of how the finer points of a poem could influence its musical setting. Considering that Beethoven set

1. In the introduction to H. Haufrecht, *Folk Songs in Settings by Master Composers* (Da Capo Press, 1977).

most of these songs 'blind' (aided by vocal lines and titles only) it is astonishing that his elaborations and arrangements (some 132 of them all in all) are as interesting and effective as they are. As one goes through the various collections of pieces there are innumerable felicitous touches, particularly when Beethoven has taken the trouble to depict the character of the music by translating the tune's title and capturing a general mood. The main source of awkwardness in this music is the result of forcing the modal lilt of many of these tunes into the major–minor tonality of the Viennese classical period.

Thomson was completely unconcerned with authenticity. If a tune had words attached to it that were unsuitably bawdy he simply arranged for new ones from the best poets of the time – Robert Burns, Sir Walter Scott, James Hogg, Joanna Baillie. There were naturally occasions when a new piece of music was so unsuitable for the traditional words that new ones had to be provided. George Thomson was a puritanical bowdleriser, but he was no folksong purist; he was mainly concerned with the music's melodic and harmonic charm. Reverence for the well-spring of melody that had sprung from Britain's soil, and from its working class, was never an issue. In fact the tunes themselves had come from a motley background: they were sometimes of genuine folk origin, but were often new compositions in a pastiche of folksong style. At that time nobody seemed to mind, and it was Thomson's lack of care in this direction, as well as the shotgun marriage between British melody and Viennese harmony, which eventually rendered his collections obsolete as far as serious scholarship was concerned. His assembled collections were soon regarded as curiosities rather than abiding classics.

A hundred years later, at the turn of the next century (the nineteenth into the twentieth), folk music, that long-ignored Cinderella, was about to go to the ball escorted by a number of young compositional princes. Britain was an important centre of a folksong revival, and this time Europe had provided an important impetus. Brahms's interest in folksong and the folk music of the Austro-Hungarian empire (gypsy music and the songs of Dvořák, which owe much to the folk tradition and Brahms's encouragement) had made the genre respectable. Rustically heartfelt music was an acceptable novelty in the drawing rooms of the cultured music lover, and raw and exciting tunes were tolerated in a spirit of ethnic broad-mindedness. There had been students of folk music for many years, specialists largely ignored by mainstream composers, but this was set to change. Tchaikovsky arranged folk melodies, while Debussy and the Russian 'Five' claimed that their whole ethos was based on a respect for the inflections of their home languages. Because the melody of folk music springs spontaneously from language, serious composers began to take an earthier interest in the medium. The stage was then set for the enthusiastic reception of the work of Kodály, Bartók, Janáček and many other composers who became absorbed in this aspect of musical history. This was indeed a new cultural theme for a new century. The Scandinavians (particularly composers such as Grieg and his followers) were increasingly aware of the treasure trove of beautiful melody that was part of their heritage. The French had long been examining their patrimony; as in other countries, it took a little time for practising composers to catch up with the scholarship of the experts.

The same was true in Britain. One of the most important people in the British folksong movement was Cecil Sharp, who was born exactly 44 years before Britten – on 22 November 1859 (he died in 1924). In 1903 Sharp heard a gardener singing 'The Seeds of Love' while mowing the lawn. This event changed his life, and henceforth he devoted his time to the collection of songs and dances in a period when it was still possible to go into the country and approach workers with a request for songs from their 'repertoire'. Sharp was amazingly industrious: he collected over 4,000 folksongs (notating them by hand) and not only from this country (he was one of the earliest students of Appalachian folksong in America). He published 1,118 folk melodies and wrote 501 accompaniments. The sad thing about this important personage was that he was no composer and had little dramatic flair. His arrangements are dull, and the great value of his musicological achievements has been undermined by this untiring worthiness. One could always argue that it was not the business of folksong (essentially an unaccompanied medium) to have 'interesting' accompaniments, and the devotees of Sharp revelled in the plainness (another means of measuring authenticity) of his legacy.

Sharp was by no means the only collector in the field. The Australian Percy Grainger (1882–1961) came to Britain in 1901. He was a busy folksong collector only a few years after Sharp, but he used a recording machine in order to capture the actual voices of his folk singers, many of whom he took the trouble to promote in his publications as unsung heroes of great nobility and dignity. It is wonderful to think of that young man, his recording contraption under his arm, approaching a farm worker in a Lincolnshire field and asking him if he knew any songs. Leaning on his hoe the labourer would comply with a stream of memorable melody matched to words as haunting as any that might have been written by that poet of the moment, Mr Yeats. It is impossible not to like Grainger, with his bright good looks and boyish enthusiasm (these qualities appealed to composers like Grieg and Delius). In turn, Britten was delighted by Grainger's achievement; he conducted a recorded 'Salute to Percy Grainger' on the Decca label

2. Decca SXL 6410.
3 Decca SXL 6872.

in the 1970s[2] and supervised another such disc when he was no longer able to conduct.[3]

Grainger was of course an original in every sense, and he composed much original music which is nothing to do with real folk music, however 'folkish' it may sound. But when he came to music he had actually transcribed himself he strove for painful accuracy, including attempts to notate phonetically the accents and dialects of the singers. The music still to be heard on Grainger's primitive recordings is completely different from the four-square, smoothed-out Cecil Sharp manner: accordingly, in Grainger's densely annotated scores we encounter songs that change time signature and metre in a meticulous, if somewhat eccentric, effort to capture the rhythmic freedom and rubato of those early singers. One of these was the venerable Mr Joseph Taylor: to hear that voice crackling over the space of a hundred years as he sings 'The Sprig of Thyme' is to be in touch with an aspect of British rural life that is dead forever. Grainger seemingly found this music at the very last possible moment in history: it is this that makes these recordings, and Grainger's transcriptions of them, sometimes unbearably poignant.

Britten's folksong settings have often been compared to Grainger's. It was certainly his admiration for the Grainger arrangements that gave Britten the confidence to make settings of his own, but the two men could not have approached this hallowed subject (and mine field) more differently. Grainger was obsessed with reproducing on the page what he had heard from his sources. He also provides a riot of harmony, but the contours of the original song, its essential dramatic conception, were seldom altered by the accompaniment, however rich in chromatic embellishment. Britten, unlike Grainger, was an opera composer, and he was far more adventurous in terms of his *mise-en-scène*, at the same time as writing music which usually made less virtuosic demands on its accompanists. By the time he came to arrange his folksong settings it was far too late to discover much of importance that was new by going out on field trips. Although some dedicated collectors such as Douglas and Peter Kennedy and A.L. Lloyd continued to discover new songs well into the post-war years, Britten was content to use songs amassed by others. Britten makes of his folksong settings a lighter thing than his older contemporaries: he is not awed by the music's provenance and he too turns to Cecil Sharp on occasion as his source. Britten's collections are surely not meant for the folksong expert, they are rather a gift, and an important one, to the recitalist. This seems to me (I refer back to my comments in Lecture 2) another example of a type of subversion – in this case of an old-fashioned, rather tweedy English tradition with lots of adherents who would have hated Britten and

66

all his doings as a matter of course. In making these settings (which included songs from France and Ireland, Scotland and Wales) Britten was refusing to accept anyone else's definition of what constituted loyalty to England, or love of its musical traditions.

With Britten we have come full circle to how folksong arrangement began in Britain in the time of George Thomson: this is an oddly similar meeting of the old and new, the rustic and the ultra-sophisticated, the conjoining of song-singing yokel and the genius composer. After exhausting his list of European contacts George Thomson had turned to British composers such as Henry Bishop and G.F. Graham; but there was no one of Britten's talent to finish the project in a way that would have improved on Beethoven. For Thomson it was acceptable, indeed it was *required*, that Beethoven's own musical ideas should entwine with the British melody and lyrics to make an international product, an art song out of an old melody – perhaps Thomson would have said a silk purse out of a sow's ear, seeing that pigs, impeccably rural creatures, must have heard many a swineherd's song in their time. Some of Thomson's contemporaries were already complaining about this awkward mixing of town and country – Vienna and, say, Lincolnshire – and there has never been a shortage of people who have bemoaned the supposed damage done to folksong by Britten's 'arty' settings. In reply to this I would say that one can permanently damage or deface the *Mona Lisa*; however, any piece of music that is written down survives any performance to live another day. If one hates the Britten folksong arrangements one can surely go back to the originals without any difficulty. I sometimes wonder, though, how many of Britten's detractors have taken the trouble to do just that …

Yes, these Britten folksongs *are* arty (in a way that Grainger's are not), and that's the fun of them. They were written to end Pears's and Britten's own recitals – a dessert course, if you like, to an evening's musical repast. These are not so much arrangements as 'liederisations' – which is why I insist on Britten's unlikely historical connection with Beethoven and George Thomson in this regard. I would venture to say that no composer who had not actually played many Schubert accompaniments (as Britten did) could have created these arrangements. Almost all the songs are strophic like many of Schubert's great songs. Almost all the accompaniments are based – as in Schubert – on a single pianistic motif which somehow encapsulates the mood of the whole, and which is capable of infinite modification and expansion in the interest of textual illustration. It is these accompanimental motifs (think of the rippling sextuplets in Schubert's 'Die Forelle' or Britten's ☉ 'The Miller of Dee') which give the songs their ☉ **CD1, track 15**

67

unity and draw the strands together. The developing of the accompanimental oak from the musical cells of tiny acorns is part of the economy and discipline, the self-imposed limits, that characterise both Schubert and Britten. And of course there are also times, in the narrative songs in particular, when we are aware that Britten is a born opera composer: a number of these arrangements are conceived, in the Italian sense, as dramatic *scene*. Britten makes these work with the minimum of fuss and the most telling effect, and we are scarcely aware how far beyond the skills of most composers a similar achievement would be.

Folksong arrangements, Volume I (1941–42)

(i) In placing 'The Salley Gardens' at the beginning of this selection Britten begins with a crossover piece – half folksong, half art song. Yeats's poem had been set by many composers – Martin Shaw, Ivor Gurney, John Ireland, for example – and cannot pass for a true folk text no matter how profoundly the words are tinged with Celtic magic. The idea of uniting Yeats's poem with this particular folk melody (the air known as 'The Maids of Mourne Shore') was that of the Northern Irish composer Herbert Hughes. His 'Down by the Sally Gardens' (note the different title and spelling) was published in 1909 as part of *Irish Country Songs* Volume 1. Britten found it there in the key of D flat; he transposed it up to G flat, transferring the vocal line into the starry-bright regions of Pears's voice. Hughes's busy accompaniment in roving quavers was replaced by a throbbing bank of softly pulsating chords, which seem scarcely to change. The effect is of a moment of time captured and preserved in a web of nostalgic memory. The left hand insinuates a mournful counter-melody in the bass – sadness, not tragedy, is evoked here. The wistfulness of the older man (who remembers his own youth and the loss of the love of his life) is softened by the passage of many years. It is the passing of time, sand slowly sifting in the hourglass (an image from *Death in Venice* incidentally) that is masterfully suggested by these seemingly static, yet inscrutably moving, quavers. I know of only one other English song as gently, yet achingly, regretful as this, and that is Gerald Finzi's 'Lizbie Brown' on a similar theme of love lost through youthful ineptitude. In 'The Salley Gardens' the flattening of harmony at the final 'young and *foolish*' is a Schubertian masterstroke. It seems unfair, however, that Hughes's role in uniting this tune with this poem is never really acknowledged.

(ii) 'Little Sir William' is a strange follow-up to 'The Salley Gardens' – it is a narrative poem about the murder of a schoolboy. It is interesting to note that this was composed at about the same time as Britten was working on

Peter Grimes – an opera that features an abused apprentice who is also (arguably) killed by cruelty. The scenario brings to mind the enormities of the schoolmaster Wackford Squeers (and his wife) in Dickens's *Nicholas Nickelby* largely because the villainess murderer of 'little Sir William' is named as a 'school wife'. In the first edition of this work we read the infinitely more controversial 'Jew-wife' – words that have been changed in every edition since.[4] There is a certain amount of anti-Semitism in old English folk poetry, but the change in sensitivity to this fact is illustrated by the difference in attitude to words such as these between 1942 (when the book of folksongs was published in a war-time edition) and following the public's awareness of the Holocaust (see Lecture 5 in this series, which discusses the composer's visit to Belsen in 1945, shortly after the camp's liberation). The conversation of the murdered boy's ghost with his mother seems uncannily prophetic of the central tragedy of Britten's first church opera, *Curlew River* (1964).

⊙ (iii) 'The Bonny Earl o' Moray' is an amazingly powerful lament at the same time as being an evocation of Scottish pomp and ceremony. The bagpipe-like drone in the bass, open fifths decorated by acciaccaturas, provides a sense of doom and heavy-hearted grandeur. This old traditional ballad has many interpretations and has been much discussed. The Queen referred to is Mary Queen of Scots, and the bonny Earl was her illegitimate half-brother James Stewart (c.1531–70). If he had been born in wedlock he, not Mary, would have been crowned as monarch of Scotland. The Catholic queen was very fond of her Protestant brother but, swayed by his own ambition, he betrayed her on more than one occasion. He was killed by one of Mary's supporters as he rode through Linlithgow. It is astonishing how Britten establishes a mourning mood, sufficiently imposing to suggest the processional of a state funeral, using the most slender musical means.

⊙ (iv) 'O Can ye Sew Cushions?'. This slender little lullaby has a marvellous melody. It is one of the pieces that was arranged by Haydn. Britten uses it as a Scottish pendant to 'The Bonny Earl o' Moray' and finds a delightfully simple two-against-three figure in the weaving accompaniment that vividly suggests the act of sewing while singing to a baby. Here is the Britten who five years later would set an entire set of such beguiling little pieces aimed at singing children to sleep – *A Charm of Lullabies*.

(v) 'The Trees they Grow so High' is unique in Britten's corpus of arranged folksongs in that it begins completely unaccompanied. Perhaps this allows

4. Despite this song's Somerset origin, the story of Saint William of Norwich comes from East Anglia. Last seen alive on the Monday of Holy Week 1144, the ritually murdered body of William, a twelve-year-old tanner's apprentice, was found in Thorpe Wood near Norwich, on the Good Friday. The body was eventually removed to the monk's cemetery at the cathedral. Within a few years, miracles were claimed and William's body was removed first to the Chapter House in 1150 and finally to the Jesus Chapel in the cathedral in 1151 where, sanctified, it became the focus of pilgrimage until after the Reformation, and was commemorated in other local churches. Not unusually for the twelfth century, the Jewish community was blamed for the murder with no basis of evidence beyond suspicion fuelled by anti-Semitism.

us to hear the beauties of a haunting little tune without any pianistic distraction, but it is hardly typical of this composer. When the piano writing begins (on the twenty-third bar) there is none of Britten's adept word-pointing, and the whole piece seems rather impersonal – that is at first glance. The influence of Percy Grainger seems strong here: the piano steals in on a single dotted minim and provides only the most discrete touches of harmony and rhythmic interest, which seem instrumentally, rather than textually, inspired. Single white notes cede to black, and the texture gradually becomes more energetic, as if other instruments were joining one by one to make a larger ensemble. Any opera-style characterisations are avoided, although it is true that the youthful energy of the 'bonny boy' is implied by pianistic rhythms that skip and jump; as he reaches the age of sixteen the accompaniment grows more rollicking and strident, but this is still more typical of Grainger than of Britten.

The words are supposedly sung by a girl (although, in the performance of folksong, such lieder-like rules of gender propriety scarcely apply). Her father has insisted on her engagement to a very young man who is the subject of the song; four or five hundred years ago children of nine or ten were betrothed in arranged marriages. The girl, who seems older, waits for her husband, denied access to him when he is still a boy. He marries her at sixteen, is a father at seventeen, and dies at eighteen, leaving her with child. At news of his death, the piano's right-hand quavers toll like church bells, chords in the treble stave that overshadow left-hand dotted minims as if tracing the slope of a burial mound.

These details are interesting enough, but the achievement of this song is less in the detail than in its charting of the broad arc of a human life through music. The nature imagery of trees – the proliferation of foliage through an ever-burgeoning accompaniment – is at the heart of the song. The boy begins life as a seed that grows into a shrub, then a tree; eventually he is in full flower, and finally, subject to the law of seasons, withers away in death. Thus the centre of the song is fully harmonised, while the beginning of his life (as if in utero), and after his death, are bare of accompaniment. And now the life-cycle will continue with a new life, the young man's son. The sheer inscrutability of that process of living and dying is perhaps what gives the song its impetus as well as its aura of slightly impersonal inevitability.

The song is dedicated to a friend of Britten's during his sojourn in America – Bobby Rothman, a teenager at the time. Even as early as this in the composer's career the pain of a Tadzio–Aschenbach scenario, particularly if the song is performed by a male voice, is reflected in the lines:

I called for my true love, but they would not let him come,
All because he was a young boy and growing.

(vi) 'The Ash Grove'. Up till now in this set of songs there is rather little to which a traditional folksong enthusiast might object. But here we have a prime example of the sort of setting which enraged the conservative listener, and delighted the admirer of Britten's music. The song which has been heartily sung time without number by many a Welsh choir (accompanied by unexceptional harmonies) is here made to seem moonstruck and anything but hearty. The bluebells are actually heard to chime in the piano writing; the impassioned song of the blackbird in throbbing right-hand triplets is brief, but almost worthy of Messiaen's ornithological excursions. The piano's counter-melody to the vocal line, a descant which summons a surprising amount of pathos, suggests the singer's disturbed state of mind. For some detractors of this music passages like these simply seemed a perverse display of wrong-note harmonies; but with the right performers this song makes the listener re-evaluate the melody and listen beyond the clichés of hundreds of uninspired choral performances.

⊙ (vii) 'Oliver Cromwell'. This is a favourite way to end a recital ('If you ⊙ **CD1, track 14** want any more you can sing it yourself!'). It goes at quite 'a lick', and many a singer has been caught up by the demands of its diction. Some years ago at the Wigmore Hall (it was a live broadcast) Dame Margaret Price got the words wrong and, without thinking, came out with an expletive ('S**T!') before she realised where she was. She expressed such an honest (and understandable) frustration that the audience howled with laughter and clapped in empathy. As for the text of the song, it seems a curious thing in the first place to need reassurance that 'Oliver Cromwell is buried and dead'; his grave was dug up after the Restoration and the return of Charles II. The new king ordered that all the corpses of the regicides responsible for the death of his father Charles I should be subject to ritual execution. Cromwell's remains were hung, drawn and quartered, but for the superstitious there was a considerable likelihood that he would be able to return to haunt his detractors. The galumphing triplets of the accompaniment suggest the possibility of just such a grotesque happening. On another level, the assurance that Cromwell, Lord Protector, puritan and killjoy, was dead signifies a lively future: it was his removal that ushered in the glorious age of Purcell. In the glee of this music Britten seems to be prophesying the arrival of the new Elizabethans. Perhaps he is obliquely informing us that there is a new age of joy and creativity ahead, that the old English puritanical attitudes and superstitions are being surmounted. The way is clear for a new post-war epoch free of dour moralistic attitudes.

Folksong arrangements, Volume III (1945–46)

Britten's second volume of folksongs was devoted to French settings (see Lecture 2). When he returned to British folk music after the appearance of *Peter Grimes* his obligations as a recitalist were ever increasing. The songs from the first book had been comprehensively aired and now new concert programmes had to be devised for recitals that were given with Pears (and others, like the great soprano Joan Cross, the first Ellen Orford) under the auspices of the English Opera Group.

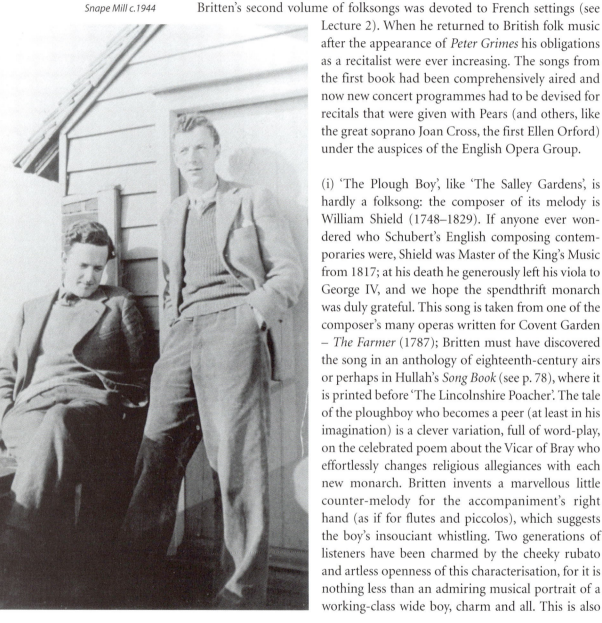

Britten and Pears at Snape Mill c.1944

(i) 'The Plough Boy', like 'The Salley Gardens', is hardly a folksong: the composer of its melody is William Shield (1748–1829). If anyone ever wondered who Schubert's English composing contemporaries were, Shield was Master of the King's Music from 1817; at his death he generously left his viola to George IV, and we hope the spendthrift monarch was duly grateful. This song is taken from one of the composer's many operas written for Covent Garden – *The Farmer* (1787); Britten must have discovered the song in an anthology of eighteenth-century airs or perhaps in Hullah's *Song Book* (see p. 78), where it is printed before 'The Lincolnshire Poacher'. The tale of the ploughboy who becomes a peer (at least in his imagination) is a clever variation, full of word-play, on the celebrated poem about the Vicar of Bray who effortlessly changes religious allegiances with each new monarch. Britten invents a marvellous little counter-melody for the accompaniment's right hand (as if for flutes and piccolos), which suggests the boy's insouciant whistling. Two generations of listeners have been charmed by the cheeky rubato and artless openness of this characterisation, for it is nothing less than an admiring musical portrait of a working-class wide boy, charm and all. This is also

72

typical of Britten's lifelong sympathy for children and their music-making. This music is closely related to another piece by Britten which is almost exactly contemporary: this is 'The Driving Boy' from the *Spring Symphony*, when the composer entwines two poems by George Peele and John Clare. Clare's 'happy, dirty, driving boy', a cousin of the ploughboy, burst out 'in fits of song' as he cracks his whip; he is also a whistler and Britten makes delighted musical use of this fact.

(ii) 'There's None to Soothe' was taken from the *Song Book* (1866) of John Hullah (1812–84), a music educationalist who assembled various vocal anthologies. As in 'O Can ye Sew Cushions?' Britten makes use of the conflict of two rhythms between the hands – three beats in the right, and two in the left. The beautiful melody, quintessentially Scottish, is underpinned by a bass line which drags its feet for two bars (rocking slowly between D flat and E flat) before making an ascent in dotted crotchets up the stave (it reaches C flat, the flattened seventh of the scale) and then, step by step, moves down again. This is the arrangement's framework and very skilfully built it is too – a peculiarly Brittenian mix of simplicity, economy and the art that conceals art.

(iii) 'Sweet Polly Oliver' is the sort of ditty that countless English children (and colonial ones in my case) were made to sing in school. Perhaps it is for this reason – childhood sentimentality – that it is often quoted as a particularly awful example of Britten's folksong 'abuse'. In actual fact it is one of the composer's best arrangements. Whenever there is an unfolding story, such as here, Britten relishes the chance to give the music a dramatic context. Thus 'Polly Oliver' is presented as a miniature dramatic opera in five scenes. The idea of Polly's wandering thoughts as she lies 'musing in bed', as well as her contrary nature in not heeding her parents' dictates, is wonderfully depicted by the way Britten makes of most of this music a deliberately awkward canon between voice and piano. In the second strophe a staccato left hand depicts Polly's exit on tiptoe from her home – here the canon suggests the furtive plotting and intrigue that Polly needs to make a success of her disguise. Suddenly, in the third verse, we find ourselves on the sergeant's parade ground. The heavy left hand, and the first appearance of strutting right-hand chords, is a marvellous sketch of military pomposity. The fourth, the scene at the bed-side of Polly's sick lover, is remarkable for how few notes Britten needs to suggest (a) grave illness; (b) Polly's nervous solicitude; (c) the shaking of the doctor's head (a simple drooping phrase that speaks volumes); and (d) the return to health (the direction of those drooping phrases is reversed – they now ascend the stave). This is all achieved with a transparency and ease that one might call Mozartian. The canon of the concluding verse (now at the fourth above) is the perfect means of suggesting the outpouring of Polly's feelings as she confides in the kind doctor. The song's brief coda even manages to suggest the joy and ceremonial of the marriage that marks the story's happy outcome.

This song is so taken for granted that it may be necessary to point out its subtext as far as Britten is concerned. Just as important as the story of Polly *en travesti*, is the idea of the young soldier's devoted love for his captain, a fact that is generously acknowledged by the doctor who sees that Polly has nursed him back to life – 'You have cherished him as if you were his wife'. Quite so, and Britten might have said the same about Pears (or Pears may have said the same about him) over many years in terms of their own relationship. Polly fools the world by going into disguise to nurse her true love; in Britain of the 1930s and 1940s thousands of similarly noble relationships were forced to be in another kind of permanent disguise. And there is one further resonance that is easy to miss: that doctor shaking his head, the terrified face of Polly believing she has lost her beloved captain. As far-fetched as it must seem one can hear here pre-echoes of the *War Requiem*: think of the anguish of 'Move him into the sun' as a young soldier hopelessly attempts to revive a mortally wounded comrade whom he cannot hope to nurse back to life. In just this way one finds in this composer's music a relatively small catalogue of scenarios (here a sympathy for soldiers and those who have loved and lost them) constantly re-visited in different, and unexpected, ways.

⊙ **CD1, track 15** ⊙ (iv) 'The Miller of Dee' is another item from Hullah's *Song Book*. The song is awash with deliberately wrong notes and sharp jabbing accents, which would make the Sharp purist wince. But the point is that the misanthropic character of the miller requires just these harmonies, just this type of grating ingratitude represented by musical discord. The poem has the same single-minded belligerence as the Burns poem 'Naebody', which Schumann set as 'Niemand' in his *Myrthen* Op. 25. The sound of the turning mill-wheel in 6/8 owes something to 'Am Feierabend' from Schubert's *Die schöne Müllerin*, as well as the anguish of 'Gretchen am Spinnrade'. Here is ample evidence of the influence of the lieder interests of Britten at this period: the Danube and the Dee are here conjoined by his genius. It is notable that song was also one of Beethoven's most successful arrangements for George Thomson (WoO No. 5, 1814–15). In this case it is the repetitive, grinding cello line that characterises the miller's cheerless occupation.

(v) 'The Foggy, Foggy Dew'. Peter Pears told me of his elderly uncle who became almost apoplectic with rage on hearing a wireless performance of his nephew singing this 'thoroughly immoral' song (it included the confessional words 'Now I am a bachelor and live with my son'). Such a reaction to man and woman living out of wedlock was common enough then: now one simply has to say '*autre temps, autre moeurs*'. Britten, like any decent song composer, had scanned the first verse for any inspiring ideas regarding the setting. His eyes alighted on the words 'worked at the weaver's trade'. Accordingly the most marvellous accompaniment is invented which suggests the act of weaving. Is it needle pulling through material that we hear with each of these right-hand staccatos, or perhaps the shuffling of a loom (see also ' O Can Ye Sew Cushions?' in Book I)? The two-against-three of the third bar of the introduction (and each subsequent interlude) depicts the meshing of two different threads of music, weaving rendered into pianistic terms. Even the marking of the song – 'Slow and regular' – seems to refer to the requirements of a serious trade. It is a miracle how Britten manages to convey the wily licentiousness of the narrator – an unrepentant sensualist and proud father; those *staccati* chords on the second and fourth beat of every bar (each launched by a left-hand acciaccatura) bring a smile to the face, as if these laugh-lines encompassed winks of complicity. It is little wonder that Pears's uncle was outraged: this music *sounds* unbelievably naughty although it is hard to analyse why. Britten himself had an idiosyncratically piquant way of playing this accompaniment, which has never been equalled. The colour he achieved on those second and fourth beats must be heard by any student who wants to attempt the piece. Pears is also wonderful here in suggesting sweet and gentle memories of a seduction long ago (*she* seduced *him*, he claims) yet he makes us realise that 'there is life in the old boy yet!' The euphemistic explanation ('just to keep her from the foggy, foggy dew') seems English dissembling at its most elegantly mischievous.

(vi) 'O Waly, Waly'. With this song Britten once again displays the full measure of his genius. Cecil Sharp made an arrangement of this song from Somerset; it has more notes than Britten's, but less inspiration. Britten takes the tune from Sharp but allows much of the vocal line to float free; each bar is launched by a simple rocking motif that establishes the ebb and flow of a slow barcarolle (as befits a rowing song with the opening words 'the water is wide'). This motif, changing harmonically in gradual but inexorable stages, makes something hypnotic of this music. What makes this arrangement particularly memorable are the tiny modifications in these chords in the last verse – the flattened seventh that is subtly introduced on the word 'new', and the devastatingly simple yet haunting discord on the word 'cold'. How a composer can musically describe in a single bar the deterioration of a relationship and the barren loneliness that is the result of abandonment is impossible to explain – but Britten does just this here. 'O Waly, Waly' is one of the most famous, and most often sung, of his folksong arrangements, and with some justification.

(vii) 'Come you not from Newcastle?' Here is another item from the Hullah *Song Book*, and one which is one of the favourites of the canon: one always seems to think of it sung most persuasively by Kathleen Ferrier, who was a Lancastrian rather than a Geordie, but who had the right sense of humour. The direction 'Fast with spirit' sets the mood for a rollicking, syncopated accompaniment in 2/2 where a minim is placed between two crotchets. The

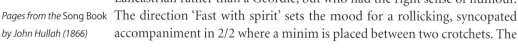

Pages from the Song Book *by John Hullah (1866)*

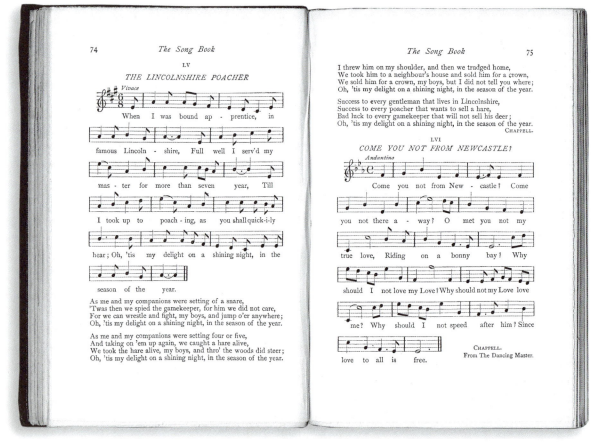

bass line accompaniment is a motif (F up to B flat, then down to the C below), which is repeated again and again – no less than 52 times, for as many bars as there are in the piece. In this folk passacaglia Britten's ingenuity is remarkably laconic: there are not many notes, certainly none too many. In the second strophe there is a marvellous dialogue between voice and piano where the vocal line waits for an echo from the accompaniment. The quizzical flattened inflection in the piano's harmony after the words 'true love' seems tellingly apt. Is this energetic search for the 'true love' the pursuit of the impossible by the rather too determined? One has the impression that one would not like to be in the pursued lover's shoes when she eventually catches up with him. For the final page Britten provides the aural equivalent of an optical illusion. Having asked her question the singer disappears down the road to Newcastle, horse and rider getting smaller as the note values of the vocal line get longer, and the sound of horses' hooves distant. An F major chord bringing the song to a full close occurs only at the very last possible moment; I wonder how many members of an audience realise that their smiles at this point are the result of unconsciously waiting for this moment of harmonic release?

Folksong arrangements, Volume V (1951–59)

(i) 'The Brisk Young Widow'. Once again Britten goes to Cecil Sharp for his material, just as Herbert Howells had gone to the same source and arranged this song in the early 1930s. Howells's arrangement is pleasing, and not without spirit, but it is Britten who has sought to make that word 'brisk' live much more vividly in terms of characterisation. He used a close and discordant canon between the hands to paint the sharp-tongued termagant who is the song's anti-heroine. Somehow or other in all this bustle the composer has managed to incorporate into this arrangement the sound of doors slamming in the faces of various would-be suitors. This widow is alarmingly energetic and likes things to be 'just so': we discern the good order of her house in the meticulously placed chords that punctuate an expanse of empty piano staves – these notes are placed at cadential points as if part of obsessive tidying-up. As we hear more about her appearance ('stout and tall' with 'fingers long and small') the fingery movement of those introductory quavers also seem part of the portrait – as if she herself were playing the spinet in a spotless parlour. The second verse brilliantly manages to suggest the diffidence of the courting farmer (the chords are marked 'heavy' and should be made to sound like the monosyllabic grunts of a man short on words and charm); in the fourth verse, after a stinging rebuff, he is roused to retaliatory eloquence to no effect. The successful suitor of the fifth verse is a 'sooty collier' – nothing like the rich man the widow has envisaged. Britten's accompaniment, an unctuous succession of pedalled crotchets, suggests that the collier, despite his crooked hat, is a smooth operator. The bass lines suggest deep, unaccountable stirrings of emotion on the part of the widow; the strength of this attraction across the social divide suggests a musical equivalent of the attraction of D.H. Lawrence's Lady Chatterley to the gamekeeper Mellors. This passage is embellished by a sudden accent in the piano writing (after the word 'swore'). This represents, no doubt, an expletive from the humiliated farmer who has lost out to a social inferior.

(ii) 'Sally in our Alley' was originally an air sung at Drury Lane on 20 May 1717 by Mrs Willis, who was dressed 'like a shoemaker's Prentice' as one contemporary notice had it. In this light the song has something in common with the *travesti* theme of 'Polly Oliver'. The composer was the immensely successful Henry Carey (1687–1743). Britten here elaborates the music of an earlier English composer (as he had with William Shield in 'The Plough Boy') rather than arranging a genuine folksong. Carey's upward musical inflections for the words 'Sally' and 'alley' is the musical key to Britten's arrangement which is pervaded with leaping intervals as if the whole accompaniment were secretly singing 'Sally' much of the time. There are five verses of which 1 and 2, then 3 and 4, are grouped in strophic pairs, with 5 as the coda. Between each of the verses there is a piano interlude original enough to startle the purists – semiquaver figurations, mainly in contrary motion, which clash in conflicting bi-tonalities. The first of these passages is marked 'freely'; between verses 2 and 3 there is a new variation on these ramblings, now marked 'more lively'; before verse 5 the interlude is marked forte and 'energetic'. These incremental changes of emphasis make us realise that the strictly disciplined apprentice's passion for his Sally is at bursting point by the end. This piano writing is remarkably appropriate for frustration mixed with longing – it simultaneously pushes and tugs.

For verse 5 ('My master and the neighbours all/Make game of me and Sally') the accompaniment is entirely made up of the rising 'Sally' motif as if constant taunts were being thrown from one end of the bass stave to the other end of the treble. This grouping of two quavers becomes so energetic that when the singer says that he would rather be 'A slave and row a galley' we have a ready-made rowing motif parting the musical waves as if under a slave dealer's whip. The last lines of the song are magical. Under the words 'I'll marry Sally' the same motif is heard in suddenly well-behaved semiquavers in an accompaniment that now winds down to a gentle and sweet conclusion. One of the joys of this idiosyncratic vocal line throughout the song has been the enormous leap of an eleventh (and a gently brushed high note on the word 'of') in the middle of the phrase 'She is the darling *of* my heart'. The penultimate phrase ('O then we'll wed and *then* we'll bed') calls for another high G in the tenor key. The pianissimo fervour of this leap on to 'then', followed by 'we'll bed', was a Pears speciality: in these few notes were enshrined a shining belief in an almost sacred consummation with the promise of long-awaited sensual delights. Those who heard this great artist will understand what I mean; for the younger generations not even fine recordings can fully convey his way with such passages where technical mastery (and I mean the *handling* of the voice rather than the more controversial intrinsic *sound* of it) seemed blended with the most tender humanity.

⊙ (iii) 'The Lincolnshire Poacher' is one of the merriest of Britten's folk- ⊙ **CD1, track 17** song settings. It is marked 'Boisterously'. This is the exception that proves the rule – a song in which Britten pushes aside his antipathy to bloodsports (see, for example, 'Tom Noddy' from the Walter de la Mare set *Tit for Tat*, discussed on p. 19) in favour of the merry japes of these laddish country folk cocking a snoot at authority. In this case the interests of badly treated humans win against the interests of the hunted hare – the same creature that is hauntingly mentioned in Britten's 'Canticle III' (1954) 'Still falls the rain' with the words 'the tears of the hunted hare'. This is proof, if any were needed, that Britten was never governed by any sense of consistently applied political correctness. The *segue* between this song and 'Sally in our Alley' is a cunning one. Ever the opera composer with a plot in mind, Britten seems to be suggesting with this juxtaposition that Sally's frustrated suitor is a poacher by night as a means of making money for the wedding: both songs' protagonists decry the tyranny of their masters. Here Britten seems to be in sympathy with the sad plight of indentured apprentices in the eighteenth century – the chimney sweepers (as in the Blake *Songs and Proverbs*) were oppressed in an even worse way. In 'Sally in our Alley' the master 'comes like any Turk and bangs me most severely' (on my advice Pears, born in 1910 and not *au courant* with how slang had evolved since Carey's time, changed this to '*beats* me most severely' for the performances we did together). In 'The Lincolnshire Poacher' the apprentice has served his time for a full seven years and has taken no pleasure in the experience.

The technique used here is one where layers of harmony, piling one on the other, reflect the exuberant and bare-faced cheek that governs the behaviour of the poacher and his mates. If these harmonisations are outrageous, so are the protagonist and his chums. The chugging rhythm continues throughout the song while prancing right-hand triplets provide an exuberant counter-melody to the vocal line. For the last verse this solo seems to have been conceived for the screech of the piccolo and Britten allows a whimsical wrong-note harmony to abound as if the whole poaching team were moonstruck (or perhaps the worse for wear after liberal doses of 'moonshine'). A key word in this setting is 'delight'. With a fine performance of this song few members of the audience can be in any doubt of the delighted exuberance felt by people who successfully break the law. Poachers flout the established laws of ownership, but they are nevertheless a part of country life. Perhaps homosexuals of the 1950s felt a similar pleasure in ignoring laws that failed to take into account the human needs of those who were the targets of establishment repression.

Britten and Pears at Glyndebourne, 1946

(iv) 'Early One Morning'. Here Britten enters the lists as a competitor to one of his idols – Percy Grainger himself. Grainger had a long-standing interest in this melody that went back to his teenage years. The final version of his setting is dated (with unusually wide parameters) 16 October 1901 to 4 August 1940. Grainger's sumptuous arrangement is very different from Britten's: it includes a twelve-bar introduction for the piano, and a coda where the voice sings a descant on 'Ah' while the piano meaningfully plays the melody in richly harmonised octaves.

By comparison Britten's setting is a model of classical purity. Grainger marks his song 'Slowly, anguished'; Britten's requirement is for a 'Gently flowing' mood. He is content to allow his music to speak for itself. Of course the distraught 'poor maiden' singing these words is the victim of a lying lover, but in verses 2 and 3 of Britten's song, the most understated mad scene ever, this anguish comes across without encouraging the singer to become musically distraught. The wandering quaver accompaniment of these two verses marvellously suggests mental imbalance in an eerie and aerial way – like an Ophelia in an underplayed production of *Hamlet*, and more succinct than any of Grainger's pointed chromatic twinges. Another song that comes to mind is Warlock's 'The Distracted Maid', the first of that composer's *Lillygay* cycle: a work that was in Peter Pears's repertory.

⊚ (v) 'Ca' the Yowes' has a wonderful melody, which was collected by Robert Burns himself in 1787.[5] Here the poem is 'Ca' the Ewes to the Knowes' (knowes are mounds or hillocks). The more verbally symmetrical version – 'Ca the Yowes to the Knowes' – dates from 1794. With a clever disposition of unexpected and subtle chords, which tellingly vary and intensify the accompanying harmony, Britten makes of this music something infinitely more profound than one could imagine. In the hands of a fine singer with a marvellous legato this can be one of the most haunting of all Britten's folksong settings.

⊚ **CD1, track 16**

5. Michael Tippett's Piano Sonata No. 1 (1936–38) uses the same melody as the basis for its rhapsodic slow movement.

The programme at the 2001 Britten festival was comprised of: **From Eight folksong arrangements for voice and harp**: 'Lord, I Married Me a Wife' (Trad.), 'Bugeilio'r Gwenith Gwyn' (Trad.), 'David of the White Rock' (Trad.); ***Moore's Irish Melodies***: 'Avenging and Bright', 'Sail on, Sail on', 'How Sweet the Answer', 'The Minstrel Boy', 'At the Mid Hour of Night', 'Rich and Rare', 'Dear Harp of my Country', 'Oft in the Stilly Night', 'The Last Rose of Summer', 'Oh! The Sight Entrancing'; **Folksongs with guitar** (Trad.): 'I Will Give my Love an Apple', 'Sailor-boy', 'Master Kilby', 'The Soldier and the Sailor', 'Bonny at Morn', 'The Shooting of his Dear'; **Folksongs posthumously published** (Trad.): 'The Crocodile', 'Pray Goody', 'Dink's Song', 'I Wonder as I Wander', 'Tom Bowling', 'The Deaf Woman's Courtship', 'Soldier, Won't you Marry Me?'. NB Only those folksongs that were performed at the 2001 festival are discussed in this lecture

Lecture 4

A miscellany of folksongs

In previous lectures I have considered Britten's folksong arrangements as they are seldom performed – in complete books, in their published order, and with a stylistic (and sometimes thematic) logic of their own. Most of the collections so far considered (Volumes I, III and V) offer a mixture of English, Scottish and Welsh music. Britten had no national agenda to promote here: his arrangements were not made to prove a parochial or partisan point about the musical superiority of any part of the British Isles; rather he was interested in finding beautiful melodies with English texts that would be useful in a recital context once he had adapted them to his purposes. They were all more or less of folk origin (I say 'more or less' because, as we have seen, he included arrangements of works by composers such as Shield and Carey under this heading, and later in this lecture we will consider a song by Charles Dibdin).

The three books of British folksongs were written for Britten's recitals with Peter Pears. The composer always had very strong feelings about all his performers, not just his chosen tenor. The artists who took central roles in his operas were of more than one generation: some died in mid-career like Kathleen Ferrier and, much later, Jennifer Vyvyan; others retired – for example Joan Cross, Nancy Evans and Margaret Ritchie – and were replaced by the younger generation of Heather Harper, Janet Baker and so on. Alfred Deller and James Bowman, counter-tenors of markedly opposite temperaments, both played Oberon (in *A Midsummer Night's Dream*); their different ways with the role reflected changing vocal fashions and a definite change in the ease with which counter-tenors took to the operatic stage. One is not really aware of a favoured baritone among Britten singers until the emergence of John Shirley-Quirk; no bass ever really replaced Owen Brannigan. From this rather selective list, only a handful of the many

Opposite: Britten and Pears, mid-1950s

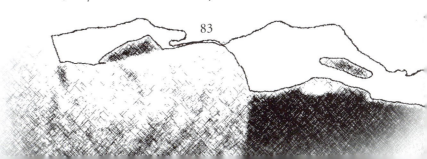

singers who peopled Britten's life, it can be seen that this composer quite simply responded to artists wherever and whenever he found sympathetic personalities for whom he could create musical possibilities.

Britten also had very determined opinions regarding instrumentalists. His admiration of Russian precision and virtuosity is discussed in Lecture 7. Amongst English pianists he valued most his old friend Clifford Curzon. His work with the English Chamber Orchestra meant that he had a long working relationship with many distinguished players, people who worked with him on his chamber operas such as the clarinettist Thea King, the double-bass player Adrian Beers and the percussionist James Blades, to name three at random across the orchestral seating plan.

Britten's music for harp is a very special case. It arose from his admiration for the work of Osian Ellis, the great harpist (b. 1928), who is also an accomplished composer, singer, and authority on Welsh folk music. Ellis featured high on the list of Britten's (and Pears's) chosen performers. The beautiful harp part of *A Midsummer Night's Dream* was written for Osian Ellis, as were the harp parts of the *War Requiem* and the three church parables. For the Aldeburgh Festival of 1969 Britten wrote a Suite for Harp. Osian Ellis's emergence as a regular accompanist of Peter Pears in recital

*Peter Pears
and Osian Ellis*

was a result of the composer's illness. The stroke Britten suffered during major heart surgery meant that in the last years of his life he was no longer able to accompany Pears, which left the tenor without a regular recital partner when still at the height of his powers (those of us who were there in the early 70s rejoiced in the glorious Indian summer of his career). In an attempt to recycle his performing options Pears established a duo with the young American pianist Murray Perahia; but it was impossible, and probably too painful, to attempt to replace Britten at the piano permanently. It was above all Osian Ellis who stepped into the breach. The folk settings with harp, as well as *A Birthday Hansel* (the Burns cycle written in

84

1975 in honour of the Queen Mother), were composed for this newly established duo. Hearing this music we realise what a wonderful accompaniment the harp is for the voice, how rich it is, how varied in colour. Unlike the piano-accompanied repertoire there is never a balance problem.

Eight folksong arrangements for voice and harp (1976)

These settings for voice and harp date from the last year of Britten's life. The dolorous and hen-pecked 'Lord, I Married Me a Wife' seems to come full circle from the very young Britten's setting of Longfellow's *Beware!*, with its warning note against dangerous women. It is notable that this is not an English folksong at all, but an arrangement from North Carolina collected by Cecil Sharp. The second song in the set ('She's Like the Swallow') is from Newfoundland, and the seventh ('The False Knight Upon the Road') is from the Southern Appalachians, also collected by Sharp. Also in this collection are two Welsh texts, arranged by Britten as a tribute to Osian Ellis and his nationality: both of these are an important part of Welsh musical tradition and Pears must have benefited from Ellis's advice as regards phrasing and style. It was Ellis himself who provided words for a second verse of 'David of the White Rock'. The music for these eight settings is charming enough and, as ever, skilful in terms of its efficacy. One must remember, however, that at this time any composition from the mortally ill composer was the result of iron will and determination. If we fail to hear in these arrangements the magic that was generated when the composer wrote music for his beloved partner and himself to perform, their very existence is a measure of his devotion to Pears, and Britten's concern for his friend's ongoing career after his own death. The most remarkable thing about these slender songs is that they were written at all.

In two of this group of songs (unofficially Britten's Volume VII), the composer allowed the printing of the Welsh text beneath the English for those (unlike Peter Pears) who were able to sing it. This express admiration of Celtic culture was nothing new. It is notable that 'The Salley Gardens', the very first song in Volume I, and probably the most famous of Britten's arrangements, is an *Irish* melody put together with a poem by the great Irish poet W.B. Yeats. Even if by chance, this underlines the fact that Irish music has always been something of a special case in the history of folksong arrangement. It is a country (one speaks of a time long before partition) that has always been exceptionally rich in folklore and its musical equivalents. George Thomson of Edinburgh had no doubt of its importance and promoted Irish folksongs with relish (many of the Beethoven sets are headed *Irische Lieder*). Thomas Moore himself (of whom more anon) in his

'Advertisement' to the Stevenson arrangements of the *Irish Melodies*, talks of music being 'the only talent for which our English neighbours ever deigned to allow us any credit'. It has always been acknowledged that the Emerald Isle has a culture that places folk music and poetry on an elevated footing where the magical and the mystical are entwined in a single poetic impulse. The songs of Erin's minstrels cut a wide swathe between depths of political oppression and flights of fantastical humour. Because of the particular tuning of the Irish harp, most violent of passions can suddenly modulate into the most abject repentance, or the lightest of laughter. The older form of Scottish song (exemplified by the immortal Burns lyrics and the work of Walter Scott) offers a soulful and touching range of emotion, but it lacks the pagan fantasy of the devout Irish. This is a seemingly incompatible mix of mythology and religion that is reconciled by an endless ability to believe in miracles – magical occurrences illumined by the votive flame of the Presence in the smallest rural church, and rendered even more mysterious by the lowering shadows of the Celtic twilight.

It has been my privilege for many years to be the accompanist of the great Irish mezzo-soprano Ann Murray; her groups of Irish folksongs have delighted audiences around the world in a completely different way from the more thoughtful pleasure with which the beauties of English folksong are received (even when performed in Britten's arrangements, which were designed to transcend national boundaries). Irish folksong has an international appeal denied to many other branches of the art. This is partly because of a persuasive charm and poignancy of the Irish personality – the effect perhaps of that notoriously powerful Blarney stone. Another example of this successful populism is the enduring popularity of the Irish tenor. There is a sensitive, pleading urgency in the work of the best of these singers, and a sweet and persuasive sound that occupies the middle ground between the stereotypes of the cultivated (sometimes churchy) English tenor, and the out-of-control, sobbing Italian. John McCormack was surely the greatest of these magicians: his early recordings of Irish ballads (issued at the same time as he was taking the world by storm as an opera singer) made him a pioneer of that musical balancing act now known as 'crossover'. One may jokingly suggest that this word referred in the first place to crossing over from serious old England (where Irish artists traditionally studied and sought employment) in order to land back 'in the garden where the pratics grow'.

Nostalgia for the old, dear home country (after having left it for reasons of poverty and famine) was also the basis of large number of songs written for the Irish émigré market in the United States. Thomas Moore wrote that 'absence ... strengthens the land where we were born and Ireland is the country, of all others, which an exile must remember with enthusiasm'. How right he was. The fanciful idea that a 'little piece of heaven could fall into the sea' (and that God should call it 'Ireland'[1]) emanates from New York rather than Dublin. The Irish-American songs written in the first three decades of the twentieth century are a separate, and remarkable, repertoire. Another of my colleagues is the Irish-American tenor Robert White. Apart from being a distinguished singer of music from Josquin to Ives, he has long been a favoured artist of the influential Irish diaspora of New York. In the late 1970s his eloquent 'Danny Boy' (the Londonderry air with a text by an Englishman named Fred Weatherley!) was issued by American RCA on green vinyl to coincide with St Patrick's Day, an idea that would seem patriotic overkill even in Ireland itself. White himself is not in the least politicised in this direction, but there was, and remains, a political dimension to this American enthusiasm for music from the old country. This is connected with the anger and humiliation, a rage passed down through the generations, at the circumstances in which starving Irish citizens left their own country two hundred years ago. The age-old theme of British oppression must be broached in an attempt to explain the otherwise inexplicable power of the IRA in the United States, and the sympathy to its cause that exists among some Americans of Irish descent. And it was only very recently, since 11 September 2001 in fact, that there has been a major breakthrough in the official re-evaluation of this dangerous alliance.

This political digression is of some significance in a commentary on Britten's music. His settings of Moore's *Irish Melodies* (Volume IV), published in 1960, were written in the last days of peace in a partitioned Ireland, just before the beginning of the so-called 'troubles', which involved the arrival of British armed forces from the mainland. His collection included at least four songs in which the poet Moore, writing at the beginning of the nineteenth century, allows himself to speak of armed struggle of various kinds where hatred of the English foe is couched in covert terms. Indeed Moore admitted that his poems were seen by many as 'a vehicle of dangerous politics'. In 1960 the intensity of these feelings must have seemed part of a distant past to Britain (and Britten), but less than a decade later the words of a song such as 'Avenging and Bright' must have seemed to take on a vivid and disturbing contemporary significance. The riots in Belfast and elsewhere, as well as IRA bombings in Britain, removed the Irish question from the realms of stirring old poetry into a horrific present. It is perhaps for this reason that these songs were scarcely ever performed when I was Peter Pears's pianist at master classes at Snape in the 1970s. Since then

1. Song by Ernest Ball (1914), recorded by John McCormack

the book of arrangements, more challenging to the singer than most in this genre, has been largely passed over by performers. This is a pity because I believe it to be the most inventive and daring of all Britten's folksong sets. The music's adventurous musical ingenuity also sadly arouses the opposition of the traditionalists who much prefer Moore's *Irish Melodies*, with their plain accompaniments by Sir John Stevenson, to be left as they are. It is interesting that Moore, in his preface to these folio volumes (1810), defended Stevenson from the charge 'of having spoiled the simplicity of the airs, by the chromatic richness of his symphonies, and the elaborate variety of his harmonies'. It seems there were folksong purists even in those far-off days. *Plus ça change …*

Thomas Moore (1779–1852) was the son of an Irish grocer. He was already a published poet in his teens. After training as a lawyer at Trinity College, Dublin, he came to London and made the acquaintance of Byron and other important literary figures. In 1803 he went to Bermuda in an admiralty post but soon returned via Canada, taking an interest in that country's folk traditions on the way. His talents as a sweet-voiced singer and accomplished musician enabled him to provide words suited to Irish tunes, mainly from the eighteenth century. Many of these originally had humorous texts, but Moore furnished them with lyrics of deeper significance. These *Irish Melodies*, issued in instalments between 1801 and 1834, were published by William Power (who had noted the success of George Thomson's project) and eventually earned the poet a good deal of money. For his *Lallah Rookh* (1817) he obtained the unheard-of advance of £3,000 as well as much public approbation (even though Lady Holland said to the author 'Mr Moore, I have not read your *Larry O'Rourke*; I don't like Irish stories'). One of this sequence of oriental-inspired tales was used by Schumann as the basis of his large choral work, *Das Paradies und die Peri*, in 1843. As a result of a financial scandal Moore temporarily fled England and lived abroad between 1818 and 1822; he spent time in Italy with Byron, and it is during this period that he composed the two Venetian poems that are set in Schumann's *Myrthen*. He was left as the custodian of Byron's *Memoirs* but, together with the publisher John Murray, he burnt these in the interest of protecting Byron's posthumous reputation. As if to compensate for this tragedy in the history of English literature, in 1830 he brought out his own life of his great friend and contemporary. He had started as a radical and a popular hero of Irish

Thomas Moore, contemporary portrait

nationalists (whose cause was given a more sympathetic ear in London society as a result of the popularity of the *Irish Melodies*) but he died in Wiltshire, on a government pension – something of an establishment figure, and the English establishment at that.

Schumann's debt to the poetry of Thomas Moore has already been noted. Among German composers the names of Carl Maria von Weber, Felix Mendelssohn, Adolf Jensen, Peter Cornelius and Paul Hindemith may be added. Slightly less expected is the influence of Moore's poems on French composers. There is a song by Henri Duparc ('Elégie'), which is Moore's plaint for his friend, the patriot Robert Emmet, who was executed by the British in 1803. A much wilder, and less performed, song is the 'Elégie' of Hector Berlioz, one of a number of Moore settings composed by Berlioz in his *Irlande* Op. 9 – the fruit of his obsessive admiration for Harriet Smithson, an Irish actress who had visited Paris in 1827 to play Shakespeare in the original language. Berlioz's 'Elégie' is quite another poem from that set by Duparc – it is nothing less than a French translation (in prose, by Louise Belloc) of Moore's version of Emmet's address from the scaffold. Another Berlioz/Moore setting, 'La Belle Voyageuse' – the only duplicate with a Britten arrangement – is discussed below. Such was the success of Berlioz's setting of Moore's *Irish Melodies* (where the piano was given a new and important role that exceeded anything known in the archaic form of the *romance*) that people spoke of Berlioz's '*mélodies*' as representing a new and special form. It is thus thanks to Tom Moore that the correct French word for the genre of piano-accompanied art song is not '*chanson*' (the usual error of English-speaking writers who, in using this word, mistakenly refer to lighter song or cabaret), but '*mélodie*'.

Britten's English folksongs seem to have been composed partly as a riposte to the more earnest settings of Cecil Sharp, Ralph Vaughan Williams, Herbert Howells and George Butterworth, *inter alia*. The fervent respect of the composers of this generation for folksong was sometimes as if courting a beautiful but untouchable paragon of virtue. Britten substituted a flair that some took to be inappropriate and irreverent, but which was in fact simply the sure touch of the practised lover. Percy Grainger was his model here, and the pupil soon took a different, more dramatic, path from that of his teacher. With Irish folksongs, however, the field of competition was quite different. Thanks to such masters of the light touch as Charles Stanford and Herbert Hughes (in arrangements notable for their charm, wit and memorable immediacy), Irish folksongs had long held the recital stage throughout the world. Irish equivalents of amusingly risqué English songs such as 'The Foggy, Foggy Dew' (Hughes's 'The Stuttering

Lovers' for example) were already firm favourites. Moreover, Hughes was successfully published by Boosey and Hawkes, Britten's own publisher at the time. There were also a number of newer, and scrupulously authentic, folksong arrangements by Britten's friend, the composer E.J. ('Jack') Moeran, which bubble with Irish *esprit*. Another factor was that Peter Pears could never see himself as anything like an Irish tenor; he would certainly have had no wish to enter the lists in a repertoire that would have required the cultivation of a cheeky brogue (he never really attempted a Scottish accent in the dialect poems in the cycle *Who are these Children?*).

All this may explain why Volume IV of Britten's *Folksong Arrangements* seems less 'fun' than the other volumes, and why the settings are also, in my opinion, often more profound. They have a different, more serious, aim: an engagement with issues especially associated with Irish music and poetry. Among these are (a) the harp seen (and heard) as an emblem of a separate national identity, (b) the continuing struggle of a small nation against a larger, (c) the laments associated with senseless bereavement (in this case the towering 'Last Rose of Summer'), and (d) the power of memory to revisit happier times. One should also remember that these songs were arranged at a time when it was reasonable (and not unusual) for someone of Britten's liberal persuasions to see the history of Ireland in the light of its subjugation at the hands of arrogant bullies. If Britten was able to insinuate into his song-writing his feelings about cruelty to animals, cruelty to people was an even stronger theme. He would certainly have known of the highly controversial trial and execution for treason of the Anglo-Irish Sir Roger Casement (1864–1916), who had sympathised with, and worked for, Irish independence. Casement's harsh treatment at the hands of the British authorities was almost certainly exacerbated by the discovery of diaries that revealed his homosexual exploits. The trial and execution of this modern Emmet (Moore would definitely have been on Casement's side) had taken place when Britten was a child, but the brouhaha surrounding the issue came to a head once more in the years between 1957 and 1960: during this time no less than five major books were published on the subject. This was of course the very period during which the composer was working on these arrangements. In more recent times the Catholic Church's intolerance of homosexuality has been unwavering (whereas, conversely, it has been insufficiently vigilant concerning child abuse by its own priests); but it is interesting to note that the most vituperative political opposition to its legalisation in Northern Ireland (a quarter of a century after the composer's death) came from the Ulster followers of Ian Paisley, descendants of those Orangemen who would have counted themselves Tom Moore's most implacable foes.

As if to be fully prepared for a task that was a touch more serious than usual in this field, Britten took great scholastic care in the preparation of the set; he even wrote a prefatory note explaining his sources: he tells us that he has examined the original Moore publications (the lesser-known *National Melodies* as well as the *Irish Melodies*) and in some cases returned to Edward Bunting's *Ancient Music of Ireland* (1796 and 1809), which had been Moore's original inspiration. The result was entirely as the composer had intended: a group of songs which by-passes the whimsy of the Irish tenor repertoire, but which is nevertheless treasure trove. If time has shown that these songs have not been taken up by those who love Irish folksong *pur sang*, they will be admired by every enthusiast of Britten's genius.

Moore's Irish Melodies (Folksong arrangements, Volume IV) (1957)

(i) 'Avenging and Bright'. Fourth number, No. 9² (1811) of *Irish Melodies*
Moore's self-imposed task was to put words to existing melodies. Here the air 'Crooghan a venee' is given a martial text and Britten increases the intensity with a setting marked 'Fast and fierce'. He invents an accompanying motif – a slew of crushed grace notes falling aggressively to an accented dotted minim held by the pianist's thumb – which suggests a minstrel's hand angrily sweeping over the strings. At the same time we can *hear* the glint of steel swords in the sunlight. In one bar, and with one vivid physical gesture, the composer establishes the entire mood of the piece. In verse 3 ('We swear to avenge them!/No joy shall be tasted') the rumbling bass line evokes the mutterings of a dangerous and unruly mob, a marvellous illustration to the composer's direction that these notes should be played as if 'in undertones'. In Britten's music it is almost unheard of to find glorification of any of the bloodier aspects of war, but – as in 'The Lincolnshire Poacher', where he allows hunting of a kind to have its day – it is clear that he was not prepared to allow his enjoyment of a rousing old tune to be spoiled by political correctness.

2. This numbering refers to the instalments in which these melodies were originally published.

(ii) 'Sail on, Sail on' (to the air 'The Humming of the Ban'). Seventh number of *Irish Melodies*.

Sail on, sail on, thou fearless bark,
Wherever blows the welcome wind;
It cannot lead to scenes more dark,
More sad than those we leave behind.

Each smiling billow seems to say,
'Tho' death beneath our surface be,
Less cold we are, less false than they
Whose smiling wreck'd thy hopes and thee.

Sail on, sail on, through endless space,
Through calm, through tempest stop no more;
The stormiest sea's a resting place
To him who leaves such hearts on shore.

Or if some desert land we meet
Where never yet false hearted men
Profaned a world that else were sweet,
Then rest thee, bark, but not till then.

The first thing that comes to mind is that this is a sailing song arranged by a composer who was always close to the sea. But this extraordinary text makes me think of the unsettled, peripatetic lives of some of the great romantic poets, above all Shelley and Byron. It was Byron of course who was Moore's close friend: the two Moore poems about Venice that were set in Schumann's *Myrthen* (in Freiligrath's translation 'Leis' rudern hier, mein Gondolier' and 'Wenn durch die Piazzetta') were written when the Irishman was in Byron's intoxicating company. The Irishman's poem set here seems to duplicate the mood of Byron's lines about 'the wanderers o'er Eternity/Whose bark drives on and on, and anchor'd ne'er shall be'.[3] The permanently displaced Shelley, who seems to have taken one dangerous sea voyage after another in his life, also quoted these very Byron lines in relation to himself.

3. Byron, *Childe Harold's Pilgrimage*, Canto iii, Stanza 70.

For this text Britten finds harmony that 'anchor'd ne'er shall be'. This is a barcarolle which looks simple enough on the page, but which is an exercise in Brittenian bi-tonality: it is as if the bass line is a tone too high for the right hand's floating chords, or perhaps the right hand is a tone too low for the bass. Whatever the means that have achieved this 'spaced-out' effect, it is an uncanny way of illustrating the prophecy of modern travel represented by the lines 'Sail on, sail on through endless space'. The enmeshing of gentle discords here seem to me music of the spheres, no longer of this world; of course the traditionalist will see the setting simply as wilful and ugly modernism. The postlude seems to dematerialise before our ears, an effect that is prescient of the final moments of the courtly pavane of Oberon, Titania and the fairies in *A Midsummer Night's Dream* ('Now until the break of day') as these luminaries evaporate before Puck's closing speech.[4]

4. These folksongs were arranged in 1957, and *A Midsummer Night's Dream* was composed 1959–60.

92

⊙ **(iii) 'How Sweet the Answer' (to the air 'The Wren'). Eighth number of** *Irish Melodies.*   ⊙ CD1, track 18

Britten's *Nocturne* for tenor, seven obbligato instruments and string orchestra Op. 60, composed August–September 1958, was written soon after these folksong settings were conceived. Night music was one of Britten's great themes, and never more potently than during this period. The composer includes in this Irish set three nocturnes of a moonlit, aching beauty. The first of these combines the ideas of blurred vision and hearing in the night hours. The main feature of the accompaniment is the occasional crossing of hands to the treble register to create a silvery and insubstantial echo – indeed 'Echo' is Moore's title for this song. For the rest of the time the murmuring right-hand chords in the middle of the stave provide a suave background to the vocal line while avoiding any definite harmonic movement that might suggest strong, visible contours. The use of strangely disorientating bass notes, as if the whole song were resounding somewhere in outer space, makes for music that seems strangely insubstantial and etiolated. All in all this is a superb acoustical depiction of a distant, answering sound; in a similar way the introduction to 'Midnight on the Great Western' ('The Journeying Boy') from *Winter Words* Britten suggests the Doppler effect as a train goes through a tunnel. Once again the presence of Britten's magical Shakespeare opera is potently evident: this is music fit for an Athenian forest as much as for an Irish glade.

(iv) 'The Minstrel Boy' (to the air 'The Moreen'). Fifth number, No. 6 (1813) of *Irish Melodies.*

> The minstrel boy to the war is gone
> In the ranks of death you'll find him;
> His father's sword he has girded on,
> And his wild harp slung behind him.
>
> 'Land of song,' said the warrior bard,
> 'Tho' all the world betrays thee,
> *One* sword, at least, thy rights shall guard,
> *One* faithful harp shall praise thee.'
>
> The minstrel fell, but the foeman's chain
> Could not bring that proud soul under;
> The harp he lov'd ne'er spoke again,
> For he tore its chords asunder;

The Minstrel fell!—but the foeman's chain
Could not bring his proud soul under;
The harp he lov'd ne'er spoke again,
For he tore its chords asunder;
And said, "No chains shall sully thee,
"Thou soul of love and bravery!
"Thy songs were made for the pure and free,
"They shall never sound in slavery."

Moore's Irish Melodies early edition, illustrated by David Maclise

And said, 'No chain shall sully thee,
Thou soul of love and brav'ry.
Thy songs were made for the pure and free,
They shall never sound in slav'ry.'

94

After a certain amount of dreaming, the collection needs a rousing interlude. The music for 'The Minstrel Boy' is, on the surface, bracing and martial. However, despite the military bluster of this march, this is nothing less
than a mini requiem for a soldier-musician, and a boy at that. One is
reminded of the many children who perished in wars of the past (and also
of the powder monkeys in *Billy Budd*, the doomed orphans of *Children's
Crusade*). The melodic line has decisive, manly contours throughout, but
the piano-writing with its chords on the weaker beats of the bar suggests
uncertainty, youth, vulnerable tenderness. The insertion of 3/4 bars in the
body of this broad march is a stroke of genius; this momentary disruption
of the rhythm suggests a stumble manfully surmounted, a tear bravely
brushed aside. The harp itself is also a key player: with the piano's help it
ripples throughout in subtly different ways – spread-chord arpeggios at
the beginning, and more eloquent sweeping figurations, which fill whole
bars in the central section. This is a remarkably subtle evocation of patriotic fervour (the first verse) and a boy's dying words (the second verse)
played out as if in a film where a small human tragedy unfolds in one corner of a larger battle scene. The point is that the fighting continues simultaneously elsewhere, and we also hear this in this setting. Other composers
would be able to write battle music and touching farewells separately; but
Britten, like Schubert (see 'Kriegers Ahnung' from *Schwanengesang*), is
able to telescope military events and personal introspection and depict
them at the same time. This is an example of how the extent of Britten's
virtuosity can go unnoticed because the results sound so natural and
unforced.

**(v) 'At the Mid Hour of Night' (to the air 'Molly my dear'). Fifth number,
No. 12 (1813) of *Irish Melodies*.**

At the mid hour of night when stars are weeping, I fly
To the lone vale we lov'd when life shone warm in thine eye;
And I think that if spirits can steal from the region of air
To revisit past scenes of delight, thou wilt come to me there
And tell me our love is remembered e'en in the sky.

Then I'll sing the wild song, which once 'twas rapture to hear,
When our voices, both mingling, breathed like one on the ear,
And as Echo far off thro' the vale my sad orison rolls,
I think, Oh my love, 'tis thy voice from the kingdom of souls
Faintly answering still the notes which once were so dear.

This is the second of the three nocturnes in this collection and one of the loveliest. It is very hard to sing, with the spinning of its long lines, and its eloquent rise and fall. The melody is almost unbearably poignant and for this reason Britten does little to disturb it. In terms of the accompaniment this is an exercise in ninths, which chime through the piano staves as if they were distant fairy bells. These bounce gently off the bass pedal notes, mainly on off-beats. At 'Then I'll sing the wild song, which once 'twas rapture to hear' the accompaniment becomes more lively and changes into a descent of rippling semiquavers. Britten keeps these details largely in the background, and little is allowed to disturb the unfolding of a remarkably touching poem and melody. Just before the end (with the words 'thy voice from the kingdom of souls') we realise that this music is that of a lover remembering his or her dead partner, endeavouring to communicate through song, hoping in vain for a sound that may return from the 'other side'. Those stretching, yearning ninths have blurred the harmony throughout and have softened the rough contours of the present. They seem perfect for this rapturous retreat into the safe haven of memory. This setting makes me think of an expansive Schubert song that creates a similar emotional effect – this is the wonderful 'Der Winterabend' (Leitner) where a widower sits and thinks of the love and companionship that has once been his. It was, as it happens, a Pears–Britten favourite on the recital platform.

(vi) 'Rich and Rare' (to the air 'The Summer is Coming'). First number, No. 10 (1810) of *Irish Melodies*.

Berlioz set this text as 'La Belle Voyageuse'; this is one of the more interesting and subtle of his nine Moore settings. His enthusiasm for Moore's poems in 1829 did not include any interest in the 'original' melodies arranged by Sir John Stevenson. He treated the poems as quite unconnected with any existing music. Herbert Hughes in his Volume III of his *Irish Country Songs* (1934) writes a new accompaniment to the old melody, which is reasonably effective.

This, on the other hand, is perhaps the least successful of these Britten arrangements; with its cruelly long phrases in the vocal line it is certainly one of the most difficult to sing. If there were ever any justice in the charge that Britten's arrangements were too 'clever' it would apply to this song. The melody is beautiful enough in its own right, and one can see how Britten would have immediately seen how well it would suit the artistry of Peter Pears. Accordingly he set about arranging it. But there seems to be a failure of will or imagination in engaging with a song which is a rapturous hymn to the beauty of the female form that incarnates Eire (because of his devotion to Harriet Smithson, Berlioz seems fired to extra lyricism for just this reason). Britten's arrangement is an impressive exercise in counterpoint, but unlike 'Polly Oliver' there are no real dramatic grounds in the text for its deployment. It is nevertheless a measure of the composer's virtuosity that each verse has a canon at a different interval beneath the vocal line, the left hand of the accompaniment always trailing the singer's melody. This dialogue changes emphasis in the last verse when it is the pianist's right hand that shadows the voice in eloquent octaves; this time the canon is placed above the vocal line and the music shimmers strangely, an appropriate harmonic aura with which to depict a magical maiden floating off into the distance. The encounter brings to mind Schumann's 'Waldesgespräch' (from the Eichendorff *Liederkreis*) except that Moore's beautiful maiden on a horse is no malign and punishing Lorelei; on the contrary, her beatific confidence in the incorruptible virtues of Irish manhood is rewarded. In the hands of an absolutely sovereign singer this song can make a fine effect, but one somehow senses the composer's heart is not completely in it.

(vii) 'Dear Harp of my Country' (to the air 'Kate Tyrrel'). Sixth number, No. 12 (1815) of *Irish Melodies.*

Dear Harp of my Country, in darkness I found thee,
The cold chain of silence had hung o'er thee long,
When proudly, my own island Harp, I unbound thee,
And gave all they chords to light, freedom and song.

The warm lay of love and the light tone of gladness
Have waken'd thy fondest, thy liveliest thrill;
But so oft has thou echo'd the deep sigh of sadness
That e'en in thy mirth it will steal from thee still.

Dear Harp of my Country, farewell to thy numbers,
This sweet wreath of song is the last we shall twine,
Go, sleep with the sunshine of Fame on thy slumbers
Till touch'd by some hand less unworthy than mine.

If the pulse of the patriot, soldier or lover,
Have throbbed at our lay, 'tis *thy* glory alone;
I was but as the wind, passing heedlessly over,
And all the wild sweetness I waked was thy own.

Britten and Osian Ellis

No composer who had not already written extensively for the harp in large orchestral pieces could have hoped to write this marvellous accompaniment. Once again the song's melodic line itself is of a beauty and interest that does not merit much interference. Accordingly Britten opts for a murmur of accompanying semiquavers, which somehow evokes the peculiarly glistening sound of the harp when nimbly plucking fingers weave a spell of sound between them. This writing is mostly in contrary motion – thirds that burble between the pianist's hands – but there are also occasional arpeggio flourishes, which propel the accompaniment to the top of the keyboard, as if the harpist's hands were sweeping across the strings when he is carried away by talk of patriots and soldiers. For the last verse there are pedal notes that resound deep in the bass, firstly at the beginning of the bar, and then at off-beat moments, creating a three-against-two hemiola. The sound of these low plucked strings remains absolutely consistent with authentic harp writing and adds a plangent majesty to the mood. In this way the accompaniment is actually the hidden star of the proceedings, the embodiment of the instrument that is being so beautifully hymned in the melody and in Moore's text. And here is evidence that not much preparation was needed by Britten to write real harp accompaniments for Osian Ellis in the years to come (albeit with a different kind of instrument in mind).

(viii) 'Oft in the Stilly Night', from *National Melodies and Airs*

Oft in the stilly night ere slumber's chain has bound me,
Fond Mem'ry brings the light of other days around me:
The smiles, the tears of boyhood's years, the words of love then spoken;
The eyes that shone, now dimmed and gone, the cheerful hearts now broken.
 Thus in the stilly night ere slumber's chain has bound me,
 Sad Mem'ry brings the light of other days around me.

When I remember all the friends, so linked together,
I've seen around me fall like leaves in wintry weather,
I feel like one who treads alone some banquet hall deserted,
Whose lights are fled, whose garlands dead, and all but he departed.
    Thus in the stilly night ere slumber's chain has bound me,
    Sad Mem'ry brings the light of other days around me.

In this noble poem (the tune is no less noble) Moore bemoans the loss of friends, some of them casualties of war and strife like Emmet and Byron, some cut off early in life by tragic accident like Shelley. That Britten was actively searching for another night piece is shown by the fact that he here chooses one of Moore's poems from the later *National Airs*, rather than the *Irish Melodies*. In that collection the sub-heading of this song is 'Scotch air', but having a cuckoo of this kind in his nest of Irish songs seems not to have disturbed Britten unduly. We would expect that this composer's ability to suggest the stillness of night would be nothing less than uncanny; but there is an added element here, which a lesser arranger could not have encompassed. These gentle, sighing triplets wafting through the song have a yearning quality that seems anything but fulfilled; they are coloured with a succession of wrong-note harmonies – nothing violent, more like strangely refracted moonlight – to colour the singer's sad memories. In depicting peace and anguish simultaneously Britten shows himself, once again, a magician. The composer directs that each of these triplets should begin with a tiny spread chord. This is the plucking of the harp I suppose, but I detect here too the hypnotic chirp of the cricket, constant companion to night-time philosophers (as in Schubert's much happier song, 'Der Einsame'). The bass line shadows the voice in the first verse; in the second, the triplets fall to the left hand while right-hand octaves add a heaviness to a texture. This is a heaviness of heart, which, at Britten's command, is made to combine with the lightness of moonbeams.

☉ (ix) 'The Last Rose of Summer' (to the air 'Groves of Blarney'). Fifth number, No. 4 of *Irish Melodies* (1813)

☉ CD1, track 19

This is by far the most famous song that Moore ever wrote, and it has triumphantly survived the centuries to surface in many a sugary performance by singers, some of them impeccably Irish, who see in it no more than the faint regret of a rueful horticulturalist as he observes he fading of a bloom. Stevenson's arrangement is not all that bad – the connecting interludes aim at poignancy in the best way that he was able. It is hardly the match for

Moore, however, who is at his most subversive. He uses domestic imagery, to which the authorities could not object, in order to voice his heartbreak at the slaughter of many young men who were lost in the summer of their lives during the struggle against the English. In a similar way the Jacobite poets had referred obliquely to the outlawed Bonnie Prince Charlie, who could not even be named in verse. The idea was surely to have everyone singing a popular song that seemed innocuous, but which had a subtext that all but the oppressors would understand.

One need not be a sympathiser to the Irish nationalist cause to respond to the intensity of a poem – and melody – that also seems worthy, for example, of the fallen young men who are the dedicatees of Britten's *War Requiem*. The grief (and guilt) of those spared and left behind to face a life without contemporaries is also a major theme of the Holocaust. If Moore subverts flower poetry here, Britten subverts all the cosy expectations of the generations who have grown up loving the melody, its original purpose long forgotten. I have heard hearty objections about this arrangement and, from the point of view of those who like their Irish songs pretty, I can see why. This rose (to paraphrase another Britten setting, this time from the *Serenade* for tenor, horn and strings) is sick, attacked by the invisible worm of the poet's anger. In acknowledging Moore's heartbroken resentment, Britten's awareness (was there ever a composer more aware of undertone and subtext?) restores the song to its historical context.

Once again it is the use of harmonic refraction, jarring chords, that speaks volumes about the poet's state of mind. The song seems harp-accompanied throughout, but by a harp that steadfastly refuses to play in tune. Shakespeare knew that this was a sign of rebellion: 'Take but degree away, untune that string/And, hark! what discord follows; …/and the rude son should strike his father dead'.[5] The sons of the Irish soil were tired of acknowledging the presence of an uninvited English patriarchy. Britten suggests not only anger, but *suppressed* anger. The introductory chords are harmonised on the clashing seventh degree of the scale (D in the key of E flat). Arpeggios ripple ominously in the lower registers of the piano while the magnificent melody flows freely across the stave. The second strophe is framed with more focussed harmonic intensity, while the third is punctuated by heavy octaves that trudge through the bass line as if Moore were bearing the weight of the whole world on his shoulders. It is with this gradual build-up, which unleashes such powerful and eloquent emotion, that Britten's arrangement pays off. Of course, to make it work the singer has to have both a command of an intense legato tone and an ability to float dreamily in the upper reaches of the stave. The magical closing phrase 'Oh

5. Shakespeare, *Troilus and Cressida* I, iii, ll.109–15.

who would inhabit/This bleak world alone' emphasises 'who' with a heart-wringing melisma. This seems a poignant echo of Peter Grimes's passionate outburst 'Who can turn skies back, and begin again?'

(x) 'Oh! The Sight Entrancing' (to the air 'Planxty Sudley'). Ninth number of *Irish Melodies.*

The work ends with a scherzo of battle fanfares marked 'Fast and brilliant'. Britten had already proved in *Gloriana* that he was a master of fanfares of every kind, including those for jousts. Here we feel all the excitement (and trepidation) of the day of battle as forces line up to fight to the death. The shrill fife and the beating drum are also incorporated into this nervous music, which reflects an itching determination to get out there and engage with the enemy. The refraction to be heard here is of brilliant sunlight glancing off highly polished weapons. The arrangement manages to work up a considerable amount of martial tension for its tiny proportions. Glorification of war is not Britten's usual territory; this should be seen rather as a tribute to the foolhardy and reckless Irish nature ready to throw their lives away for a cause in which they believe. The final piano ritornello is a stirring peroration in bounding octaves, which may seem to depict the start of the battle in earnest. This makes a brilliant postlude to a remarkable set of songs – certainly much more remarkable than is generally acknowledged.

Folksong arrangements, Volume VI ('England') (1956–58)

Like Osian Ellis, and long before him, the guitarist Julian Bream (b. 1933) was an established part of the Aldeburgh scene. Unlike Ellis he was not recruited to play under Britten's baton – the guitar is obviously not an orchestral instrument. For Bream in 1963 Britten wrote the *Nocturnal after John Dowland* (a reflection on the song 'Come Heavy Sleep') for solo guitar Op. 70. That work is dedicated to him. As Pears's accompanist (on both the lute and guitar) Bream had already performed numerous programmes of Elizabethan music, as well making various recordings. I believe that *Julian Bream in Concert*, which includes six lute songs by Dowland, sung by Pears and recorded live at the Wigmore Hall, is one of the most compelling of all performances of this great repertoire.[6] Britten's *Songs from the Chinese* (Op. 58 – 1957), settings of Arthur Waley's translations of Chinese poetry, were written for the same duo. Here the fragile but telling sound of the guitar exactly conveys a sonority – one might imagine precious Ming porcelain translated into music to sound like this – that somehow brings ancient China to life. The *implied* harmony, rather than a full harmonic palette

6. RCA Victor SB6646.

(such as would be provided by a piano) gives this music a timelessness, like Roussel's flute-accompanied settings of poems evoking ancient Greek poetry, for example. Britten's Chinese excursion has a remarkable travel itinerary, both in terms of time and geographical distance.

The six arrangements contained in Volume VI of the folksong arrangements date from 1961. For his sources Britten seems much less relaxed than in his earlier volumes, when there seems to have been a conscious effort to avoid such collectors as Vaughan Williams and Cecil Sharp; both make an appearance here. The subtitle of the collection is 'England', but as we shall see this is not completely accurate: 'I Will Give my Love an Apple' is from Dorset (collected by H.E.D. Hammond and Vaughan Williams); 'Master Kilby' is from Somerset (Cecil Sharp); 'The Soldier and the Sailor' is from Oxfordshire (Sharp); 'Bonny at Morn' is from Northumberland (W.G. Whittaker); and 'The Shooting of his Dear' is from Norfolk (E.J. Moeran). This leaves 'Sailor-boy', which is unaccountably from Kentucky – a song gathered by Cecil Sharp during his American visits to the Appalachian mountains.

Of course this inconsistency does not matter a jot to the musical quality of these remarkably effective arrangements. The guitar's luminous and transparent sound seems to remind us of just how clumsy and opaque the piano can be as an accompanying instrument in the wrong hands. (i) 'I Will Give my Love an Apple' is underscored by a teasingly off-beat accompaniment, which makes the guitar seem to be playing in a different time signature. It gives a subtle new dimension to what is perhaps an over-familiar melody. The jauntiness of (ii) ⊙'Sailor-boy' recalls the jubilant fourth Choral Dance (entitled 'Country Girls') from the opera *Gloriana* ('Sweet flag, Sweet flag and cuckoo flower'). The swagger of this music is delicious, as is the ten-bar postlude, which seems to paint a picture of seduction where the girls' initial hesitation is replaced by gleeful capitulation. (iii) 'Master Kilby' boasts a very beautiful melody, which the guitar accompanies in the most simple way possible, always elegant and filled with subtle harmonic touches in response to the ebb and flow of the words. (iv) ⊙ 'The Soldier and the Sailor' is quite simply the most masterful depiction of gradually deepening inebriation that I know of in the entire song repertoire. The successive pronouncements of 'Amen' get more and more comically lugubrious, and the guitar figurations devised by Britten are marvellously expressive of the giggly smiles of the drinkers, and their hiccups of delighted drunkenness. The last eight bars of the song are marked 'Freely', and the guitar's postlude seems to totter unsteadily on its pins as the singer sinks under the table. His final 'Amen' has all the solemnity of those who are well and truly drunk.

⊙ **CD1, track 20**

⊙ **CD1, track 21**

(v) 'Bonny at Morn' is the only folksong known to me that Britten chose to set twice, each time quite differently. The second setting is to be found as No. 4 of the *Eight Folksongs* (a selection from which is discussed at the beginning of this lecture). That version for voice and harp is much more simple, and more of a unity, than this ornate and highly worked guitar setting, which seems devised to show the contrasting moods of the various strophes. There is the suggestion here of leaping trout and birdsong in the second strophe, and of pleasurable licentiousness in the last section, where Britten makes the guitar depict a fluttering shudder of sexual excitement more effectively than most other instruments could.

(vi) ⊙ 'The Shooting of his Dear' was collected in his native Norfolk by the   ⊙ **CD1, track 22**
Anglo-Irish composer E.J. Moeran (1894–1950) some time before 1924. As settings go it is far from Moeran's most interesting: he leaves large swathes of melody unharmonised, and the piano writing is lacklustre. Britten delights in a text that revisits an anti-hunting theme first broached in the early cycle *Tit for Tat*. There the oaf named Tom Noddy (in a Walter de la Mare poem) has been shooting rabbits; here the singer is a fowler. There has been a dreadful accident that would never have happened if it had not been for guns and their everyday use in the countryside. Polly (the girlfriend who has been shot) makes an appearance at the trial which, in Moeran's version, is musically unexceptional. She begs that her lover be excused for his mistake and explains that her apron had been bound around her making her look like a swan. Britten on the other hand understands that Polly makes this appearance as a wraith. This fact is vividly communicated by the other-worldly shimmer of the guitar writing in demi-semiquavers, which suggests the transparency of a ghostly apparition. Before this episode the martial dotted rhythms of the accompaniment at 'So the trial came on' suggest the gravity of the charge (see also the dotted rhythms of the trial scene at the very beginning of *Peter Grimes*); in terms of musical atmosphere alone we are left in no doubt that the trial will be followed by an execution. The differences between Moeran's meandering arrangement and Britten's are astonishing. The thirty-seven years that separate the two pieces represent the mighty changes that had taken place in English song: this can be summed up in a single phrase – the move, via opera, towards a greater dramaturgy in word-setting. Britten's genius for sharpening the focus of a text, his flair for changing theory into practice, and narration into drama, is never clearer than here.

Folksongs posthumously published
So far in this book we have considered all six Britten folksong collections, as well as four of the eight harp-accompanied songs. This lecture concludes

with a selection from the ten folksongs published posthumously, as recently as 2001. Some of these date from 1941 – the period when the composer lived in America and began to make folksong settings – and others from as late as the end of the 1950s.

'The Crocodile' is one of the longest of Britten's folksong arrangements, as befits a tall story that becomes taller with each verse, each modulatory turn of the tonal screw further straining any shred of remaining credulity. Its textual provenance is English (Broadwood and Fuller-Maitland's *English County Songs*) but its style is somehow American. Composed in 1941 this piece is audibly related to the ballad style of Britten's operetta *Paul Bunyan*.

'Pray Goody' is another of Britten's several settings from Hullah's *Song Book*. The melody is originally by Charles Burney (1726–1814) and, as such, is part of an ongoing mini-tradition whereby Britten, quite apart from his Purcell realisations, paid homage to important, if forgotten, English composers of the past (such as Shield, Carey and Dibdin) by furnishing their melodies with new accompaniments. (Paul Kildea, in his introduction to the Boosey and Hawkes edition of these songs, claims that 'Tom Bowling' 'was Britten's first realisation of a song by someone other than Purcell',[7] but this honour must surely belong to Britten's arrangement of William Shield's 'flaxen headed ploughboy' in Volume III of the folksongs.) Britten's chattering accompaniment to 'Pray Goody' (marked 'Presto') was almost certainly accomplished in a matter of minutes, but the goodwife's 'rancour of tongue' is admirably, and amusingly, depicted.

'Dink's Song' is another fruit of the American period, and it sounds it. This is as near as Britten ever came to setting a spiritual. The publication of this music makes sense of something I once heard Pears say to Britten at the end of a telephone conversation with the composer who was sometimes consulted, then and there, during our rehearsals for *Death in Venice* in London. This was the phrase 'Fare thee well, o Honey' which occurs with an exquisite high note for floated head voice in 'Dink's Song'. At this stage (in about 1972) even *Paul Bunyan* was part of a private world of allusion and memory (going back to the beginning of their relationship) which belonged to singer and composer alone, and was not yet public property. I was once in the car with Britten and Pears when the latter began singing a beautiful melody completely unknown to me. Britten then identified it, with a wonderful smile, as coming from *Paul Bunyan*; he later told me that Peter had copied the vocal score for that work ... partly by candlelight. This seemed so poetic that I did not ask why there was no electricity in the America of the time. A power cut perhaps, unpaid bills, or simply a house without electricity in rural New York State in the 1940s ... ?

7. Paul Kildea, Preface to Britten, *Tom Bowling and Other Song Arrangements* (Boosey and Hawkes, 2001).

104

The story of the arrangement of 'I Wonder as I Wander' reveals Britten's ingenuity when faced with a copyright problem. This beautiful melody was not collected by the American John Jacob Niles (1892–1980) as is stated in the Boosey and Hawkes edition, but was in fact an original song by him, which was always mistaken for a folksong – or so states his biographical article in the *New Grove Dictionary of American Music*.[8] This article makes clear that 'I Wonder as I Wander' was so often mistaken for a folksong (and thus assumed to be in the public domain) that Niles put an embargo on its publication and recording shortly after 1940. This was almost certainly as a reaction against Britten's interest in arranging it, and would explain why the work often appeared in recitals by composer and tenor, but took so long to reach print. Britten's solution was that his own contribution should leave Niles's vocal line untouched. Britten's eloquent piano writing on one stave simply frames Niles's music as prelude, interludes and postlude. Where else in Britten's songs is the accompaniment reduced to a single treble line? The answer is in *Winter Words*: in 'At the Railway Station, Upway' the boy with a violin shows compassion, through music, to the handcuffed convict. A reading of the poem of 'I Wonder as I Wander' shows a similar open-hearted and childlike devotion. Even unconsciously the composer seems to have linked the image of compassionately offering to help a convicted criminal, and surrendering one's heart to Jesus, as similar gestures of artless, single-minded (thus single-staved) goodness.

⊙ 'Tom Bowling' is from the table entertainment *The Oddities* (1789) composed by Charles Dibdin (1745–1814). The original Tom was apparently this composer's brother. To Britten goes the credit for a grave and simple arrangement, which, in its prelude and postlude, manages to suggest the drum-beats accompanying a funeral at sea, and the sad ceremonial of committing a body to the deep. Paul Kildea points out the naval connections between Tom Bowling, Billy Budd and the cabin-boy in the vaudeville *The Golden Vanity*.[9] The 'beauty, handsomeness, goodness' of the eponymous hero of *Billy Budd* is found again in the hymn to Tom Bowling, which has, at least to twentieth-century ears, homoerotic overtones. The work was one of the duo's recital items for many years, and its inclusion in recitals is typical of their dual means of coping with the opprobrium of some sectors of society regarding their relationship: this was verbal discretion (and discretion of lifestyle – theirs was never a household for wild parties or scandal) counterbalanced by *musical* openness, indeed defiance, of just this sort. This audacity-in-art seems to have been more comprehensible to the composer's friends than his enemies, and this must have been precisely its intention.

'The Deaf Woman's Courtship' is a duet (another from Cecil Sharp's

8. H. Wiley Hitchcock and Stanley Sadie (eds), *New Grove Dictionary of American Music* (Macmillan Press, 1986).

9. Kildea, Preface to Britten, *Tom Bowling*.

⊙ **CD1, track 23**

Appalachian collection) arranged for a series of recitals that Peter Pears and the composer gave with the English mezzo-soprano Norma Proctor (b. 1928) – the character and humour of that kind, but redoubtable, artist is somehow built into this music.

⊙ **CD1, track 24**

⊙ 'Soldier, Won't you Marry Me?' is an effective duet, drawn yet again from Cecil Sharp's Appalachian songs. The text was set by the young Peter Pears when he still had composing aspirations; this setting – not very different from Britten's as it happens – was performed at a Songmakers' Almanac concert at the Wigmore Hall in 1984 honouring the great singer. The song reveals the unreliability and deviousness of the male suitor, but it is also one of those songs that might be seen to have another agenda. In finally refusing to marry the girl, the soldier gives her the perfect excuse of having another wife and baby at home. But this refusal to marry and become tied down might have had any number of other reasons. (There is a story, possibly apocryphal, that Alma Mahler pursued Britten and proposed marriage to him!) This declaration of independence is typical of Britten's music where the normal romantic conventions are seldom celebrated at any length. (The marriage of Polly Oliver and her captain seems to have received the composer's imprimatur mainly as a result of her devoted impersonation of a young male soldier.)

The volume of posthumous folksongs (published in 2001 under the title of *Tom Bowling and Other Song Arrangements*) contains three further items. There is a not particularly original arrangement of 'Greensleeves' (a tune that Britten seems to have approached in 1941 with uncharacteristic diffidence, as if he were encroaching on the property of Vaughan Williams). An arrangement of 'The Holly and the Ivy' (also 1941) is strangely banal and lacking in the original word-to-music responses we have come to expect from this composer (we have to acknowledge that even a great composer like Britten was correct in withholding a few of his works from publication).

The final arrangement for voice, piano and cello entitled 'The Stream in the Valley' is an oddity, and not only because of the instrumental obbligato. It was composed for a BBC broadcast in 1946 with the cellist Maurice Gendron. At that time, so soon after the war, it might have seemed odd for an English composer to explore German folksong, but this was the period when Germany, defeated and occupied by the vengeful Russians among others, was in the greatest need of compassion. The anguish of the cello interludes in this song set in a valley in which the waters run 'troubled and sad' seem to go beyond a personal commentary on a failed love affair.

Britten might have taken this melody from its best-known source – the folksongs of Johannes Brahms, where it was published as 'Da unten im Tale', No. 6 of that composer's forty-nine arrangements. Was this really sung in an English translation as printed in the new Faber edition? It seems a pity not to have there the original German words.[10] The composer's flowing quavers, increasingly chromatically disturbed, provide a portrait of unease and anguish, but they have not replaced those of Brahms whose touching arrangement remains a beloved fixture of the recital platform. It might not have pleased Britten to know that the composer whose music he seems to have most disliked has got the better of him, at least on this tiny issue.

10. The manuscript source for this at the Britten–Pears Library is in English; no trace of a German version has been found.

The programme at the 2001 Britten festival was comprised of: **From *Gloriana*:** The Second Lute Song of the Earl of Essex (Robert Devereux, Earl of Essex); *Lachrymae - Reflections on a song of John Dowland* **Op. 48**; *Canticle I - My Beloved is Mine* **Op. 40** (Quarles); *The Holy Sonnets of John Donne* **Op. 35**: VI 'Oh My Blacke Soule', XIV 'Batter my heart', III 'O Might those Sighes and Teares', XIX 'Since she whom I loved', VII 'At the round earth's imagin'd corners', I 'Thou hast made me', X 'Death be not Proud'

Lecture 5
Britten the Elizabethan, Britten and the Baroque

In Act One of Britten's opera *Gloriana*, the Earl of Essex is ushered into Queen Elizabeth I's presence. She commands him to sing a song to lift her spirits. He takes up the lute to do so, and the orchestral harp springs into action. This 'First Lute Song' opens with the words 'Quick music is best/When the heart is oppressed, Quick music can heal/With dancing, by night and by day'. The tonality of this merry dance in triple time is a bright E major; but its carefree mood is undermined by a jarring E flat in the bass. A similar lingering undertone of disquiet destroys the sentimental complacency of that famous Irish tune ⊙ 'The Last Rose of Summer' in Britten's unusual arrangement. (It is ironic that the Earl of Essex's unsuccessful attempt to subjugate Ireland was the cause of his downfall.) With this discordant harmony the composer encapsulates the Queen's bad mood and the disparity of temperament between older monarch and young courtier that is at the heart of their twinned tragedy.

⊙ **CD1, track 19**

The Queen's opinion of this first song is withering: 'Too light, too gay:/A song for careless hearts' (one would scarcely imagine that this had been Elizabeth II's verdict on Britten's opera, which was dedicated to her!). 'Gloriana' then further commands the Earl: 'Turn to the lute again/Evoke some far-off place or time/A dream, a mood an air/To spirit us both away'. In using words about the evocation of 'a far-off place *or time*', the librettist William Plomer succinctly defines one of this opera's principal aims, an ambition that was wonderfully realised thanks to Britten raising pastiche to a higher power and turning it into a new art form – there are moments in this music where it is as if Dowland himself had been 'spirited away' to the twentieth century and lent his pen to the younger composer, one of his musical heirs.

Opposite: Britten and Joan Cross rehearsing the première of Gloriana, *Covent Garden, 1953.*

'The Second Lute Song' is one of the most evocative set-pieces in all

109

*Britten and the Queen
Mother at the Red House,
Aldeburgh, 1975*

Britten's output, full of harmonic felicity and period detail. When I hear the tenor embark on the ornate melisma on the word 'brambleberry' I am reminded of another masterful evocation, an opera aria written seven years later, which also manages to sound simultaneously ancient and modern (and quite unlike a hymn!): in Oberon's aria 'I know a bank' from *A Midsummer Night's Dream* the word 'eglantine' is set as a roulade that twirls and rises, and then dips to the bottom of the counter-tenor's vocal range at the last moment (in contrast, 'brambleberry' aspires to the heights). Both are similarly perverse, similarly delicious. In these phrases the flowering semiquavers, like the unruly tendrils of plants that grow proudly in the wild, seem to disdain the constrictions of the trellised stave. This unruly curvaceousness is the planned anarchy of Baroque ornamentation, or rather Britten's version of it. If architecture is frozen music (as Schelling had it)[1] then music is liquefied art: these passages, and many more like them in Britten's realisations and stylisations, might solidify into tangible form as wood carvings by Grinling Gibbons.

1. Friedrich Wilhelm
Joseph Schelling,
Philosophie der Kunst
(Wissenschaftliche
Buchgesellschaft, 1980),
pp.576, 593.

The Second Lute Song of the Earl of Essex, from *Gloriana* (Robert Devereux, Earl of Essex)

Happy were he could finish forth his fate
In some unhaunted desert, where, obscure
From all society, from love and hate
Of worldly folk, then might he sleep secure;
Then wake again and give God ever praise;
Content with hips and haws and brambleberry;
In contemplation spending all his days,
And change of holy thoughts to make him merry;
Where, when he dies, his tomb might be a bush
Where harmless robin dwells with gentle thrush.

110

This lecture aims to explain how Britten coped with, and built on, his own country's various musical pasts. The composer's visits, both actual and imaginary, to such countries as Italy, France, Germany and Russia (and the musical fruits of these explorations) are commented upon in other lectures. Here we concentrate on Britten's travels within his own country – not in any geographical sense, but in terms of how the musical style and literary culture of the sixteenth and seventeenth centuries enriched his compositions and gave him another framework in which to define, and celebrate, his Englishness. The two composers' names that shine as twin beacons in any discussion of Britten's musical forbears are John Dowland (1563–1626) and Henry Purcell (1659–95) – two great masters of English song in a triumvirate where Britten is the arguable third. These two figures are book-ends framing a period of English musical history that extends from about 1580 to 1700. Between these two stellar points appear any number of poets: Shakespeare naturally, but also John Donne, Francis Quarles, Robert Herrick, John Milton. These were all set to music by Britten (though not all for voice with piano) at a time when, already famous for his foreign excursions, he seems to have become increasingly determined to explore the literary heritage of his own country. The late 1940s and early 1950s were also a time in his career and development when it was easier (particularly in terms of copyright problems and expenses) to embrace the rich literary legacy of the past – an area where he need never fear the argumentative acrimony of contemporary collaborators.

At the time when the young Britten set Victor Hugo, Arthur Rimbaud or Michelangelo it was unusual for an Englishman to embark into foreign territory; Britten's determined steps in this direction remain an important part of his achievement – an early statement of international intent, which refused to be hemmed in by English tradition. The 'olde English' way of doing things had long included a patriotic tendency to travel into the past, more specifically into the Elizabethan era (some of the English composers who were enthusiastic 'Elizabethans' are discussed later in this lecture). From relatively early on Britten was a part of a long-standing tradition of time-travelling in English music, but it was only gradually that he approached the Elizabethan age – more or less moving backwards in time as he did so. He refrained from Elizabethan evocation in the earlier part of his career, and one may say that his position in 1953 as a proud new Elizabethan, Companion of Honour and composer of *Gloriana* (a commission which all but openly acknowledged his position as Britain's premier composer) was reached in various stages – above all via realisations of

Henry Purcell (beginning in the middle to late 1940s) and of a complete reworking of John Gay's *The Beggars' Opera* (1947–48).

The most overtly significant preparatory work for *Gloriana* is undoubtedly the beautiful ⊙ *Lachrymae* for viola and piano (1950) – the only solo work for the composer's preferred string instrument (of which he was, incidentally, an accomplished player) that was published during his lifetime.[2] When Britten and Pears left for the United States in 1939, Frank Bridge, the composer's teacher, drove with his wife to Southampton. At this leave-taking Bridge gave Britten his own viola as a sign of his devoted admiration. This was to be the last time that the younger composer was to see Bridge, who died in 1941. He had been a leading professional violist, and the gift could not have been made lightly.

⊙ **CD2, track 1**

2. Viola works subsequently published include *Reflection* (1930; pub. 1997), *Elegy* (1930; pub. 1985), No. 2 of *Two Portraits* for viola and string orchestra (1930; pub. 1997) and the Double Concerto for violin and viola (1930; pub. 1999).

Pears and Julian Bream, 1956

Reflections and realisations: Dowland and Purcell

Succinct chamber music pieces of this distinction are rare in the English repertory; solo chamber music pieces of any kind are even rarer in the mature Britten's output, that is until the advent of the Russian cellist Rostropovich in the 1960s. The choice of Dowland as the source of the melodic inspiration for ⊙ *Lachrymae – Reflections on a song of John* ⊙ **CD2, track 1** *Dowland* Op. 48 (1950) seems apposite and natural. Peter Pears had known and loved the lute song repertoire long before the establishment of his relationship with Britten; he had been an accomplished consort singer with the English Singers, and had toured America with this ensemble in 1936, performing Elizabethan madrigals. Dowland, specifically, was to be a composer whom Pears served marvellously if not in his voice and piano duo with Britten, then in his later partnership with the lutenist Julian Bream.

Lachrymae is a skilfully unconventional set of variations from a composer who was on his way to becoming an acknowledged master of variation in all its forms. The first eight bars of Dowland's song 'If My Complaints Could Passion Move' serve as the basis of ten 'reflections', which are heard one after the other, without a break. These are preceded by a very cunning *lento* introduction based on the opening of Dowland's theme. A fuller appearance of this is partially concealed in the bass of the piano writing, beginning in the ninth bar of the piece. The composer's choice of the word 'reflections' is justified by Britten's determination to devise a construction that avoids the patchwork-quilt fragmentation of many sets of variations – this piece is a continuous piece of music. The appearance of another Dowland song, 'Flow, O My Tears', in the viola part of the sixth variation enriches the proceedings. But this work is planned in such a way that twentieth-century clouds gradually clear to reveal a soft ray of Elizabethan sunlight: this is the almost miraculous unveiling of something we had not realised we had been waiting for – the *second* half of Dowland's 'If My Complaints Could Passion Move', which serves as a coda. Intimately reflective, while majestically eloquent, this is the jewel that has been waiting to be placed in its setting. It is also the focal point to which the whole work has been leading in a steadily graded progress from complexity to extreme simplicity. By the end this retrogression has almost physically drawn us back into the clutches of a far-off century: it is as if we were listening to the strains of a chest of viols floating down a wooden-panelled corridor in a Tudor palace. It is in this music that we discern, albeit in the bud, the enormous emotional scale of *Gloriana*.

Dowland's influence at one end of the historical spectrum of Britten's

3. CDA 67061/2.

time-travelling is counterbalanced by that of Purcell at the other – a composer who might have merited a separate lecture in this book. In Britten studies, the many Purcell realisations are almost as rich a field as the folk-song arrangements. Hyperion issued a recording of this composer's complete Purcell realisations in 1995,[3] and I was proud to have been an instigator of the project. Amongst some of my contemporaries it was sometimes an *idée reçue* that Britten's arrangements were anachronistic and flawed, as if one adjective automatically went with the other. But it was interesting how many new converts these realisations (some of them fifty years old) made during the recording sessions. There was a roster of wonderful English singers for these discs (John Mark Ainsley, Ian Bostridge, James Bowman, Simon Keenlyside, Felicity Lott, Anthony Rolfe Johnson, Sarah Walker); most of them had sung this composer in more scholastically accurate editions. And yet they admitted, time and again, that they were 'spirited away' by the very arrangements that had come in for a great deal of opprobrium in earlier years. I was a student at the Royal Academy of Music in the early 1970s; the principal of that school, Sir Anthony Lewis, one of the great Purcell experts of the age, was horrified by Britten's realisations. I tried to draw Britten himself on this point: he simply said that Tony Lewis knew a great deal more about Purcell than he did. That was accurate no doubt, but not really the point. At the beginning of my musical career the battle still raged between the devotees of the sober song realisations of the Purcell Society (which never put a foot wrong, however leaden the feet of the various arrangers), and those, like me, who admired Britten's blatantly free arrangements (using all the resources of the piano, as well as pungent harmonic anachronisms). Somewhere between the two stood the Tippett–Bergmann arrangements, which were taken to be less offensive by the purists. I was of the 'in for a penny, in for a pound' school of thought. If one acknowledged that the use of the piano in accompanying Purcell was in any case an anachronism, it seemed to me that 'authenticity' was no longer the burning issue. Instead of allocating the Steinway harpsichord writing, it was surely more important that the excitement of playing the harpsichord, as well as an evocation of its actual *sound* (and somehow the reckless, colourful quality of Purcell's epoch) should be recreated in pianistic terms. (It is fascinating to see how Britten achieves just this, in the opening bars of his versions of 'Lord, What Is Man?', and the third version of 'If Music Be the Food of Love'.) Admittedly, this was at a time when the average accompanist would not have had sufficient knowledge, or experience, to make performing versions of his or her own.

Times have changed. Since the 1970s, the flowering of the early music movement has enabled us to take scholastically accurate recordings of Purcell's music more for granted. At last modern listeners have easy access to as much 'authentic' Purcell as they wish to hear. This has freed them, perhaps, to re-assess Britten's Purcell's realisations for what they really are: musical fireworks to set post-war Britain ablaze with that mix of 'clarity, brilliance, tenderness and strangeness' to which Pears and Britten refer at the beginning of their published editions. 'If you think *we* are strange', Britten and Pears seem to be saying, 'here is evidence that Purcell was too … he has much more in common with people like us than with the Puritans who would have harassed and prosecuted Nell Gwyn, or the Earl of Rochester, for immoral behaviour.' A number of Britten's works seek to strike off the rusty manacles of the Victorian age, but they do so without an openly confrontational agenda. The Purcell arrangements are bolder than most of Britten's statements, as are the folksong arrangements: they challenge the worthies of the musical establishment with a flair that was considered outrageous at the time. This confrontation was as near as Britten got to 'camp' – that lethal weapon which (when cleverly handled) has done much in recent times to deflate establishment pomposity on the subject of gender stereotypes. The composer's aesthetical rebellions in these areas enraged some people certainly, but they encouraged others to re-think the entire framework of their tastes and sympathies. It seems to me that Britten's hope for his listeners was not only a sharpening of the musical ear, but also a conversion to a state of mind that was more liberal and inwardly free. We will encounter another example of this in the love music considered next in this lecture.

In sheerly musical terms the Purcell realisations, or re-workings, belong to that very special, and usually audacious, world of transcriptions (typified by those larger than life *maestri* Liszt and Busoni) where old wine is poured into new bottles. Another metaphor involves glass of a different kind, this time lenses: familiar musical shapes are refracted prismatically through spectacles belonging to composers of equal, and sometimes greater, genius and imagination (thus the short-sighted Stravinsky arranged the music of Pergolesi for his far-sighted *Pulcinella*). At their best these conjunctions take our breath away by fusing the creative spirits of two great composers. The Britten–Purcell arrangements (as accurate a billing, I think, as Purcell–Britten, and one which perhaps makes more sense on the programmes of today) may have lost their ability to shock (no one objects to Bach on the piano any more), but they can still excite. In certain cases they get closer to the nerve-centre of the Purcellian powerhouse, in terms of word-setting and visceral response to text, than any other realisations before or since.

Francis Quarles,
contemporary portrait

The life and the career of the poet Francis Quarles (1592–1644) stand chronologically between those of Shakespeare and Purcell. He was twenty years younger than John Donne, and must have been much influenced by that master. Quarles, like Donne, was a staunch Royalist who would have ardently hoped, during his bleak later years (when Oliver Cromwell was anything but 'buried and dead') to see the victory of Charles I. He could not have realised Charles's son, Charles II, would be restored to the British throne only in 1660. Quarles did not live to enjoy the excitement of the return of the Stuart dynasty, although he would no doubt have been shocked by the excesses of the court. Quarles was a devout Anglican, almost exclusively taken up with religion as his subject matter. In the narrowness of his range (his posthumous reputation, such as it was, was attacked mercilessly by Alexander Pope) he was undeniably a minor poet, but one with particular gifts. His use of English for his biblical paraphrases, in its richness of metaphor, and in its passionate use of hyperbole, is of a kind that made Britten reach for a musical style influenced by the melismatic freedoms of Purcell. The mannerism of this exalted text 'My Beloved Is Mine', suggests the powerful sweep of a seventeenth-century sermon, and this must have been one of the reasons that it attracted Britten to select it as the text of his first *Canticle*, the prototype of five works written over a thirty-year period to different texts, each of them religious in a different way.

The piece, a setting of Quarles's meditation on the biblical *Song of Solomon*, otherwise known as *The Song of Songs*, was written for the Dick Sheppard Memorial Concert given at the Central Hall, Westminster, on 1 November 1947. Dick Sheppard (his name is mis-spelled as Shepherd in the printed dedication) was Vicar of St Martin-in-the-Fields; he was a clergyman-activist and leading figure in the Peace Pledge Union, to which

Britten and Pears belonged. He was much admired by many people for his courageous pacifism at a time when such a stance required the courage of one's convictions. In retrospect one is astonished by Britten's sheer nerve in selecting a text which combines a commitment to God, and an equally committed devotion to 'the beloved' in emotional, and physical, terms. It was a commitment mirrored by the depth of Britten's own relationship to Pears. Whether Quarles's poem had any homosexual intent, at least consciously, is doubtful. The tone of this ecstatic hymn of spiritual unity between God and man, the worshipped and the worshipper, is not unusual in literature of the period. This would have been appreciated by any member of the educated audience at the work's first performance, and making a fuss about the profusion of masculine pronouns in the piece would simply have been taken as a sign of ignorance of religious literature (Sir Philip Sidney's famous 'My True Love Hath My Heart, and I Have His' – set to music by Britten's deeply closeted teacher John Ireland incidentally – has usually been excused moral censure for the same reason). And yet here is an absolutely typical example of the composer's ability to be subversive. Ambiguity is the key. The full verbal impact of his Michelangelo songs (dedicated to Pears) had been deliberately disguised through distancing proclamations of love by voicing them in Italian. Here, a modern reading of this Quarles text easily (and naturally) encompasses an ecstatic hymn to the male lover. No modern heterosexual reader could doubt the eroticism of *The Song of Solomon* despite its biblical provenance, but its biblical status protected it, at least partly, from the censorship of the Victorian era. Here Britten's cloak is neither the Italian language nor the Bible, but the earlier conventions of English literature, and the use of passionately homoerotic metaphor in high-minded metaphysical poetry. Britten's use of this rather Anglican ambiguity for his own purposes (and these included both an honouring of Dick Sheppard's memory, and a reaffirmation of his love for Pears) is the type of subversive masterstroke that this composer carried off time and again.

Canticle I – My Beloved is Mine Op. 40 (1947)

Ev'n like two little bankdivided brooks
   That wash the pebbles with their wanton streams,
And having ranged and searched a thousand nooks,
    Meet both at length at silver-breasted Thames,
      Where in a greater current they conjoin,
So I my best beloved's am; so he is mine.
Ev'n so we met, and after long pursuit,

Ev'n so we joined; we both became entire.
No need for either to renew a suit,
  For I was flax, and he was flames of fire.
    Our firm-united souls did more than twine;
So I my best beloved's am; so he is mine.
If all those glittering monarchs that command
  The servile quarters of this earthly ball
Should tender, in exchange, their shares of land,
  I would not change my fortunes for them all;
    Their wealth is but a counter to my coin;
The world's but theirs; but my beloved's mine.
  …
Nor time, nor place, nor chance, nor death can bow
  My least desires unto the least remove;
He's firmly mine by oath, I his by vow;
  He's mine by faith and I am his by love;
    He's mine by water, I am his by wine;
Thus I my best beloved's am; thus he is mine.

⊙ CD2, track 2 ⊙ He is my altar; I, his holy place;
  I am his guest, and he my living food;
I'm his by penitence, he mine by grace;
  I'm his by purchase, he is mine by blood!
    He's my supporting elm, and I his vine;
Thus I my best beloved's am; thus he is mine.
He gives me wealth, I give him all my vows;
  I give him songs, he gives me length of days;
With wreaths of grace he crowns my longing brows,
  And I his temples with a crown of praise,
    Which he accepts: an everlasting sign
That I my best beloved's am, that he is mine.

The opening of the *Canticle* (marked 'Andante alla barcarola') is a remarkable study in bi-tonality. The verbal wordplay of the first strophe, and beyond, is water imagery worthy of the Schubert of *Die schöne Müllerin*. The courtship of the lovers, or of Christ and his adoring acolyte, is described as the watery progress of 'two little bankdivided brooks', one in each hand. Rocking left-hand quavers establish the barcarole movement while the right flows free in off-beat or syncopated quavers which flower into flurries of semiquavers. The interaction of these two musical strands is lyrical but awkward, as if perfect alignment is sought, but not yet achieved.

The struggle to become perfectly 'conjoined' is the theme of the first part of the canticle. This tugging of two different directions is emphasised by the rhythmical struggle between the hands, one in an imperturbable 6/8, the other in a dragging 2/4. At the end of the first strophe we first hear the words that become a refrain justifying the preceding imagery: 'So I my best beloved's am; so he is mine'. This is set as an almost unaccompanied recitative followed by a resolute modulation from G minor to G-flat major. The intensity of the wooing becomes more heated. At 'After long pursuit' the pianist's two hands chase each other down the keyboard; the right moves faster than the left and they actually catch up and collide as they land on the same E flat deep in the bass.

The moment when the key-signature changes again, this time to E-flat major, on 'we *joined*', is the climax of this whole section. 'Joined' occasions a mighty melisma, three bars long, ecstatic semiquavers in an almost sexual explosion of joy and energy. The words 'entire' and 'fire' are vocally decorated in a similarly extravagant way. The model seems to be partly the Elizabethans, partly Purcell, all via Michael Tippett, an influence here discernible not for the first time in Britten's music, and which will be discussed later in this lecture.

The second strophe begins with a series of recitative passages punctuated by mini-fanfares in the piano writing. One can hear in this music for 'those glitt'ring monarchs that command/The servile quarters of this earthly ball' the birth of several ceremonial patterns of fanfares in *Gloriana*, a 'glitt'ring monarch' if ever there was one. Quarles's abdication from a desire for earthly bounty seems at one in mood with the poem for the Earl of Essex's 'Second Lute Song' (in both songs the lover dreams of withdrawal from pomp and circumstance; this would have meant retiring from life in London – a town from which Britten also chose largely to withdraw). The third strophe is a scherzo marked 'Presto', where every trick of counterpoint is aptly deployed to depict the playful interaction of two personalities mirroring each other's devotion. The fifth strophe is suddenly marked 'Lento'. The levity of the preceding section is banished by a holy affirmation punctuated with rich chords in Scots-snap dotted rhythm. These throbbing impulses, when played softly and gently, denote the yearning and submission of the lover; but they can also appear proclamations of one's love to the outside world. The sixth, and last, strophe abandons chordal accompaniment in favour of a gentle weave of two-part harmony; the writing here is for hands which are placed closely together, almost as if entwined at the keyboard. This is music of intimacy, and music for the making of sacred vows. The vocal line is so exactly tailored for Pears's voice (the tessitura, the sinuous line, the required mastery of *mezza voce*) that it almost seems indecent to require anyone else to sing it.

This musing meditation seems to make time stand still. But Britten has one more masterstroke up his sleeve. The words 'an everlasting sign' call for a blessing to descend on the music that Britten duly provides (there is at least one such 'miracle' in each of the canticles). As the word 'sign' is held for three beats, the spare piano writing beneath melts into the warm effulgence of rich G major chords and another new key signature. This tonal metamorphosis lifts the music into a plane that is other-worldly – simultaneously metaphysical, and also deeply sensual. This duality is, after all, Britten's reading of the text. The progress of this grand musical arch from the G minor of the opening, to the G major of the coda provides an amazing sense of a promise fulfilled; it also demonstrates this composer's total control of tonal architecture.

Canticle I is a short work, but it makes a surprisingly powerful effect; its elusive appeal is derived in part from Britten's ardent response to Quarles's early seventeenth-century text. In the composer's output it stands between the *Holy Sonnets of John Donne* and *Gloriana*, an extraordinarily fertile period in Britten's career for time-travel. Of course there was nothing new whatever about evoking past centuries in original music. The recital repertoire is full of stylisations based on what one may term musical 'costume drama', where the disguises are of varying degrees of efficacy. Piano-accompanied song is a medium usually denied the theatrical trappings that help capture the attention of the public in operatic works. These extra-musical factors include moves for the singing actors (decided upon during an extended production period); a complicated lighting plot; a coherent story line (something lacking even in *Winterreise* for example); a varied cast of characters, and so on. Costumes also play an important role in any production. But it is sometimes possible to 'costume' songs with material no more substantial than style and harmony. It has long been the delight of certain composers to use archaisms of various kinds in order to clothe their works in a garb which is meant to evoke the past: a florid cadence with an opportune *tierce de Picardie* might trace the contours of an exaggeratedly courtly bow; a deliberately simple and archaic texture can help place a song in medieval times.

Time-travel at this less sophisticated level is within the reach of almost any composer with flair and an imitative ear: a tinkling Alberti bass and we have 'un po' de Mozartino' (as E.F. Benson's Lucia would have it); a few thundering chords in 'Sturm und Drang' mood, and gloomy Ludwig can be made to appear, or at least a passably decent look-alike. At one time such pastiche exercises in various composers' styles (particularly the dressing up of nursery rhymes) were published by Victor Hely-Hutchinson, Michael Diack and Herbert Hughes. There has never been any shortage of musical journalists or composers of film-music who can arrange things 'in the style of' by cottoning on to some of the more obvious mannerisms that characterise composers of all periods. As far back as 1936 Britten had composed music for a documentary film entitled *The Way to the Sea*, which included a historical sequence requiring various types of pastiche; the following year he composed the song 'Let the Florid Music Praise!', which opens with piano figurations that suggest neo-classical pomp. These were probably the earliest instances of this composer's own time-travelling.

I remember discussing with Britten something of a *cause célèbre* of the time: the case of Mrs Rosemary Brown, a medium of musical acuity, who claimed that she was daily visited in her flat in Balham by the ghosts of many great composers. The dictated musical results of these visits proved beyond doubt that an extended state of death had done nothing to burnish the talents of the departed masters who, without exception, seem to have slipped below their most convincing form. Schubert, as it happened, had chosen not to visit Mrs Brown's Balham abode. I wondered at the time whether this could have been because Schubert, of all composers, is the hardest to imitate with any authenticity. Britten agreed. At the time I did not realise that many years previously he had attempted to complete a lied (the Goethe setting 'Gretchens Bitte' D564) that Schubert had left as a fragment. Even Britten had not found that task at all easy.

Time-travel in song: a European digression

On the whole, the German lieder repertoire is not especially attuned to, or attracted by, time-travel. There are of course some exceptions, but the journey is more likely to encompass fifty years rather than two hundred. In 1802 Beethoven set the early eighteenth-century poet Gellert; the simplicity of the old-fashioned style suggests the rigours of a monumental faith where musical frills are out of place. The last song, 'Bußlied', might have been composed by C.P.E. Bach. When Schubert sets eighteenth-century poets (such as Hölty, Klopstock or Claudius) one can sense that he makes their music less 'modern' than if he were setting contemporary figures such as Goethe or Heine. In the deeply Catholic verses of F. von Schlegel's *Vom Mitleiden Mariä* he deliberately broaches the archaisms of the 'learned' old style.

On a number of occasions Schumann allowed the influence of his revered Bach to enter his music – the counterpoint in his duet 'In der

Nacht' is an example. The Gothic grandeur of Cologne cathedral is evoked at the opening of 'Im Rhein, im heiligen Strome' from *Dichterliebe*. The same composer's 'Stirb, Lieb' und Freude' from the Kerner *Liederreihe* Op. 35 is set in Augsburg cathedral; here Schumann allows himself to write in portentous breves – how ancient they look on the page! – for the only time in his songs. Some of his late songs to poems of Mary Stuart have an austere texture that suggests that the composer has taken some trouble to try and place the Queen in a sixteenth-century context (a drawback is that almost no German poetry from the sixteenth century lends itself to the lied form). Brahms, in setting the *Schöne Magelone* poems of Ludwig Tieck, allows himself a tone of ancient minstrelsy. This is hard to pinpoint unless these courtly Tieck songs are compared to settings of more modern inspiration. Hugo Wolf's 'Philine' (the poem is from Goethe's *Wilhelm Meister*) is a delicious eighteenth-century gavotte. Strauss's *Der Rosenkavalier* is an evocation of the eighteenth century on a much larger scale. But here we have suddenly returned to the subject of opera where an elaborate set (and costumes) can play as large a part in evoking the Vienna of Maria Theresa as the music itself.

Far richer in the field of pastiche, and more complex in its various gradations ranging from inspired to banal, is the repertoire of the French *mélodie*. The chaotic France of the post-revolutionary period could look back to various historical pasts with pride and pleasure, something that the Germans (as a not yet united nation) were unable to do. The medieval period is evoked in Claude Debussy's highly atmospheric (and rigorously austere) settings of Charles d'Orléans and François Villon – afterwards the dying composer, horrified by the First World War, chose to call himself 'Claude de France', taking refuge in a cloak of medievalism. This exploration of the fifteenth century seems to have been the long-delayed result, as much else in Debussy's creative life, of his friendship with Erik Satie. At about the same time Reynaldo Hahn set the amorous 'Quand je fus pris au pavillon', a rondel by Charles d'Orléans which calls for a romp in madrigal style. Forty years later, and oppressed by the prospects of a second European war, Francis Poulenc turned to Charles d'Orléans for his hieratic 'Priez pour paix', a stained-glass window in song.

Another period for re-visiting by musicians was that of the Valois kings. The glorious chateaux of the Loire valley remain a testament to the richly creative reigns of François I and Henri II. The great poet of this period, one might almost say France's Shakespeare, was Pierre de Ronsard (1524–85). There were also other contemporary poets who belonged to a starry group of writers known as *La Pléiade*. Almost every time that a French composer sets the words of Ronsard or his contemporaries we encounter a time-travelling stylisation. This is the case with Charles Gounod's enchanting 'O ma belle rebelle' (the words are by Baïf, a *Pléiade* member), Georges Bizet's 'Sonnet' (Ronsard), Ravel's two settings of Clément Marot (one of which evokes the sound of the spinet to delightful effect), to name only a few from a much longer list (Saint-Saëns, Duparc, Sévérac, D'Indy *et alia*). Chabrier's opera *Le Roi malgré lui* is a remarkable piece of time-travel, with sixteenth-century Poland as its destination. Reynaldo Hahn's increasingly popular song 'A Chloris' – its nearest musical relative is Bach's *Air on a G string* – is a setting of Théophile de Viau, a poet who was banished during the reign of Louis XIII for the irregularities of his morals. This choice of text by Hahn, the lover of Marcel Proust, has something of a Brittennian air of quiet subversion about it. In more modern times Poulenc's lute song pastiche 'A sa guitare' (words by Ronsard) comes to mind, as do numerous choral settings, and some piano pieces, in which this composer evokes the sixteenth century. George Enescu's Marot settings are fluently successful examples of successful sixteenth-century stylisation. The composer Jacques Leguerney (1906–97) made almost an entire career from exploring every possible musical aspect of illustrating the period of the *Pléiade*.

Perhaps the most recent period on which a Frenchman of the late nineteenth century may have looked back with some nostalgia is that of the *ancien régime* – the France of the Bourbon kings at Versailles. The most astonishing and enduring pastiche of this period is Jules Massenet's opera, *Manon* (1884). Paul Verlaine's evocations of the *bergerette* games of courtiers in Louis XV's reign were inspired by the paintings of Antoine Watteau; Verlaine's poems were issued under the title *Fêtes galantes* (1869) and these were seized by a number of French composers who set them in various ways. That immortal song 'Clair de lune' of Gabriel Fauré (1887) is as subtle a piece of time-travel as is to be found anywhere in the repertoire – the grace and the inordinately complex manners of another age come to vivid musical life in a setting remarkable for its underplayed musical language and style – a perfect embodiment of passion beneath the surface in a courtly world where the strictest of etiquette controls all emotional responses. Perhaps because this mood happens to chime with Fauré's own temperament, a number of his songs were cast in this mould – something which has been dubbed his 'madrigal' style. Among the best known of these is 'Chanson d'amour' ('J'aime tes yeux/J'aime ton front/O ma rebelle/O ma farouche'), which is a setting of a poem by the composer's contemporary, Armand Silvestre. This music, where the piano imitates a gently plucked lute, evokes a courtly antiquity which is deliberately ageless, a vagueness which is something of a Fauré speciality. His incidental music for Edmond de Haraucort's play *Shylock* (after the *Merchant of Venice*) is his charming contribution to Shakespearian characterisation. Berlioz and Chausson had set this writer in their time, but Fauré's music sounds positively Elizabethan in comparison.

Back to England …

Shakespeare! The Elizabethan age! These are proud calls to arms for the English artist. If the French had a more active musical life in the nineteenth century than our own, nothing can hide the fact that the sixteenth and seventeenth centuries were a more glorious part of English musical history. There is little in French music truly to compete with the great lute songs and church music of Elizabethan times, and the vigour of Elizabethan theatre and poetry was also *sans pareil*. This had long been a factor in the musical pride that had almost wilfully turned many British composers away from an Armada of European influences. Their response was along the lines of 'we have been great before as a threatened island, and we can be great again'. After we had emerged from the Victorian age, and from being in the thrall of Mendelssohn, Brahms and Wagner, it is noticeable how Elizabethan stylisations began gradually to creep into English song, and with slowly increasing evocative accuracy. One of the earliest of these is 'Queen Mary's Song' ('Low, low my lute') by Edward Elgar (1887). The text is taken from Tennyson's play about Mary Tudor and one can hear the composer making a real effort to capture an appropriately historical inflection. Edward German's operetta *Merrie England* was written in 1902, a work that achieved as much popularity as Gilbert and Sullivan, and is now notorious for its simplistic view of England's merriness in days of yore. Far more serious work was done by Vaughan Williams in researching real Elizabethan sources: this resulted in such works as his *Fantasia on a Theme of Thomas Tallis* (1910), and his Shakespeare opera *Sir John in Love* (1924–28), from which comes his *Fantasia on Greensleeves*. Ivor Gurney (1890–1937) spoke of his five songs to Elizabethan texts (1920) as his 'Elizas'. At least three of these are in styles convincingly evocative of the sixteenth century, both perky ('Under the Greenwood Tree' and 'Spring') and soulful (the beautiful 'Sleep'). The real master of Elizabethiana before Britten was Peter Warlock (1894–1930). I know of nothing more piquant in English song than such virtuoso pieces as the dazzling 'The Lover's Maze' of 1927 (the piano part seems to come straight from the more devilishly difficult pages of the *Fitzwilliam Virginal Book*), nor more moving than the justly famous 'Sleep' – here the part-writing of the accompaniment suggests a chest of viols. In this style Warlock is prodigal with his viols, less so with his vowels. The extravagance of his inspired pastiche is confined to a relish for false relations, and a delight in the dexterity of his accompaniments; the fetching melodies sometimes suggest the old style, but the word-setting, apart from changes of metre (as in 'Sleep'), remains free from melisma. In this way Warlock held true to the tenets of his time; the prevailing rule of one syllable per note overrules the verbal freedoms of the past.

One should also mention here an interest in great seventeenth-century poets, although John Donne is conspicuously absent: Herrick was lovingly set by Quilter in his cycle *To Julia* (1905); 'To Gratiana Dancing and Singing' by W. Denis Browne (1888–1915) is a gravely beautiful setting of Richard Lovelace where the sound of the accompanying harpsichord floating across the centuries is evoked in extraordinarily luminous terms (at the time many poets were moved by the performances of that pioneer harpsichordist Mrs Violet Gordon Woodhouse, 1872–1948). Less original, but still very charming, is Herbert Howells's 'Gavotte', which has more in common with the pastiches of the French composers, Hahn say, in summoning up a time of 'lords and ladies' that is impossible to date precisely. However, Howells's music for clavichord – e.g. 'Lambert's Clavichord' (1926–27), 'My Lady Harewood's Pavane' (1949), 'Finzi; His Rest' (1956) shows this composer to have been a serious scholar of Tudor music.

The stage was now set for a second Elizabethan age, although in musical terms it dawned a decade before the accession of the new Queen. When Britten had left for America his main English rival had been William Walton (the latter's contributions to the genre of musical time-travel with his film music for Olivier's *Henry V* could be the subject of another discussion). When Britten returned to England in 1942, his new opera under his arm, he was certain of his ascendancy among English composers. But in his absence a new genius, albeit eight years older than him, had begun to make his mark. Imprisoned in Wormwood Scrubs as a wartime conscientious objector, also homosexual, good-looking and charismatic, Michael Tippett (1905–98) could not be written off as another establishment figure blocking musical (and social) change. On the contrary, he forced the pace of change, not least as a writer and a teacher – he gave inspiring classes at Morley College, which included study of the Elizabethan repertoire. For a crucial period between 1943 and 1953, Tippett's music was a major influence on Britten's work and vice versa. Theirs was a friendship inevitably shot through with friendly rivalry, but a competitive element between them had crucial consequences for English song.

Tippett wrote a new piece for the Pears–Britten duo almost as soon as the couple had returned from America. This was the cantata *Boyhood's End* (1943), surely one of his greatest, and most ground-breaking, works (it is obvious that the continuous cantata form of Britten's *Canticle I*, written four years later, derives from this piece). In this music we can hear all the fruits of Tippett's profound, and intuitively visceral, response to the Elizabethans. *Boyhood's End* bristles with modern versions of the complexities of the greatest madrigals and music for viols. The use of extended melisma is astonishing (for example on the three-fold repeated word 'dance' which, in this setting, truly lives up to its meaning); the performers also have to negotiate a hemiola minefield. The virtuosity of the piano-writing (despite the fact that Tippett was no pianist) is spine-tingling, and the final section (despite quite unreasonable vocal demands on the tenor) is visionary in a way that is unique in English song. This work was written at full pelt, and it has to be performed with similarly extravagant commitment. When Tippett handed over the manuscript to his dedicatees it must have been clear that Pears had a great many notes to learn, and that Britten was in for a lot of piano practice.

What else did Britten think? I can imagine a mixture of admiration, dismay and genuine puzzlement. Quite apart from a certain unrelenting density in the writing, which would not have been to Britten's taste, why, for example, had Tippett decided to marry this extraordinary neo-Elizabethan style with words (in prose) by W.H. Hudson about his boyhood in Argentina of all places? This passage from *Far Away, and Long Ago* about Hudson's nostalgia for the beauties of the Pampas, is powerfully evocative but, knowing Britten, I can see that he must have thought it a mismatch with the music. This exalted style surely called for Elizabethan texts, poetry (not prose) contemporary with the spirit of the musical evocation. Here, surely, lies the birth of the idea behind the musical style of *The Holy Sonnets of John Donne*.

It is an almost legendary fact that this great work was written in a week or so in August 1945. The composer was ill with fever, but nevertheless composed the cycle at a feverish pace. He had just returned from a tour of the recently liberated German concentration camps. There he accompanied Yehudi Menuhin in music for violin and piano performed for the surviving inmates; the duo gave up to three short recitals a day. After seeing the unimaginable sights of genocide (about which the world in general at that time was still ill-informed) it was inevitable that Britten should have been deeply affected. The Holocaust was the catalyst that made him rise to what might be thought of as Tippett's challenge – to write a really important work that drew on the greatest manifestations of Britain's musical past. But there was a further purpose to this counterblast to European disintegration and decay. After having just seen such evidence of Nazi atrocity, any English artist might be excused a moment of patriotic insistence on his own national identity. One of the greatest English poets, John Donne, would give voice to the composer's despair at the barbarity of modern times. Which living poet could have been asked to write words adequate to such a task? None. Up to this point Donne was a more or less an unset poet, scarcely, if ever broached by musicians (apart from the famous 'Hymn to God the Father' by Pelham Humfrey). Donne's slate was clean of other musical associations, and his searing poems were classics that could appear universal and relevant to all ages.

The new work that came out of this experience was one of Britten's finest, a pendant to his other cycle of sonnets by Michelangelo. The great themes of love and death are thus reflected in Britten's output by the words of two artists who seem to pass the torch one to the other – Michelangelo died in 1564, only eight years before Donne was born (1564, incidentally, was also the year of Shakespeare's birth, another coincidence). One might believe that Britten was aware of a kind of symmetry in his choice of poets; both works are dedicated to Peter Pears.

The Holy Sonnets of John Donne Op. 35 (1945)

John Donne (1572–1631) was one of the greatest non-theatrical poets of the age. He was born into a recusant Catholic family and only gradually embraced Anglicanism. As a young man he took part in the Earl of Essex's successful attack on Cadiz (in Britten's *Gloriana* the Queen greets the Earl with the words 'Victor of Cadiz'). In 1601 Donne secretly married Lady Anne More without her father's consent, which cost him much trouble in his career. As a result of the marriage, his hopes of a life in politics gradually receded; on the advice of James I he eventually entered the church. He became one of the great preachers of the age; his majesty of diction is evident in the use of language in the Holy Sonnets. His devotion to his wife remained constant; she died in 1617, giving birth to their twelfth child (who also died). This painful circumstance is reflected in the sixth *John Donne,* sonnet in this cycle. Donne was much preoccupied with the theme of death *contemporary portrait* throughout his career – sometimes with almost suicidal fear, at others with doughty optimism in the immortality of the soul. Nicholas Stone's effigy of Donne in white marble survived the destruction of the old St Paul's in the Great Fire of 1666 (the only monument to do so). It can be seen in the South aisle of the present cathedral.

The piano writing in this set of songs is probably the most difficult of any of the Britten works for voice and piano. Many of these pieces are dominated by a single accompanimental motif. In this way Elizabethan freedom and intensity are tempered by Schubertian economy, a distinct difference from the aesthetic governing Tippett's much more pianistically 'busy' cantata.

⊙ CD2, track 3

⊙ (i) Oh My Blacke Soule

Oh my blacke Soule! now thou art summoned
By sicknesse, death's herald, and champion;
Thou art like a pilgrim, which abroad hath done
Treason, and durst not turne to whence hee is fled,
Or like a thiefe, which till death's doome be read,
Wisheth himselfe deliver'd from prison;
But damn'd and hal'd to execution
Wisheth that still he might be imprisoned.
Yet grace, if thou repent, thou canst not lacke;
But who shall give thee that grace to beginne?
Oh make thy selfe with holy mourning blacke,
And red with blushing, as thou art with sinne;
Or wash thee in Christ's blood, which hath this might
That being red, it dyes red soules to white.

In the first song hammered double octaves call the soul to account as if in the most solemn legal process. The voice weaves its address in wideranging intervals. Here and elsewhere in the cycle the oratorical inflections of Donne the celebrated preacher are wonderfully captured in the wideranging contours of the vocal line. For nine bars the accompaniment is centred on repeated F sharps; at 'Thou art like a pilgrim' the rise of a semitone in the accompaniment (to a G natural) seems like the beginning of a portentous journey – the song seems suddenly launched on its magnificent progress. In the last four lines of the poem unremitting octaves are replaced by softer, more inward harmonies. Black, red and white are evoked in this concluding section, and the accompaniment follows suit with chords successively murky, rich and finally drained of colour to match the phrase 'it dyes red souls to white'.

128

⊙ (ii) Batter my heart

Batter my heart, three person'd God; for, you
As yet but knocke, breathe, shine, and seeke to mend
That I may rise, and stand, o'erthrow mee, and bend
Your force, to breake, blowe, burn and make me new.
I, like an usurpt towne, to another due,
Labour to admit you, but Oh, to no end,
Reason your viceroy in mee, mee should defend,
But is captiv'd, and proves weake or untrue.
Yet dearely I love you, and would be loved faine,
But am betroth'd unto your enemie:
Divorce mee, untie, or breake that knot againe,
Take mee to you, imprison mee, for I
Except you enthrall mee, never shall be free,
Nor ever chaste, except you ravish mee.

This is the first of three songs that are framed as challenging piano études – in this case semiquaver triplets that dart up and down the keyboard like the feverish shivers that probably assailed the composer as he wrote the music. Here the vocal line, charged with the delivery of many vehement words, is hardly melismatic at all (the final 'ravish mee' is an exception). Instead the music is propelled forward by a menacing and muttering parlando – a terrific challenge for both performers.

⊙ (iii) O Might those Sighes and Teares

O might those sighes and teares returne againe
Into my breast and eyes, which I have spent,
That I might in this holy discontent
Mourne with some fruit, as I have mourn'd in vaine;
In mine Idolatry what show'rs of rain
Mine eyes did waste? what griefs my heart did rent?
That sufferance was my sinne; now I repent;
'Cause I did suffer I must suffer paine.
Th'hydroptique drunkard, and night-scouting thiefe,
The itchy Lecher, and self tickling proud
Have the remembrance of past joyes, for reliefe
Of coming ills. To poore me is allow'd
No ease; for, long, yet vehement griefe hath beene
Th'effect and cause, the punishment and sinne.

This is a slow and eloquent song that finds its counterpart many years later in the *Elegia* movement of the Britten Cello Sonata. Both voice and accompaniment roll lugubriously from side to side in semiquaver intervals, a musical metaphor for sighing and weeping. Keening quavers are gradually replaced by semiquavers; these in turn lead up to desperate vocal outbursts, grotesque pictures of drunkards, thieves and lechers, accompanied by shivering *tremolandi* as if played by strings *sul ponticello*. The music then returns to those pivoting intervals (rocking between C and B natural) that seem to indicate obsessive introspection and mental imprisonment. There is something about this music which also depicts the merciless passing of time: staccato notes (both sung and played) can be heard as the dropping of tears, but the tick of a clock never seems far away (compare this, for example, with 'Lines Written During a Sleepless Night', the last song of *The Poet's Echo* – see p.203).

(iv) Oh, to vex me

Oh, to vex me, contraryes meet in one:
Inconstancy unnaturally hath begott
A constant habit; that when I would not
I change in vowes, and in devotione.
As humorous is my contritione
As my profane Love, and as soone forgott:
As ridlingly distemper'd, cold and hott,
As praying, as mute; as infinite, as none.
I durst not view Heav'n yesterday; and today
In prayers, and flatt'ring speaches I court God:
Tomorrow I quake with true feare of his rod.
So my devout fitts come and go away
Like a fantastique Ague: save that here
Those are my best dayes, when I shake with feare.

This is another piano étude fit to describe the 'devout fitts' of a 'fantastique Ague'. The ceaseless twisting and turning of the babbling figurations seems directly inspired by the nervy, energetic slews of notes that characterise Tippett's piano writing in *Boyhood's End*. At the same time, the image of 'contraryes meet in one' is wonderfully caught by the opposite directions, first up, then down, in which the piano writing moves in the opening bars of the accompaniment. This song contains the work's most extravagant melisma: for the word 'shake' no fewer than thirty-seven notes descend in sequences of triplets, which twist and turn in a mixture of tones and semitones. After this ordeal, the simplicity of 'with fear' (two staccato notes, a syllable apiece, separated by a rest) is a masterstroke of contrast.

(v) What if this present

What if this present were the world's last night?
Marke in my heart, O Soule, where thou dost dwell,
The picture of Christ crucified, and tell
Whether that countenance can thee affright,
Teares in his eyes quench the amazing light,
Blood fills his frownes, which from his pierc'd head fell.
And can that tongue adjudge thee into hell,
Which pray'd forgiveness for his foes fierce spight?
No, no; but as in my idolatrie
I said to all my profane mistresses,
Beauty, of pitty, foulnesse onely is
A signe of rigour, so I say to thee,
To wicked spirits are horrid shapes assign'd,
This beauteous forme assures a pitious minde.

The culminative power of this march is related to the 'Dirge' from the *Serenade* for tenor, horn and strings. Its gawky and grotesque aspect is the result of heavy and insistent staccato quavers punched out in the bass while the right hand roves wild and free with trills, semiquavers, sextuplets and demi-semiquavers. The thrust of this music, its driving impulse, suggests abandoned sexual congress while being tormented with guilt personified by 'wicked spirits' and 'horrid shapes'. The poet speaks of his panic (and self-revulsion) at the thought of being caught in lustful activity as the Last Trump sounds and brings him to account. Like some of the other songs in this cycle it has a Schubertian link: Britten seems to have imagined the 'world's last night' as cold, stormy and windy. Under his or her fingers the pianist feels the ghost of the second song from *Winterreise* ('Die Wetterfahne') with its shuddering trills and unhinged semiquaver figurations, which trace the whiplash movement of a weather-vane. In that song the villain is the 'rich bride' whose fickle affections have led to the winter traveller's betrayal and madness. The final sextet of the poem is in another mood altogether – a bridge passage into the love music of the next setting. The ghost of the march continues through the music, like the rumble of distant drums while the vocal line calms into the rapt contemplation. It is as if those abandoned exclamations of 'No, No' had been climactic in every sense; only the relief of subsequent detumescence (the music also softens) brings the anguished poet any relief from his lust. The song ends in a mood of touching emotional dependency on 'this beauteous form' (perhaps the poet's wife as opposed to one of his 'profane mistresses'). But for most of the sonnet the entwined t(h)rills and tremors of sex and guilty self-laceration are hair-raising.

(vi) Since she whom I loved

Since she whom I lov'd hath payd her last debt
To Nature, and to hers, and my good is dead,
And her Soule early into Heaven ravished,
Wholly on heavenly things my mind is sett.
Here the admyring her my mind did whett
To seeke thee God; so streames do shew their head;
But though I have found thee, and thou my thirst hast fed,
A holy thirsty dropsy melts mee yett.
But why should I begg more Love, when as thou
Dost wooe my soule for hers; offring all thine:
And dost not only feare least I allow
My Love to Saints and Angels things divine,
But in thy tender jealosy dost doubt
Least the World, Fleshe, yea Devill putt thee out.

If the previous sonnet has been profane love, this is a hymn to sacred love. It is one of Britten's greatest songs, an instinctively heartfelt response to Donne's bereavement on the loss of his wife. The accompaniment is in gently oscillating triplets throughout, shaped in such a way that the ear sometimes hears them in duplets. This is one of the very few Britten songs that calls for a type of lieder rubato seldom encountered with such potency in his music – that is, hesitations and placements to mark harmonic turning points, surging forward at times, and pulling back at others. Even the singer's melody has a lieder-like lyricism; the highly placed, and highly strung, vocal line is anguished and calm in turns. The way the composer accompanied this song himself was wonderfully flexible, imbued with an understanding of song traditions other than English. The elegiac tone of Mahler's *Kindertotenlieder* comes to mind here, an unlikely alliance between the English neo-Baroque and the Viennese Successionist. It would not have escaped Britten's notice that the concentration camps from which he had just returned enfolded millions of stories of similar family tragedy and bereavement – that is if there was a family member left alive to grieve. The reconciliation of such cruel loss with continuing religious belief, the dilemma at the core of Donne's poem, is also one of the great themes of the Holocaust.

(vii) At the round earth's imagin'd corners
At the round earth's imagin'd corners, blow
Your trumpets, Angels, and arise, arise
From death, you numberlesse infinities
Of soules, and to your scattr'd bodies goe,
All whom the flood did, and fire shall o'erthrow,
All whom warre, dearth, age, agues, tyrannies,
Despaire, law, chance, hath slaine, and you whose eyes,
Shall behold God, and never taste death's woe.
But let them sleepe, Lord, and mee mourne aspace,
For, if above all these, my sinnes abound,
'Tis late to ask abundance of thy grace,
When we are there; here on this lowly ground,
Teach me how to repent; for that's as good
As if thou hadst seal'd my pardon, with thy blood.

This is a companion piece to the fifth song in this cycle, and another nocturne. No less than the Second Coming promised in *Revelations* is the theme. Britten is at his most boldly illustrative at the opening. But, as in a number of the other settings, there is a clear distinction, a thesis and antithesis, between the two parts of the sonnet – octet and sextet. Here the first eight lines are brightly illumined with the glow of blazing trumpets – there is a majesty and pomp and circumstance about this music that prophecies *Gloriana*. On the other hand, when it is time for Donne to make his own personal reckoning with the Almighty, Britten somehow superimposes the intimacy of the confessional on a much broader musical canvas depicting the end of the rest of the world. The trumpets now resound in the bass clef of the accompaniment while the vocal line breathlessly echoes the outline of their distant fanfares. The final line, addressed to God, is unaccompanied. The sounds of the Last Trump no longer pursue and accuse the poet. This is a marvellous line conceived, like so much else, for Pears's voice alone – a single long-spanned musical arch that achingly rises to the words 'sealed my pardon' before it falls back to its starting point – a genuflection in sound. It is surely here that the final unaccompanied phrase of the Agnus Dei from the *War Requiem* ('Dona nobis pacem') had its beginning.

(viii) Thou hast made me

Thou hast made me, and shall thy worke decay?
Repaire me now, for now mine end doth haste,
I runne to death, and death meets me as fast,
And all my pleasures are like yesterday;
I dare not move my dimme eyes any way,
Despaire behind, and death before doth cast
Such terror, and my feeble flesh doth waste
By sinne in it, which it t'wards Hell doth weigh;
Onely thou art above, and when t'wards thee
By thy leave I can looke, I rise againe;
But our old subtle foe so tempteth me,
That not one houre my selfe I can sustaine;
Thy Grace may wing me to prevent his art,
And thou like Adamant draw mine iron heart.

This is the last of the three études in the cycle, a devilish pianistic construction where the left hand chases the right – or is it vice versa? – in shuddering octaves up and down the keyboard. The kinetic energy of the Creation of Man ('Thou has made me') is expressed here (see also the flurry of creation of bird life in the wild triplets of 'Proud Songsters', the fifth song in the *Winter Words* cycle) as if handfuls of clay were simply being thrown at the potter's wheel. Partly defiant, and partly cravenly fearful, the poet veers dizzily between radiant faith and tearful supplication. The way the vocal line rises to the top of the stave (we are made to follow Donne's upward gaze with the words 'Onely thou art above') is extraordinary. Britten seems to have no difficulty in limning in expressive details (the soaring arpeggio resurrection on 'I rise againe' is a case in point) while allowing the *moto perpetuo* to tread water, as it were, while doing so. The last two lines of the poem are set on a long succession of E flats – the musical equivalent of the vocal line having the unbending strength of Adamant. It is as if Donne is hanging on for dear life, seeking his final refuge by holing up at the top of the stave. This determination is shaken only at the very end. The coda is surely the most stormy of any Britten song.

(ix) Death be not proud

Death be not proud, though some have called thee
Mighty and dreadfull, for, thou art not soe,
For, those, whom thou think'st, thou dost overthrow,
Die not, poore death, nor yet canst thou kill mee.

From rest and sleepe, which but thy pictures bee,
Much pleasure, then from thee, much more must flow,
And soonest our best men with thee doe goe,
Rest of their bones, and soules deliverie.
Thou art slave to Fate, Chance, kings and desperate men,
And dost with poyson, warre, and sicknesse dwell,
And poppie, or charmes, can make us sleepe as well,
And better than thy stroake; why swell'st thou then?
One short sleepe past, wee wake eternally,
And death shall be no more; death, thou shalt die.

After the depiction of so much fear, so much horror and revulsion, so much grief, it was important that the clinching song of the cycle should have a different message. The words 'Death be not proud' at the beginning of this poem must have immediately appealed to Britten. The Allies had just defeated an overwhelmingly proud enemy whose insignia was death – literally so in the case of the SS. Donne's defiance of death in this poem can be heard (in the context of this cycle) as a defiant rejection of the dark forces that had gripped Europe for so many years. The composer's visits to Belsen and other camps revealed to him a new scale of horror in man's inhumanity to man, but the fact that he and Menuhin had played to survivors, however few, was a triumph over the Nazi death machine, and over death itself. Life would go on, and this horror, too, would pass. Here Britten calls on Purcell's favourite device, the ground bass, or passacaglia, to make his point. The music has the grandeur and dignity of a broad march that also manages to be elegiac. The time-signature is 4/4, but there are times when a hemiola in the vocal line is superimposed on the implacable progress of a bass line that repeats itself every five bars. The music is a set of extremely cunning variations: the gentleness of 'From rest and sleepe', the strident accusatory tone of 'Thou art slave to Fate' (where the voice is jagged and disjointed), and the triumphant climax of 'And better than thy stroake'. As a coda, the augmentation of 'One short sleepe past' (where the melody suddenly expands into minims) is one of those many moments in this cycle when technical wizardry astounds us, but never at the expense of our emotions. One only notices how clever Britten has been after he has profoundly moved us.

After we have heard this cycle we ask ourselves whether this music is pastiche, stylisation, or Baroque evocation. It is none of these, yet they have all played their part in the music's genesis. The refiner's fire has burnt away the

Michael Tippett

4. From C. Palmer (ed.),
The Britten Companion
(Faber and Faber, 1984).

residual traces of anything copied or unoriginal. But the service to Donne *does* encompass imitation and stylisation of a kind. Because these are great seventeenth-century words, Britten has a way of suggesting, whether through vocal or pianistic virtuosity, those flights of exalted fantasy that make the Baroque what it is. The role of Tippett in this sound-word is crucial as I have said, but it was Britten who balanced neo-Purcellian music of this kind with poetry that was meant for it. Allow me to quote the words of a friend of mine, that fine poet Peter Porter:

I had read John Donne but had responded to his baroque exaggeration very imperfectly until I heard Britten's music for nine of the *Holy Sonnets*. There, in his equally extravagant declamation, and his quick-changing moods, its matching imagery with musical virtuosity, and its reliance on a range of vocal devices from bitter parlando to saturated melisma, I found a way into Donne's world. Donne's universe of 'auto-angst' spoke to me for the first time. Britten's settings are not alien to Donne's poetry: on the contrary, they show how poetical Donne is, and they underline that in linking itself to poetry music may be returning to its true home – at least when the composer has a genius for song.[4]

We end this lecture with many points left undiscussed: Britten's Second String Quartet, for example, dedicated to the memory of Purcell and bristling with all the wonderful things of which that composer's technical resources were capable – above all in the mighty concluding Passacaglia. Some years after the *Holy Sonnets* were composed, Tippett responded to Britten's challenge with another song cycle, *The Heart's Assurance* (1950–51), which, in turn, owes much to Britten's example. The influence of 'Death be not Proud' on 'Remember your Lovers' is particularly clear (Peter Pears often spoke of Tippett's indebtedness in this case – proof, if any were needed, that this 'exchange' of competitive rivalry between two young composers was an unofficially thorny issue). This new Tippett cycle, a setting of verses by war poets of World War Two, Alun Lewis and Sidney Keyes, was also dedicated to Britten and Pears, who duly gave its first performance. Perhaps it was at this time that Britten stored away a determination to set war poetry one day in a way that would astonish even Tippett.

Eight years after the *Holy Sonnets*, the crowning of a new Queen Elizabeth in 1953 was the perfect incentive for Britten to show what he could do, if he chose, to outdo all other 'Elizabethans' in terms of scale and skill. By this time, Imogen Holst (1907–84), that remarkable musicologist and choral conductor who had long been conversant with the Elizabethan repertory, was at the composer's right hand as his music assistant. The disgraceful story of the hostile reception of *Gloriana* by the critics belongs to another article; this would have to discuss the establishment's hostility to Britten's lifestyle as much as to his music.

And now, a final point. Britten's last and greatest stylisation – *A Midsummer Night's Dream* (1960) – undoubtedly owes its power and fluency to all those years of assimilating (while enriching and subverting) the English tradition – including all the Purcell realisations, revising *The Beggar's Opera*, and composing *Gloriana*. And just when we imagine that we have identified this great Shakespeare opera (the most successful by any English composer) as being thoroughly English, Britten embarks, in the final act of that opera, on the most devilishly cunning comic pastiche of Italian *bel canto* opera that could ever be imagined. But here we must stop for fear of never finishing. It seems there is no end to the laying on of hands between countries, and between centuries, in this composer's work.

The programme at the 2001
Britten festival was comprised of:
***On This Island* Op. 11 (Auden):**
'Let the Florid Music Praise!',
'Now the Leaves are Falling Fast',
'Seascape', 'Nocturne', 'As It Is,
Plenty'; 'The Sun Shines Down'
(Auden); 'To Lie Flat on the Back'
(Auden); 'Fish in the Unruffled
Lakes' (Auden); 'When You're
Feeling like Expressing your
Affection' (Auden); *Canticle V - The*
Death of St Narcissus Op. 89 **(Eliot);**
Canticle IV - The Journey of the Magi
Op. 86 *(Eliot);* 'Underneath the
Abject Willow' *(Auden);* **Cabaret**
Songs *(Auden): 'Tell me the Truth*
about Love', 'Funeral Blues', 'Johnny',
'Calypso'

Lecture 6

Beginnings (Auden) and ends (Eliot)

This lecture is given over to two of Britten's, and Britain's, most important poets. Indeed one may say that Eliot and Auden (for this is their chronological order of seniority) were two of the greatest, if not the greatest, of all twentieth-century English poets. There is about some aspects of their very different lives a curious mirror-image symmetry. Thomas Stearns Eliot (1888–1965) was born and raised in America but became a quintessential Englishman. Wystan Hugh Auden (1907–73) was born English but, despite his middle-class background and public-school upbringing, became a naturalised American who thrived, for a time at least, in the louche bohemian atmosphere of New York. He once said that he preferred to live in that city because the things he hated most were more obvious there and he was in no danger of succumbing to their neon lures.

T.S. Eliot looked the part of the English civil servant to such an extent that he went to work (at Faber and Faber in London – he was, incidentally, also Auden's publisher) in a bowler hat. The late Queen Mother, in a possibly apocryphal conversation with A.N. Wilson, recalled a poetry reading at Windsor arranged by the Sitwells during the war. A very stiff gentleman 'who looked like a banker' gave incomprehensible readings from something called *The Desert* (Wilson gently suggested to his royal interlocutor that this was probably *The Waste Land*), which caused barely suppressed hilarity among the entire royal party. On this embarrassing occasion (and, to be fair, the Queen Mother described it as such) Eliot must have been easily the most patrician presence in the room. And so well he might: he was a lord of literature, and no poet who followed him, including Auden, could claim to be free of his influence. In 1948, a short time after this episode at Windsor, he was awarded both the Order of Merit and the Nobel Prize for Literature.

Opposite: Britten and Auden, New York, c. 1941

139

W.H. Auden (one wonders whether his use of his two prefatory initials was inspired by Eliot's example) blithely disregarded most aspects of outward respectability. Apart from an obsession with punctuality, he had few of the social graces that are supposed to typify the English gentleman. He had nicotine-stained fingers by his middle twenties, and became increasingly unkempt (and craggy-faced) as the years wore on. Benzedrine was taken like a morning vitamin in the middle years of his life, and booze was an ever more constant companion. (Paul Johnson has recently revealed however[1] how T.S. Eliot's widow confided that 'Journey of the Magi' was written one Sunday morning after church with the help of half a bottle of Booth's gin.) For a time Auden spent his springs and summers on the Italian island of Ischia, and then in Kirchstetten in Austria where his passion for opera could be indulged by visits to the nearby *Staatsoper* in Vienna. German became his second language, and he was described in later years as a 'transatlantic Goethe'. Eliot's expertise, on the other hand, encompassed the French symbolist masters Mallarmé and Laforgue; his study of Dante is also considered a masterpiece.

1. In the *Spectator*, 13 April 2002, p. 32.

Auden returned to England towards the end of his life and took a 'grace and favour' cottage at Christ Church, Oxford, where he shuffled around the university in carpet slippers. Eliot was twice-married; the first caused him untold anguish, the second was happy. His posthumous privacy (Peter Ackroyd had to write an unauthorised Life without permission to quote from the sources) has been protected to a degree that is almost unique in modern letters. Auden was an unashamed homosexual – although this adjective, if not the adjectival noun to which it is attached, inordinately simplifies the emotive life of a complicated man.

On the surface Eliot was ascetic by nature and Auden a voluptuary (at least as a younger artist) but at a deeper level this, too, is over-simplification: Auden was only a bohemian on the surface. He had a strongly developed religious side like Eliot, and also like Eliot he had iron will-power and artistic discipline. It is thus, after all, that both men occupy their important places in literary history. In their relationship to Britten's music they occupy polar positions: Auden was the poet of Britten's youth; and Eliot – even if only in two poignant works – was the poet of the composer's final period. It is a paradox that Britten knew, and admired, Eliot's poetry as a young man without seriously thinking of turning it into music; as a dying older man he looked back on his Auden period with no desire to return to setting the poetry – and this despite the fact that news of his former friend's death brought about, in Donald Mitchell's words, 'a storm of tears'.

If this lecture is more concerned with Auden it is because Britten was not a personal friend of Eliot. Auden, on the other hand, was Britten's confidant, mentor and librettist. They met in July 1935 when Auden was working as a schoolmaster at the Downs School, Colwall to supplement his writing income (Colwall is a village on the Herefordshire–Worcestershire borders, home of Elizabeth Barrett Browning as a girl, and later of Jenny Lind). At the Downs Auden taught English, arithmetic, French, gymnastics and biology. Britten, aged 22, had left the Royal College of Music eighteen months earlier and had begun work for the General Post Office Film Unit under John Grierson. Auden was also part of this team for a while, and thus it was that the two men suddenly became colleagues. By chance, they had been to the same school (Gresham's, in Holt, Norfolk), but this seems to have played no part in their bonding. Auden was older by six years and had already

Britten, Auden and Coldstream as the 'Three Graces' at The Downs School, Colwall, Herefordshire, June 1937

141

experienced far more than the younger man; a gap of six years makes a big difference at that age, although one suspects that even if the two had been exact contemporaries Auden's temperament would have already led him to bolder adventures than those which might have been enjoyed by Britten. The poet, unlike the composer, had lived in the second half of the 1920s as an adult – he was 19 at the time of the General Strike. The search for a different means of ordering the world economy was the preoccupation of the idealistic younger generation, and many, including the young Auden, looked to Russia and the writings of Marx and Engels as a solution to the collapse of capitalism. This generation was a politicised one, while remaining close enough to the First World War (where many had lost close relatives) to recoil from another such conflict. Unlike Britten, however, Auden was no pacifist. By the time the composer became truly politically aware Fascist governments were already in place in Italy and Germany; but Auden had seen the early growth of Nazism at first hand during the year he spent in Berlin (1928–29). Later he was concerned enough by the Fascist threat to Spain to be determined to join the ranks of the Republican forces even if only as an ambulance driver (Auden, son of a doctor and a nurse had had a perpetual fascination with all things medical).

In 1935 the precocious Britten was already admired by musicians in the know, but Auden's career was much more advanced. He was, in Eliot's opinion, the established leader of his generation – that group which later became known as the MacSpaunday poets: Auden, Louis MacNeice, Stephen Spender and Cecil Day-Lewis. Auden's *Poems* were published in England in 1930 (the first American edition dated from 1934), and his play *The Orators* was first published in 1932. *The Dance of Death* had been produced by Rupert Doone's Group Theatre in February 1934. His play *The Dog Beneath the Skin* was published a few months later (he had already established a tradition of collaboration with his lovers by writing this work with Christopher Isherwood). A fortnight before Auden met Britten he had married Erika Mann in the Ledbury Registry Office; she was Thomas Mann's daughter and, exiled from her home country by the Nazis, desperately needed a British passport. Auden had never met his 'bride' until the day of the wedding. His famous remark on this compassionate arrangement was 'What are buggers for?' Still in the future were visits to Iceland with Louis MacNiece (1937), and to China with Christopher Isherwood (1938); both of which were also to result in memorable poetry (and prose).

When Britten went to meet a 'schoolmaster' in Colwall (Herefordshire) on 5 July 1935 he encountered a man whose already legendary knowledge of literature was reinforced by sophisticated experience of the outside world. Auden's Berlin period (in the company of Isherwood) had been enlivened by the easy availability of young men in the most permissive country in Europe – inflation-ridden Germany in the dying years of the Weimar Republic. For Isherwood in particular this was a rich source of his own artistic invention, inspiring *Mr Norris Changes Trains*, and the creation of the unforgettable Sally Bowles, the latter character much later to be turned into an even greater icon by the musical *Cabaret*. By the time of that meeting with a talented young composer, Auden had both thoroughly established his artistic presence and had come to terms with his sexual nature. And Britten had done neither, at least in terms of the outside world.

How Britten must have felt about meeting Auden for the first time invites comparison with a diary entry he made after being invited to lunch by the older composer William Walton: on that rather uncomfortable occasion he felt himself to be the new boy of the school, while Walton was the slightly patronising school prefect (Britten extended the analogy in his diary by musing that Vaughan Williams might have been headmaster of such a school, and Elgar on the board of governors). Moving ahead in our story to search for reasons for the eventual breakdown of the Auden–Britten friendship, the composer never completely got over the fact that Auden was another 'prefect' – a seniority in years mightily accentuated by the poet's command of language, and his seemingly inexhaustible knowledge. There was a side of Britten that always felt inadequate in Auden's company; he was one of many people who felt wrong-footed by the poet's intelligence and his conversation, which sometimes resembled an overwhelming monologue.

But there was a huge difference between Walton and Auden, and it was that the first was a rival composer (who became increasingly discomforted by Britten's success) and the other a poet who took it for granted that his words (or some of them) should be set to music. Auden was always on the look-out for talented collaborators, and composers were as important to him as they had been to Goethe (even if the latter badly blundered in ignoring Schubert). If Walton had seemed a head prefect, Auden was head of house, and it was the one to which the composer belonged in terms of temperament and inclination. 'W.H.A.' (as Britten sometimes referred to him) looked at the newcomer and liked what he saw. He accorded him a special status – as if a new boy were discovered to be a world-class athlete and, however young, allowed fast-track entry to the top echelons of the house hierarchy. English public schools lavish honours on those gifted at sport; the musically gifted, however, are another matter – at least in those days. But Auden was no sportsman (his teaching of gymnastics is hard to imagine); his criteria for welcoming new people into his circle (and like many bossy and gifted creators he aspired, even if unconsciously, to the creation of his own *Musenhof*) were talent and attractiveness. In Britten he saw someone young and sensitive, attractive in an unconventional way, 'of the same sort' as Isherwood would have put it (and as Auden's own sexual intuition would have told him), and, moreover, someone with an unusually developed musical talent. This must have been a well-nigh irresistible combination to Auden, a passable pianist in his youth, for whom music was a lifelong passion. Like Goethe he had no real gift in this field, but a fascination for those who did. Britten quickly proved himself in Auden's eyes as an adept and highly gifted composer, and this excused him, as if by papal dispensation, from all the books he had not yet read, and all the ideas about life he had not yet formulated.

It would have been fascinating to overhear the means by which Auden persuaded Britten to confess his sexuality – thoughts that had hitherto been preserved only in hints in the pages of the composer's diary. Whether this was coaxed or cajoled out of him, or whether Auden simply bluntly questioned his new young friend, we shall never know. There is no evidence that the composer had discussed this matter with anyone else by 1935 (although it would be surprising if he had not met some like-minded people). But even if he had had crushes and felt attracted to other young men, he suddenly found himself in a milieu where the gay (or 'queer') way of life was completely taken for granted. His sense of relief must have been palpable. Young men and women drawn to a way of life which is, by definition, different from that of their parents, lack a set of inherited values; even today they can feel out on a limb in a hostile world. A moment such as the introduction to Auden and his friends must have been like the discovery of a new family. Britten did not belong with the Royal College of Music set, or the Walton set; but he was now more than happy to be part of Auden's circle, particularly as it involved a combination of hard work and mental enrichment. He was suddenly part of a community with all the camaraderie of a large network of ready-made contacts and cross-references. By this I mean that Auden's friendship gave Britten his historical bearings as a homosexual. He would have been encouraged to see himself as one of a long line of gifted, artistic and *productive* like-minded people going back to Socrates and Plato, Leonardo and Michelangelo, a line that continued into every area (and some most unsuspected corners) of modern life. The young composer's acceptance into Auden's group (and we must remember that homosexuals were still proscribed by law, and subject to blackmail) was a coming in from the cold.

Both Peter Pears and Christopher Isherwood denied that there had ever been a physical relationship between composer and poet. But it is possible that at the beginning there was a passing moment of attempted intimacy – attempted, that is, on Auden's part: much points to the fact that he found the younger man attractive for reasons that went far beyond the physical. Of their shared mental intimacy there is no doubt; though here, again, one realises the impossibility of being 'intimate' with such a single-minded character as Auden, and this was one of the great problems of the relationship. It is enough to say that they were close collaborators and friends, and that Auden's influence on Britten was the most important exercised on him by anyone between Frank Bridge and Peter Pears – the first of these men was his teacher as an adolescent, the second his lover as an adult. Auden's role in Britten's life was transitional – that of a teacher who groomed the emerging composer into an intellectually engaged human being, though sadly for the poet (and I will develop this theme later) it was not his role to be the composer's lover, much less his life's companion. But Auden was the person who helped Britten to grow up intellectually as a man and artist, and as such he occupied a central place in the younger man's life and career.

When he first met Auden, Britten was, in physical terms, still almost certainly a virgin: 'cold', 'frozen' or 'suspended' are common descriptions of his attitude to love and sex at this point in his life. Auden seems to have taken it upon himself to 'unfreeze' his younger colleague into a state of emotional responsiveness. In taking the composer under his wing, Auden felt a real sense of affectionate responsibility, something that has emerged, I think, only as result of various documents published since Britten's death. In some ways Auden was louche and loose-living, in others remarkably strict and old-fashioned, and loyal too. It is clear that once Britten felt confident enough, some time later, to embark on affairs of his own, Auden was his confidant and advisor. But the poet's fatherly advice on matters of the heart (marvellously preserved for us in the poem 'Underneath the Abject Willow') is only one aspect of their friendship. Irretrievably lost to us are the exchanges between composer and poet during the many hours spent in each other's company where the conversation must have been 'glorious' (the word Britten used in his diary to describe a morning spent talking with Auden at Lyon's Corner House before the poet's departure to war-torn Spain). The composer absorbed a huge amount from Auden and his attitude to life changed as a result; the great poet fashioned for him a custom-made university course whereby the sheltered provincial, who had gone straight from school to music college, completed his education.

Britten, who was already touchy when faced with criticism, already impatiently dismissive of unmerited (in his view) musical reputations, in short already a 'star' in his own field, accepted everything Auden said with the greatest humility – at least in these early years of the friendship. In the period after the meeting Britten's diary is full of what Auden had said or done: he was intellectually dazzled by his new friend. In the political and philosophical areas some of his diary observations sound, almost touchingly, like *idées reçues*, but they soon became his own. On one hand he felt inferior to the poet, but he also must have known, deep down, that he, like Auden, possessed real genius: despite the discrepancies of intellectual background and verbal articulation he was the poet's artistic peer. The composer had an array of very gifted librettists in later years, but he was never again to be in such close contact with another creator *on his own level*. Auden could, with a matching virtuosity and ease, produce words that, like Britten's music, seemed magical – 'a delight cascading/The falls of the knee, and the weirs of the spine'.[2]

2. W.H. Auden, 'The Composer', *Collected Shorter Poems 1927–1957* (Faber, 1966), p.125.

We have mentioned that Britten felt intimidated in Auden's company, but it was just this company that gave him the confidence to be stronger and more opinionated when he was with other people. Auden's influence produced a huge growth in the composer's ability to stand his ground. It was working on Auden settings that encouraged Britten to establish his independence from Frank Bridge (however much the younger composer owed to the older) and it was surely Auden who enabled a shy and rather reticent young man to cut himself free from England's apron strings and go to America – an important aspect of Britten's maturing process. In this book I have on a number of occasions discussed the 'subversive' side of Britten's nature, his ability to remain himself while cleverly undermining the narrow-minded premises of English middle-class respectability. Starting with the controversial *Our Hunting Fathers*, the orchestral song cycle to an Auden text composed for the Norwich Festival, I think that this was a game for which Britten acquired a taste, thanks to the poet's incomparable self-possession and sense of purpose. Britten became (however briefly) sympathetic to communism; but he remained perpetually anti-Fascist, and aware of a much wider range of literature:

3. From an interview between Britten and Lord Harewood broadcast on 23 June 1960 (BBC Home Service, 10.15 p.m.) for the series *People Today*.

I remember he showed me Chaucer for the first time. I'd always imagined that was a kind of foreign language, but as he [Auden] read, which was very well, I understood almost immediately what it meant, and I find now that it isn't so difficult to read – one must just have confidence and read ahead and then the meaning comes very strongly, very easily.[3]

The meaning of a lot of things came more strongly, more easily, thanks to Auden's persuasive presence, an influence which lingered. For the rest of his life Britten remained left-of-centre, anti-establishment, sympathetic to most things Russian, more sympathetic to German culture than to French, down to earth about his work (a passionate belief in no-nonsense, professional graft), and essentially unashamed (sometimes defiantly so) of his homosexuality. On the negative side he was capable of black and white opinions, a cutting 'them and us' view of the world, which also seems to have been typical of Auden in dogmatic or bullying mode. Above all the composer believed in the power of his own partnership with a fellow artist to be a productive and fruitful source of art. As we shall see this was to be perhaps the poet's greatest philosophical gift to the composer, at the same time as being one of the reasons for their estrangement.

We turn to the most important piece for voice and piano that came from the Britten–Auden collaboration – a song cycle premiered by the composer and Sophie Wyss at a BBC contemporary concert on 19 November 1937.[4]

On This Island Op. 11 (1937)

(i) **Let the Florid Music Praise!** (October, 1937)

Britten himself told me that Frank Bridge had disapproved of the opening of 'Let the Florid Music Praise!' as he had originally conceived it. Apparently the original version was an exuberant downward glissando in the opening bars, which Bridge pronounced to be 'not really music'. This criticism removed what would have been an inappropriately jazzy opening to a piece which, in its revised form, marvellously evokes the pomp of seventeenth-century 'florid music' rather than the 'swing' of the twentieth century.

If Britten had already made Purcell realisations by this time we would ascribe this composer as the inspiration for these formidably ornate opening pages. Another possibility is Handel. But although he never spoke of it later in his life, surely this is Britten's bow to Stravinsky, a composer he admired in his youth, but came to loathe, not least because of that composer's (or Robert Craft's) derogatory remarks about him in the *Conversations*.[5] This is not the Stravinsky of *Le Sacre du printemps* of course, but the neo-classical Stravinsky of the violin concerto, the ballet *Apollon Musagète* (the title of Britten's own *Young Apollo* for pianos and orchestra comes to mind in this regard) or even the ballet *Pulcinella*. For the pianist who has to play this song, Britten's own version of neo-classical articulation unmistakably prophesies the exuberance of his later Purcell realisations – his very own, home-grown, neo-classicism.

4. Readers may notice slight differences between Auden's texts as printed in his collections of printed poetry and the versions set by Britten. This is due to Auden polishing his own verse for subsequent editions after it had been set by Britten. Thus Britten's songs represent pure Auden, but not the 'final' versions, which sometimes changed more than once.

5. Igor Stravinsky with Robert Craft, *Conversations*, University of California Press, 1980.

The poem is a hymn of praise to one of Auden's lovers, but praise is tempered by regret; this is not a relationship that has a future. The fact that this boy is dazzlingly attractive is shown by the poet's imagery: 'Beauty's conquest of your face' makes clear that the good-looking are not responsible for their beauty, nor is handsomeness the result of any conscious achievement (we can even be the victims of our own beauty). Beauty is exciting, but this 'land of flesh and bone' tells us nothing of the heart or mind of its possessor. The empty pomp of the music (all glittering arpeggios) suggests beauty's imperial ability ('imperial' is not a flattering word in Auden's vocabulary) to dictate its own terms to its haplessly enthralled (or colonised) admirers. The hot sun shining on (in Britten's song this is set to elaborate, but essentially heartless, melismas) represents the radiant and tyrannical power of 'hot' physical attraction to excite and lead us on. The poet's surrender, however temporary, to this attraction is vividly depicted by Britten's music.

This yields to a *minore* section, *poco più lento*, where the 'unloved' are introduced with the cautionary word 'but'. Auden's imagery seems to equate the beauty of *jeunesse dorée* with the 'imperial' upper classes; on the other hand the plain looks of the unloved represent those who are less advantaged. The words 'weeping and striking' are ambiguous: in a domestic context they betoken sorrow and physical violence; in political terms 'striking' means something different – the withdrawal of labour. Some people have it all (in terms of money, looks, power) and others have nothing. It is clear in this scenario that Auden regards himself, at least personally if not politically, as belonging to the latter category – unloved and unbeautiful. 'Oh! but the unloved *have had* power' Auden says (the italics are mine) as if he were suggesting that the tyranny of beauty had drained him of his power like a shorn Samson seduced by Delilah. Almost sounding a revolutionary note he says that 'time will bring their hour'. He, like the working class, will survive, still keeping his intelligence; physical beauty, on the other hand, like all aristocracies, must surely decay.

The following lines, which we will discuss more fully later, are crucial to an understanding of Auden's expectations in a relationship: 'Their secretive children walk/Through your vigilance of breath/To unpardonable death/ And my vows break/Before his look'. The 'secretive children' who go 'to their unpardonable death', quite apart from a political reading of the poem which would have one thinking of poverty and death in poor families, seem to me to refer to the still-born shadows of a failed collaboration. The beautiful lover has given nothing of himself (hence his 'vigilance of breath') to make a fruitful exchange possible; Auden is a worker and creator, the lover is not. 'Children' in many a gay relationship are the dual achievements that are born as a result of love – spiritual children, a phenomenon acknowledged in such relationships by Plato in *Phaedrus*. It seems to me that 'my vows' are promises made by the poet to himself to end an unproductive relationship and search for something more fruitful. But one look from that beautiful, alluring face and his resolve to end the romance evaporates.

Auden's struggle (and this includes a struggle with himself) to find a meaningful collaboration, a productiveness to make sense of his emotional life, is an important theme in his biography, and particularly his friendship with Britten. In the circumstances described in this song such a collaboration with the loved one is impossible – there is too large a gap between the object of the poet's sensual affections, and the needs of his own intellectual idealism. He laments that he is transfixed in the web of beauty (note the swooning descent of Britten's setting of 'And my vows *break*' which seems entangled and rooted in a poignant sequence of harmonies).

The theme of hopeless enslavement to love based on beauty alone (and its dire consequences) is that of Thomas Mann's *Tod in Venedig* (*Death in Venice*) of 1912. It is a work that Auden certainly knew, and probably in the original – he was after all the son-in-law, albeit for the most unusual reasons, of the work's author. This novella was, in turn, the basis of Britten's opera of 1973. In that work is to be found both the reckless admiration of beauty that Gustav von Aschenbach feels for the Polish boy Tadzio, as well as the sad and woeful introspection of a great writer who is aware of what he is giving up in embarking on this unrequited passion. Conscious talent is counterpointed with unconscious beauty – the first acquired by hard work, the second a gift of nature. In 'Let the Florid Music Praise!' a number of the opera's themes are prefigured in miniature, with Auden assuming the role of a youthful Aschenbach. It is interesting that the same theme – that of the older man and the younger lover – is covered in yet another song, this time from the composer's maturity: 'Sokrates und Alcibiades' from the *Sechs Hölderlin-Fragmente* (1958). This poem was known and quoted by Auden on a number of occasions.

Eric Blom in an early review of *On This Island* referred to the 'Handelian dignity and buoyancy' of the music, and I think he must have meant 'Let the Florid Music Praise!' in particular. The coda is launched with the words 'Before his look'; there is a sadness in this ornate, but crestfallen, music, where trills and roulades (florid music indeed) are shot through with real feeling – quite a different mood from the opening. The first half of the song is utterly brilliant and unaware, unfeeling; the second half all too aware, and sadly so. This places Auden in his typical position of the waking observer. One of his most famous poems is his immortal lullaby 'Lay your sleeping head my love/Human on my faithless arm'. In this poem the lover is asleep and it is Auden who keeps vigil, aware and articulate. And so it is in 'Let the Florid Music Praise!' as well as in the 'Nocturne' later in the cycle.

(ii) Now the Leaves Are Falling Fast (May, 1937)

This describes in a single song why both Auden and Britten felt the need to leave England for the United States. The poem is an unflattering 'state of the union' address as far as Britain is concerned: autumn approaches with ever darker skies; through the leafless wood the fascist 'trolls' advance hungrily, the rottenness of the body politic has allowed them to go on the rampage. Part of the overall malaise is the sexual hypocrisy of what Auden would later call a 'Low, dishonest decade'.[6] In the repeated, urgent quavers of the accompaniment, and in the ominously snakings of the vocal line, we sense a one-way journey to a doomed destination. In the trudge of the music we also discern the composer's awareness of the politicised Brecht settings of composers such as Kurt Weill and Hanns Eisler.

6. From 'September 1 1939', first strophe.

The poet uses the quintessentially English images of nurse (or 'nanny') and 'prams' (perambulators for infants) to symbolise the Victorian attitude to life, which still inappropriately held modern Britons back from their 'real delight'. The phrase about frozen hands 'lonely on the separate knees' betokens the sexual repression which, in other poems (such as 'Miss Gee'), Auden suggests can be the cause of cancer. In this case the diseased organism is the country itself. 'Dead in hundreds at the back' describes the force of the example of earlier generations; their 'false attitudes of love' are the rigor mortis of a tradition that stifles the younger generation. The ineluctable forward impulse of these words and music might describe a conveyor belt to an emotional abattoir; the tension screws ever tighter, the music ever louder, as we approach the chopping chords that accompany 'And the angel will not come'. There is no rescue from this fate, and the music suddenly breaks off after this point.

The song had been introduced by a strange and haunting sequence of four minims marked '*Lento*' (a note to performers: the ensuing passage of rolling semiquavers is marked '*più mosso e commodo*' – a speed which is faster than that initial *Lento*, rather than being fast in itself. This song is almost always rushed and garbled; it is much more effective if the mood is measured and ominous, rather than hysterical). These four minims reappear on the song's final page as the harmonic basis for a hushed epilogue. 'The mountain of instead' (as Auden calls it in a later version of this poem) is a vision of what Britain might have been, and might still be, in another time. But a mention of 'travellers in their last distress' is a clear sign that the poet believed that the problems the younger generation experienced on this island could only be solved by leaving it.

(iii) Seascape (October 1937)

It is perhaps appropriate that a song all about the poet's disillusionment with his country should be followed by 'Seascape', a paean to its marine beauties. As far as Britten was concerned, who returned to Britain from America after three years, an opera about the sea in his head if not actually in his suitcase, it was this more optimistic view of course that would prevail. Auden wrote the poem for a documentary entitled *Beside the Seaside* and seems to have been influenced by the E.M. Forster of *Howard's End*. In this novel Auden's 'stranger' equates to Forster's 'foreigner'. Passages from Forster such as these must have influenced Auden: 'If one wanted to show a foreigner England' ... or 'It is as if a fragment of England floated forward to greet the foreigner' ... 'Does she belong to those who have ... seen the whole island at once?' [7]

As if a schoolboy let out on holiday, Britten delightedly responds to a poem which is neither a dissection of love nor a lecture about philosophy or politics. The sea is something he knew about at first hand – in fact a great deal more than the poet who was born, and grew up, inland. The poem's mention of the 'chalk wall' that 'falls to the foam' suggests Kent rather than Britten's native Suffolk, but no matter. Although the whole cycle is dedicated to Auden's companion and on-and-off lover Christopher Isherwood, this song is separately inscribed to another Christopher – Kit Welford, the composer's future brother-in-law.[8] This accords well with music that has the confident swagger of a young man.

The accompaniment to this song (*Allegro molto* – and, in contrast to the preceding song, often performed not quite fast enough) is made up of swirling semiquavers which marvellously suggest waves rushing forward to break on the barrier of the bar-line. As if holding this force at bay the syncopated left hand of the piano represents the opposing tug of the tide. The perpetual undulations of this music, formed (and foamed) from a single idea announced in the opening bar, are an indication that Britten was already a master of an unified, and unifying, accompanying style, which took Schubert as its model (that composer's second *Suleika* song comes to mind, where the restless semiquavers represent the rustling of the west wind). This music may be a very distant relation to the *Sea Interludes* from *Peter Grimes*, but it is conceived by the same hand. In the middle section of the song 'the pluck and knock of the tide' is depicted with awkward and

7. As pointed out in John Fuller, *WH Auden, A Commentary*, Faber and Faber, 1998.

8. He married Britten's sister Beth on 22 January 1938.

151

insistent syncopations between voice and piano and aggressive *sforzarti*. After mention of the shingle, which 'scrambles after the sucking surf', a seagull makes its appearance, not only in the poem but in the high-pitched wailing piano interlude which rises to a dissonant cry before dissolving into the final verse.

For this the 'camera' of the poet's eye pans out to a broader picture, a change of perspective that is brilliantly caught in Britten's music (now marked '*Molto tranquillo*') where the immediacy of crashing waves is replaced by the crests of distant sea-horses (the force of the right-hand piano writing is now etiolated, glistening gently in a higher octave). Little ships are seen like 'floating seeds' in the water; their movements are 'urgent' but 'voluntary', for this is still Britain at peace, something which is soon to change. The nonchalant movement of the clouds in the mirror of the water occasions one of Britten's most lovely (and difficult to execute) melismas in quasi-Purcellian style – the most perfectly apt setting of the word 'saunter' that could be imagined, particularly if the singer has the breath-control to throw it off with graceful insouciance.

WH Auden Look, Stranger! book cover, 1936

It is worth mentioning that *Look, Stranger!* (the words taken from this poem) was the title chosen by the firm of Faber for Auden's first collection of poetry. The poet himself disliked this intensely and the first American edition (of the same collection) was re-titled *On This Island*. This almost quotes *Seascape* again … 'Look, stranger at this island now', using 'on' rather than 'at'. It is notable that the blurb on the dust-jacket of *Look, Stranger!* was written by T.S. Eliot himself; he refers to Auden as 'a leader of a new school of poetry'.

(iv) Nocturne (May, 1937)

'Nocturne' is an early (though not the earliest) example of Britten's interest in music of the night. It was a theme that was to return throughout his life with the *Serenade* for tenor, horn and strings, the *Nocturne* for tenor, orchestra and seven obbligato instruments, the *Nocturnal* for solo guitar, the *Night Piece* for solo piano, and the opera *A Midsummer Night's Dream* (this is far from a complete list). This *Nocturne* (marked *andante piacev-*

ole) is a beautiful hymn addressed to an anonymous lover; the poem is a choric part of Auden's play *The Dog Beneath the Skin*. As Auden watches the beloved sleep beside him (the poem ends with the words 'Calmly till the morning break/Let him lie then gently wake') the controlling poet, a self-appointed Prospero with powerful verbal spells, enters into his dreams, imagining the topsy-turvy world they represent. Auden's imagery is extraordinary: the idea that night touches the rotating globe with a 'caressing grip', lover-like, is instantly memorable (one remembers another immortal line by this poet: 'The earth turns over, our side feels the cold').[9] Night reverses all truths: the proudly attired become naked, the unjust become just, sexual reticence turns into welcoming sensuality, the loser wins – all these transformations seem to spring from *A Midsummer Night's Dream* where the four lovers' eyes, as well as Tytania's, have been streaked by Puck's magic juice at Oberon's behest.

One finds similar paradoxes in surreal poetry of the time, and the French song enthusiast treasures a similar poem in the closing song (entitled 'Nous avons fait la nuit') of Francis Poulenc's cycle *Tel jour telle nuit* to the words of Paul Eluard. It is a piece of music, incidentally, that was composed more or less at the same time; the pre-war collaboration of the middle-class Britten and the left-leaning Auden is uncannily mirrored by that of the bourgeois and well-to-do Poulenc, and the communist Eluard. In 'Nous avons fait la nuit', also a visionary nocturne, the poet rhapsodises about how his wife Nusch constantly surprises him and enriches him with her perceptions, which are always revealing, always new (the kind of collaboration between spouses of which Auden dreamed): she elevates the poor and scorns the rich, she respects the opinion of those whom others think deranged. These dream-like inversions, a type of divine madness stronger and truer than reality, are also at the heart of 'Nocturne'.

The accompaniment to this piece is deceptively simple: dotted minims throughout, until the closing moments of the song when these blossom into a sprinkling of melodic crotchets – a *dolcissimo* touch which seems to spread a musical blessing over the sleeping lover in the song's closing moments. Otherwise this piano writing, as constant and repetitive as the Purcellian passacaglia form it evokes, is the foundation on which the long-arched vocal lines are built. This is one of Britten's most taxing vocal pieces – there are very few singers with the technical control to encompass the recurring six-bar span without a second breath. The rise and fall of this music represents the slow inhalation (3 bars) and exhalation (3 bars) of someone in a very deep sleep. The shape of the phrases, climbing to a point where a note is held, and then falling to a harmonic resolution, recalls

9. No. XVII of Poems 1931–1936, in *The English Auden*, ed. Edward Mendelsson, (Faber, 1977).

153

Schumann's sublime 'Mondnacht' from the Eichendorff *Liederkreis* Op. 39. As it happens, the 'Nocturne' is composed in the relative minor (C-sharp minor) of that E major masterpiece. A sovereign performance of either work is rare and elusive, but when achieved the musical effect is similarly hypnotic.

⊙ **CD2, track 6**

⊙ (v) As It Is, Plenty (October, 1937)

'As It Is, Plenty' takes its idea from a short story by Somerset Maugham (yet another homosexual artist, but of an older generation than Auden and Britten) entitled 'His Excellency'. It is the most awkward of the songs of *On This Island* in that it does not seem to fit in with the rest of the cycle. It is nearer to the *Cabaret Songs* in idiom – there is an undeniable jazz influence here – but it is not quite jazzy enough to sing in a manner that abandons recital formalities altogether. The text is a serious one despite the manner in which it is presented. The theme, like that of the first song in the set, is about a failed relationship. In this case it is the state of marriage, which is a respectable veneer for a tragic situation where wife and husband have all the superficial trappings of prosperity (children, a car – something to be proud of in the 1930s – money, in short, success) while sacrificing happiness and spiritual fulfilment. This is an observation typical of the younger Auden who is inimical to comfortable bourgeois institutions such as marriage. This reaction is understandable at a time when the outraged objections to his own lifestyle were most likely to have come from those who claimed for themselves blameless respectability, often behind a curtain of hypocrisy. Then, as now, those who parrot 'family values' as the excuse for intolerance are particularly vulnerable to any close investigation of their own unblemished righteousness.

In this song we are invited behind the scenes of a marriage. In Maugham's story Sir Humphrey Witherspoon is an ambassador who admits to an affair with Alix, a music hall acrobat. The deliberately ambivalent name[10] (Alex?) suggests that, in the author's mind, the ambassador's lover is a man; Auden himself thought so at any rate. The ambassador has married a beautiful woman from a good family, but the excitement of his clandestine affair makes him realise just how lifeless are his own domestic arrangements. The downbeat and rather bored tone of the setting is determined by the way Britten sets the words 'And the car, the car/That goes so far/And the wife *devoted*' (my italics mark the composer's musical emphasis, which superbly conveys sarcasm). The song's American musical flavour, and its air of aimless *ennui*, makes one feel that one should be chewing gum as one sings and plays it. Perhaps one should imagine 'going for a spin' in

10. See Fuller, *WH Auden, A Commentary*, p.162.

154

the 1930s – mindless driving for the sake of it – showing off the new car, with a married couple having nothing to say to each other as they do so. The swinging dotted rhythm interlude (marked *molto marcato*) between 'Give thanks, give thanks' and 'All that was thought' is reminiscent of a big-band break. When young singers sang 'When nothing is enough/But love' Peter Pears used to urge them to think of 'lurv' as an American crooner may have pronounced it. Love itself is now parodied because it is no longer real.

The wife has started off with high ideals and expectations, but she has turned a blind eye to her husband's infidelities (sins he himself writes off as 'venal', a word which Auden changed to 'venial' in later editions) in order to preserve the dignities and advantages of her comfortable life. These are, in turn, made possible by 'the profits larger', a phrase which suggests shady financial deals. In this song Britten allows himself the glissando, rather sleazy in this context, a device which had been excised from the first song in the set. The song's final two pages suggest a jazz combo: the spread left-hand chords, also marked staccato, evoke the sound of a plucked double bass while wire brushes stroke a snare drum.

The words that condemn the marriage to major and final loss are sung to a background of deliberate musical banality. This is a relationship on automatic pilot and doomed to crash, somehow and somewhere, most horribly. Brassy big-band chords punctuate four repetitions of the word final. And then a crowning sixteen-note melisma on a fifth 'final' unwinds like a tightly coiled spring up the stave. There is now another pianissimo chord by way of interjection, then a last 'final' (also pianissimo) with a downward inflection like a door clicking firmly shut. Truly finally, a huge chord in both hands descends on the keyboard like a fly-swatter, something which often raises a laugh in performance. This whole section is comically world-weary. It is clear that the Auden's protégé of 1935 is no longer subscribing to middle-class values; by 1937 Britten has become almost as cynical as his mentor.

Four settings of W.H. Auden (1935–38)

We now move to four further Auden songs: three of these were only published fairly recently. We might ask why the composer had held them back from publication; he may of course have been simply dissatisfied with their musical quality, but one suspects that in this case there were other, more personal, reasons. Britten was never ashamed of being biographically revealing in his music, but one senses that this part of his biography contained an element of pain and embarrassment, as well as various loose ends. There was to have been a second volume of *On This Island*, but this came to nothing, partly because of the war and Britten's three-year American sojourn.

(i) The Sun Shines Down

This is a setting of a poem from 1932, which Auden included in his *Look, Stranger!* volume but excised from later editions of his work. It is the most recent of Britten's Auden settings to have emerged, reaching print only in 1997, and not having been performed before that time. Britten's song has an attractive momentum that successfully encompasses Auden's sardonic observations of contemporary British life. This is a song in honour of a young man's twenty-first birthday; in welcoming him into manhood and citizenship the poem depicts British society in disintegration – 'History seems to have struck a bad patch'. Everyone goes on with their dishonest work seemingly oblivious of the various forces (class warfare, a moribund legal system, capitalism linked to the arms trade) that threaten society's destruction. Part of this lyric ('The journalist writing his falsifications') seem prophetic of lines in Auden's famous *The Fall of Rome* (1947). And Britten's music aptly suggests the merriment of fiddling while Rome burns. The final succession of 'La la las' at the end of the piece are the composer's own; they strike just the right ironic note, nonchalant and pointed at the same time. The end of Debussy's light-hearted song 'Mandoline' comes to mind. This is also the only song known to me to include a setting of the word 'Gosh'; one can surely get no more English than this, certainly in terms of the song's date of composition and the shared public school education of both poet and composer.

⊙ CD2, track 7

⊙ (ii) To Lie Flat on the Back

'To Lie Flat on the Back' is surely the most openly erotic text that Britten ever set. The poem, a sonnet (the form giving an old-fashioned stylistic discipline to words that assume a new and free sexual order), dates from 1934. The words chart the build-up of erotic tension between two people who are sunbathing next to each other, talking casually, and increasingly flirtatiously, as they do so. This conversation is not face-to-face of course (the potential lover is a person 'at whom you dare not look') and the final question ('Do you know why?') – set as a heady octave leap in Britten's vocal line – supposes that the person addressed (by thoughts, not openly spoken words) is less aware of the undertones in this courtship than the narrator. Britten's interest in this poem seems to be personal: he was still at a point in his life when he was diffident about seduction and preferred the oblique approach (Auden gave the composer step-by-step counsel on this very sub-

156

ject: one of his letters stressed the importance of playing the piano a great deal to the object of his affections in order to make the desired effect). The capricious melisma on 'boy' is notable, as is the use of the American word 'sidewalk' before the poet went to America. Britten seems unsure how to set this, stressing the second syllable ('walk') by placing it on the first beat of the bar. This word reveals the poem to be something of an American, and specifically Hollywood, fantasy; the weather that enables such casual sun-bathing also seems to be part of the scenario. It is significant that Christopher Isherwood, to whom Auden first sent the poem, chose to take up residence in California. And there is no doubt that Auden thought of the United States as a more likely source of romantic adventure than England. He was to meet his partner Chester Kallman there in 1939.

Britten's music requires imaginative performance to make it work well – above all in the sense of rubato in the piano's triplets, which have to suggest the quickening pulse of excitement, as well as a flickering barometer of hopes and fears, first rising and then falling away. The melismatic setting of the word 'casual' (casual indeed) is an augury of the later composer. The middle section, where the voice intones twelve bars of repeated E naturals while the piano embroiders in triplets (wandering hands to depict wandering thoughts), seems accurately to describe the breathless excitement of the inexperienced suitor who fears to turn thought into action. At more or less this time the composer Lennox Berkeley, who was ten years older, appears to have proposed a relationship with Britten. But Britten continued, nevertheless, to take an interest in men younger than himself. At this time he also became infatuated with Wolf Scherchen, the son of the famous German conductor. This song reflects Britten's diffidence in the more active role of seducer and lover, rather than the pursued beloved.

(iii) Fish in the Unruffled Lakes

This was regarded by its composer as sufficiently successful to publish it in 1947.[11] It was composed in early 1938 at a fluid time in Britten's emotional life – after he had met the tenor Peter Pears, but long before their relationship had developed into love. Other friendships, in particular that with Lennox Berkeley, were closer on the horizon. This is a beautiful poem set to wonderful music, though very difficult to sing and tricky to play. The semiquaver figurations at the top of the piano are inspired water music: the poem calls for lakes not rivers, and the composer manages to suggest that the darting movement in the inner reaches of the *delicato* piano writing represents the glistening of fish (with their 'swarming colours') beneath an essentially 'unruffled' surface. The complete success of Britten's translation

11. A new edition of this, using Sophie Wyss's manuscript, has recently come to light, and was published by Boosey and Hawkes in 1997 under the title: *Fish in the Unruffled Lakes and other songs.*

157

of Auden's imagery into such a subtle musical equivalent is an indication of his future Schubertian mastery. Both hands are bidden to the heights of the treble clef: the key is F-sharp major, which places much of the piano writing on the black keys. These sounds tinkle in such a high tessitura that we feel harmonically unanchored in a calm, watery expanse of sound.

The vocal line, almost *bel canto* in its demands, is full of graceful and extravagant melismas, expressive first of the movement of fish, then the gliding of swans and the striding of the great lion. This bestiary equates the beauties of nature with spontaneous action, everything stemming from guiltless instinct: 'Lion, fish and swan/Act and are gone/Upon time's toppling wave' (the last image must also have played its part in inspiring Britten's accompaniment where those semiquavers brim over the barlines in cascades of accidentals). By contrast, mankind is haunted by his 'shadowed days'; he is obsessed with time (here the 'devil in the clock' is aptly represented by those incessant semiquavers, now ticking away in the bass of the piano writing) and constrained by religion and superstition. He is aware that everything is mortal. And he can only envy the ability of the animal kingdom to live, without feeling sorry for itself, in the joy of the present. Animals do not look back with regret on mistaken events in their lives.

But then comes the twist in the song that reaffirms, and redefines, the unique joy of being human. Only human beings can exercise conscious choice, and when two people come together, when the heart and the head are as engaged as much as the body, love-making is a matter of volition and selection; spiritual as much as natural. This makes the recipient of this gift of love feel both grateful and proud:

> Sighs for folly said and done
> Twist our narrow days;
> But I must bless, I must praise
> That you, my swan, who have
> All gifts that to the swan
> Impulsive Nature gave,
> The majesty and pride,
> Last night should add
> Your voluntary love.

In Britten's song the first two lines of this verse are accompanied by restless semiquaver figurations; then 'I must bless, I must praise' is set as a slow unaccompanied chromatic scale that rises from E to the B a fifth higher.

The word 'that' is a *tenuto* B sharp full of anticipation, and then the radiance of 'you' on a C sharp coincides with the recapitulation of the opening music (*Tempo primo, tranquillo*) in F-sharp major. The conjunction of those rustling semiquavers with the word 'you', and the return to the home key, is a magical one. By now we have forgotten the watery imagery that had initially prompted this accompaniment; we hear instead the whispered intimacy of the venerating poet who is awe-struck by his luck. The physical gifts of his new lover, the 'majesty and pride' equal to any of that in the animal kingdom, has been matched by 'voluntary love', a gift which only a human being can make to another. The conjunction of that *macho* word 'pride' with the yielding inherent in 'voluntary love' is especially poignant. Britten prepares the setting of 'Last night' most beautifully; his music implies that the poet is making a sacred diary entry to mark a new phase in his life. This lovemaking, a union of twin souls, has been no favour granted out of pity; it is a result of neither well-planned seduction, nor surrender to momentary lust. The key to the poet's joy is human consensuality. This journey into erotic, and spiritual, bliss is marked by the extraordinarily wide ranging, and quietly ecstatic, melisma on the word 'voluntary'.

Whether or not this poem (and song) referred to a specifically biographical situation for either poet or composer is unlikely. The words were written in March 1936 (set to music in 1938) and we do not know to whom they refer, if anyone. To me they signify a fantasy – what Auden would have liked to find in his life, what he was looking for: someone good and unaffected, talented and strong, lusty and yet intellectual, someone who would be the perfect companion, perfect lover, and *muse and collaborator*. I put those words in italics because these seem to encapsulate the poet's strongest needs. We know this above all from the fact that when he met the young poet Chester Kallman in 1939 he invested a huge amount of energy over many years to collaborate, and to be seen to collaborate, with Kallman on many projects, including all the opera libretti they wrote together. In some respects this relationship was far from ideal for them both, but it was one to which Auden adhered through thick and thin.

When focussing on the Britten–Auden relationship it is all too easy to forget there were countless other forces (and people) in both their busy lives. But something must explain the later course of events and the fact that theirs was 'the only friendship of Auden's life that ended bitterly' in the words of the poet's biographer Richard Davenport-Hines.[12] Although there is nothing in the documents to suggest anything approaching a love affair, I think it likely that Britten became the subject of an emotional obsession for the poet, and 1936 seems to be have been a high-point of that crush, as

12. Richard Davenport-Hines, *Auden* (Vintage, 1999).

well as being a period when Auden wrote more love poetry than at any other time of his life. At this time the poem 'Night Covers Up the Rigid Land' was also written with the superscription 'For Benjamin Britten'; it was set by Britten in 1937 and its message is clear, even if the experts tell us to beware linking Britten personally with the poem simply because of its dedication. By further irony it was set by Lennox Berkeley at the end of 1938, who seems to have appropriated Auden's mourning words for the same reason that the poet had almost certainly written them: the impossibility of a reciprocated relationship with Benjamin Britten. The poem ends with these lines:

> For each love to its aim is true,
>   And all kinds seek their own:
> You love your life and I love you
>   So I must lie alone.
> O hurry to the fêted spot
>   Of your deliberate fall;
> For now my dream of you cannot
>   Refer to you at all.

'My dream of you' is indicative of the poet's huge interest in the significance of dreams and their Freudian interpretation. But one can also dream of the person for whose arrival one has long awaited. I believe that Auden must have regarded his meeting with a young musical genius in the summer of 1935 as potentially very significant for his own future. He had a dream that included collaboration with someone resulting in artistic 'children'. In this respect he was positively broody. (His determination to work together with Chester Kallman later on was not a new manifestation of his needs.) Britten was simply not interested in such a relationship *with Auden himself*. I place these words in italics because I believe that, as in much else, Britten was profoundly influenced by Auden's aesthetic, including his attempts to dignify his otherwise barren sexuality (in terms of the ability to father children) with work and creative fruitfulness. Britten, probably with Auden's encouragement, also came to realise that it was more important for a partner to be talented and creative than it was for him to be a vision of loveliness 'in that land of flesh and bone'. But as far as Britten was concerned Auden himself, for a number of reasons, did not fit the bill.

In the beginning the poet might have ascribed Britten's reticence towards him as physical inexperience and inhibition. There might have been an element of self-interest in his helping Britten through this phase with constant

160

advice help and encouragement, in counselling the composer about confronting these hang-ups. He must have hoped that he could 'warm' the disdainful Britten into action, and that he might then become physically close to the composer, as well as mentally. How long this phase of longing on his side lasted it is difficult to say. But any tension brought about by an inequality of feeling at an early stage would explain much in the break-up of this relationship much later on.

I remember Peter Pears talking about this episode; he said that Auden had never been jealous of him *physically* – he emphasised that word. It is clear that after a while Auden accepted that poet and composer were not destined to take the world by storm as a partnership where private love and public work were to be united. But in the American years I do think that he must have felt a pang of envy concerning the relationship with Peter Pears because it must have soon become obvious that this blossoming collaboration between composer and interpreter had, to a certain extent, appropriated, even stolen, Auden's ideal. That it was a partnership which was to be almost unique in musical history could hardly have been easy for Auden either. The letter that Auden wrote to Britten before the composer left America (discussed later in this lecture) was a perspicacious one, particularly when read with hindsight. It was well meant, but I believe it was badly received by Britten partly because he imagined he perceived behind it Auden's resentment, even jealousy, regarding Peter Pears's role in his life. In any case, Britten, when counselled and supported by Pears, was infinitely less amenable to Auden's advice; the singer had, to a large extent, replaced the poet as Svengali, and he knew a lot more about practical music-making. The depth of their collaboration was further strengthened, from 1941, by a flourishing physical relationship. It was a friendship that was destined to set standards for countless other partnerships, both gay and straight, throughout the world.

⊙ (iv) When You're Feeling Like Expressing your Affection ⊙ **CD2, track 8**

'When You're Feeling Like Expressing your Affection' is the only probable Auden setting to appear in *The Red Cockatoo*, a collection of previously unpublished songs that appeared in 1994. 'Probable' because there is no proof that these words are by Auden (no manuscript of the poem survives) and the song is undated. But the style of this advertising jingle – obviously for the General Post Office, with its telephone monopoly – is in Auden's lighter mode in which he typically links technological advances with an American 'hip' casualness. Britten reflects this by aping a jazz style in his slinky music. The product that is promoted could not be more English

161

however: the red kiosk containing the black metal telephone with its 'A' and 'B' buttons. The first of these was pushed only when the caller heard he or she had got through to the right number (this meant that any coins that the caller had inserted fell irretrievably into the metal strong-box, and the government's hands); pressing button 'B' refunded the money in the event of an engaged signal or a wrong number. The GPO was obviously considering an advertising campaign to encourage the British public to make long-distance calls, but there is no record that the song was used for that purpose. Many such modernisations were deferred by the gathering storm clouds that would eventually lead to war.

The entry of that great literary mandarin T.S. Eliot into Britten's creative life comes as something of a late surprise. Apart from the work of his librettists, of course, after Auden we associate the music of Britten's maturity with words from earlier times – Hardy, Hölderlin, Blake, Pushkin. An exception was the work of the Scottish poet William Soutar; the cycle based on his 'Who are these Children?' dates from shortly before *Canticle IV*. Eliot had been dead for six years when Britten decided to set his words for the first time, although we do know that he had admired Eliot since the 1930s. The composer does not seem, however, to have earlier made any effort to meet Eliot personally. A link between them might have been their shared publisher, but Britten's collaboration with the firm of Faber and Faber (through the foundation of Faber Music specifically to publish his music) was established only at about the time of Eliot's death. The point is that in stark contrast to the Auden settings this music is nothing to do with friendships and connections and collaborators. The fact that poet and composer did not know each other seems a positive advantage. Eliot's words had become as much part of the literary canon as if they were holy writ: in Britten's mind they seem completely separated from the personality of their creator, or any biographical aspect of their composition. This perhaps is a factor in the music's translucent purity, certainly in comparison to the Auden settings even the lightest of which seem weighed down by complicated personal 'baggage' and allusion. As Arnold Whittall says[13] of the Eliot canticles 'The progression away from Auden was complete'; this lecture charts the contrasts – beginning and ends – acknowledged in Whittall's observation.

13. Arnold Whittall
The Music of Britten and Tippett: Studies in Themes and Techniques (Cambridge University Press, 1982), p.255.

Canticle V – The Death of St Narcissus Op. 89 (1974)

This is the second of Britten's Eliot settings, also one of the composer's last works. It is probably the trickiest text the composer set in his whole career. This poetry seems to have suited the mood of his post-operative illness in

162

a way that no one could have foreseen. Donald Mitchell remarked that Eliot's poetry was 'one of the few things Britten felt himself able to read' at this time of preoccupation with, and gradual preparation for, his own death. In *Canticle IV* the three kings explore the idea of birth-in-death, and this last canticle is also suffused with the almost unearthly valedictory tone of Britten's last works, including the Third String Quartet. It was written in the shadow of death and of course it deals with the extinction of a strange creature, St Narcissus, a hybrid of the Christian Saint Sebastian and the pagan shepherd boy Narcissus who is hymned in famous English songs by Butterworth and Ireland in words from A.E. Housman's *Shropshire Lad*:

> A Grecian lad, as I hear tell
> One that many loved in vain,
> Looked into a forest well
> And never looked away again.

The martyred St Sebastian was slain with arrows and Narcissus, transfixed with the reflection of his own beauty, was changed into a jonquil. These polar points of background orientation melt into an intricate mass of imagery where each reader (including Britten himself) must, and should, experience different things. The failure of Narcissus to be anything other than he is, his attempts to change himself only to encounter his heart-breaking mortality, are all the more poignant when set by a dying man. There is in this music a sense of the eroticism of the grave, the composer's last, and inevitably failing, attempt to define and hold on to beauty, and the bitterness of bidding it, together with all things of the flesh, farewell. Here he is not an old man looking at a beautiful boy, but an old man who is still, somewhere within, still that beautiful boy himself.[14]

In this music a gallery of characters, like fading photographs, seem evoked from the composer's own past: most recently, Mann's Tadzio of course, who is an agent of Eros. I also think of *The Persian Boy* by Mary Renault, which Pears had read to Britten some time earlier (this was the story of the eunuch Bagoas and his attachment to Alexander the Great). The strangely alluring 'gracieux fils de Pan' from 'Antique' in the Rimbaud *Les Illuminations* is at last re-visited in Britten's oeuvre (the echo is in Eliot's words 'his ancient beauty/Caught fast in the pink tips of his new beauty'). And Britten's attachment to Schubert's Mayrhofer setting 'Atys' D585 also comes to mind, a rarely performed song of unearthly beauty recorded by Pears and the composer for their last Decca LP in November 1972. This is perhaps the strangest poem ever set by Schubert: the themes are taken from

14. Recent publications have explored the homosexual side of T.S. Eliot and his infatuation with Jean Verderal in Paris between 1910 and 1911. There is also unproven speculation about such inclinations in London from the mid-thirties. See Carole Seymour Jones, *Painted Shadows: The Life of Vivienne Eliot, First Wife of TS Eliot and the Long-Suppressed Truth About Her Influence on His Genius* (Talese/Doubleday, 2002).

Greek mythology and deal with castration and suicide (Eliot's 'bloody cloth and limbs').

'St Narcissus' is surely Britten himself, catching a sight of himself in the mirror of death. In writing this piece at great cost to his own energies he himself 'danced on the hot sand/Until the arrows came'. In the music's fragility (where the nineteenth-century piano has been replaced by the timeless sound of the harp) one encounters a mixture of light and dark, old and new, Christian and pagan, which is the composer himself. If he had been Aschenbach searching for sunlight and forbidden pleasures he was also 'a dancer for God', a deeply humble servant of that blessed St Cecilia who appears 'In visions/To all musicians' and who startles 'Composing mortals/With immortal fire'. I am happy to quote these lines by Auden in this context because I believe that, despite their debt to Dryden, they could never have been written without Eliot's example. It is only here that the two poets of this study briefly join hands with Mallarmé's poem about St Cecilia entitled 'Sainte', so admired by Eliot, an intermediary link, which was set to music by Maurice Ravel. Otherwise the two pieces by Eliot in Britten's oeuvre are hermetically sealed and lie apart from the rest of his output.

⊙ *Canticle IV – The Journey of the Magi* Op. 86 (1971)

The fourth Canticle, *The Journey of the Magi*, was written in early 1971. It was the period of *Death in Venice*, and the three artists for whom it was conceived, James Bowman (counter-tenor), John Shirley-Quirk (baritone) and Peter Pears, were all part of that opera's cast. This canticle was thus an off-shoot of the opera: the haunting words about birth and death with which it closes reveal the underlying links between the works. I remember the first rehearsal at Britten's Halliford Street flat in Islington; such was the respect of these singers for the composer, and such was their standard of preparation, that this run-through was almost perfect. I still vividly remember the quality of the *tremolando* passages (pp. 18–19 in the score) as Britten played them; I have never heard these colours in other performances of the piece – it was as if the sounds were being made on an array of ancient and exotic instruments – bells and woodwind. The Iranian camel bells I later gave Britten as a birthday present (in November 1971) still hang suspended from the ceiling at the foot of the staircase in the Red House: the composer liked to shake and chime them in passing.

Britten's second canticle (*Abraham and Isaac*) is for two characters where

T.S. Eliot

⊙ **CD2, track 9**

a third, the voice of God, is evoked by the combination of the two voices (I will discuss this work in the last lecture of the book). In this fourth canticle the narratory 'we' of the poem is obviously that of the three Magi – Melchior, Balthasar and Caspar. Britten casts three singers where the presence of the counter-tenor adds a note of eastern exoticism. There are colours in this eastern *Winterreise* that seem to have been derived from the second of his church operas, *The Burning Fiery Furnace*, where the pagan panoply of Nebuchadnezzar's court is richly evoked. We might tend to forget the royal background of these travellers, but evidence of their high-born origin is heard in the luxurious and sinuous lines of 'There were times we regretted/The summer palaces on slopes, the terraces,/And the silken girls bringing sherbet' (the last word in that phrase joins 'brambleberry' and 'eglantine' on the list of Britten's most extravagant melismas). At another point the eponymous hero of *The Prodigal Son* comes to mind: for the passage beginning 'At the end we preferred to travel all night' the accompaniment recalls his slow trudge through the desert, uncannily evoked (in the opera) by percussion effects that suggest sand-filled shoes.

The comparison with *Winterreise* (the most trudging of song cycles) is not an idle one: travel as such seems a constant theme in Britten's later works, including of course *Death in Venice*.

The singers relate the story as if from long ago – old men attempting to remember, and differing slightly with each other as they do so. The ensemble writing suggests a slightly querulous triumvirate: many of the three-part passages are not in exact unison, and one would not expect three crotchety and ageing despots to sing in exactly synchronised harmony. There is also a vivid sense that they are remembering details on the spot as they put their heads together in order to contribute their memories of the story, completing each others' phrases as they do so. This is a brilliant addition of another dimension to Eliot's understated poem, the provision of a musical dramaturgy. The Magi recall struggling through all sorts of hardships to get to the stable in Bethlehem, one of which – marvellously evoked in the sheer sound of this setting – is the coldness of the desert nights. With the words 'A cold coming [coming] we had of it' the scoring and spacing of the three voices produces a sound that is as unearthly and cool as a distant star. The audacious repetition of Eliot's 'coming' (and the insertion of a 5/8 bar to accommodate it) is another feature that continues throughout the canticle. This adds significantly to the mood of the piece, an asymmetry where these verbal repetitions suggest the pontificating of the aged Magi as they ransack their dimming collective memory for the truth behind a momentous event. Throughout the piece the undulating bass line of the

165

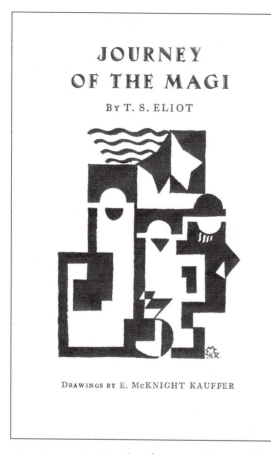

JOURNEY
OF THE MAGI

BY T. S. ELIOT

DRAWINGS BY E. McKNIGHT KAUFFER

Cover design for T.S. Eliot's
'Journey of the Magi'

accompaniment, first heard in the introductory bars, perfectly paints the sway of a camel train moving across the uneven desert terrain.

In that extraordinary (and famous) Eliotian understatement they find the result 'You may say, satisfactory'. No words in the poem describe the scene in the manger, but Britten adds something to the picture that only a musician can. The melody in the piano on pages 22 to 24 is that of *Magi videntes stellam*, the Antiphon before Magnificat at First Vespers for the Feast of the Epiphany (this recalls the composer's use of the hymn-tune 'St Ephraim' as a basis of 'The Choirmaster's Burial' in the *Winter Words*). This melody is heard like a radiant peal of bells with multiple repetitions of 'satisfactory' sung against the chant: having told the story more or less in unison, each of the kings is given the chance separately to ponder the consequences of this world-shattering event. Once again this lack of unanimity adds an extra layer of commentary to Eliot's poem. It is as if the kings are given time, during those repetitions of 'satisfactory', to voice different thoughts, thus leaving open the whole question of whether their journey had really been worthwhile and beneficial to mankind. This underlines and amplifies Eliot's single and ambiguous 'satisfactory' to a remarkable degree, and one cannot be certain he would have approved. The composer's solution makes it appear that the whole subsequent history of Christianity is covered by that one word, and by that Antiphon chiming in the piano part.

⊙ CD2, track 10

⊙ Underneath the Abject Willow (17–18 November, 1936)

From the sublime to the not quite ridiculous; we return to Auden for the remainder of the lecture. The first of these is a duet setting of the poem 'Underneath the Abject Willow'. The poem is like a message left under Britten's pillow, the advice of a friend to 'lighten up' and '*carpe diem*'. A summary of the poem shorn of its marvellous imagery might be: 'Please don't get into a state about what you are. Simply be who you are and enjoy it'.

166

Underneath the abject willow,
Lover, sulk no more;
Act from thought should quickly follow:
What is thinking for?
Your unique and moping station
Proves you cold;
Stand up and fold
Your map of desolation.

And the last verse continues…

Geese in flocks above you flying,
Their direction know;
Brooks beneath the thin ice flowing
To their oceans go.
Coldest love will warm to action,
Walk then, come,
Into your satisfaction.

It must be difficult to know what to do with a great poem when it has been written *about* you, as well as for you. Haydn set Mrs Anne Hunter's laudatory 'O Tuneful Voice' without too much embarrassment. When Johann Mayrhofer wrote a hymn of praise for Schubert ('Geheimnis an Franz Schubert' D491) the composer set it to music simply because that is what composers are expected to do. This was not an act of vanity, but the only way he knew of saying 'thank you' to the poet. This duet, however, seems to me to mark, if not an act of rebellion against Auden on Britten's part (he was still enthralled by the poet's friendship in 1936), then a strong difference in personality between the two men which is evident from early on. The tone of the poem seems to me to be elevated rather than flippant, persuasive rather than merry. But Britten treats it as a mere invitation to naughtiness. He makes the two female singers chortle away in thirds and sixths. The only other music like this in his output is that for the two 'Nieces' in *Peter Grimes* composed at least six years later; these are ladies of easy virtue, kept by 'Auntie' in the pub for the delectation of the sinners of Aldeburgh. Britten thus responds to Auden's masterpiece of a poem (for I believe that is exactly what it is) by setting the music for two bohemian girls, fly-by-nights, whose music cajoles and flirts with the man to whom the poem is addressed.

Could the composer really have so misunderstood Auden's intent? It is as if Britten has completely deflected the words' application to, and significance for, himself in relation to the text's author. Auden's attempted thrust is parried with music of charm (which seems to me to owe something stylistically to that of the Piano Concerto, including the song's middle-section waltz) but the serious, and loving, intention behind the words has been glossed over. This is surely an early sign of embarrassment at the intensity of the poet's interest, and a quiet declaration of independence. It is as if the composer were saying 'When I write my love music it won't be to words like these'. If Auden had been more musically sophisticated he may have hoped for music of a different tone, but the *Seven Sonnets of Michelangelo* were some years in the future, and when that cycle was written it was not for him.

In 1997 a solo version of 'Underneath the Abject Willow' was published, which had been previously unknown; this dates from 1941. It is an arrangement of the duet for single voice and piano rather than a new composition, and was probably made by the composer for a recital in America with Peter Pears.

Cabaret Songs (1937–39)

Britten was a terrific jazz pianist after his own fashion. He admired Cole Porter's songs ('Night and Day' was a favourite) and he loved improvising in light-hearted company. Like the similarly shy Schubert he made for the piano at parties, and with a few drinks he would enter into the spirit of fun with the greatest relish. These *Cabaret Songs* (apparently there are others yet to be re-discovered) are as near as we can get to hearing the composer in this relaxed mood; they were written for the singer-*diseuse* Hedli Anderson, wife of the poet Louis MacNeice. She was an attractive red-head, leader of the chorus line at the late-night cabaret at the Trocadero Grillroom, Piccadilly Circus, and also associated with Rupert Doone's Group Theatre. She sang the original version of 'Funeral Blues' in the Group Theatre's production of Auden and Isherwood's play *The Ascent of F6* in February 1937.

These songs have become very well known since their publication. This is the side of Auden's relationship with Britten that came back into public view only at the end of the composer's life, when he allowed the pieces to re-emerge. This was only after the poet's death. The same applies to the revision and revival of the Auden operetta from the American period, *Paul Bunyan*. There was probably an element of making peace with Auden's shade in so doing, but Britten would also have had a horror of approaching Auden for permission to revive, and publish, these old works during the poet's lifetime.

168

I remember accompanying Peter Pears in May 1972 in three of the songs (the text of *Johnny* is unsuitable for a male singer) while the composer listened in a wheelchair at the back of the Jubilee Hall in Aldeburgh. This was the first public airing of the pieces for thirty-three years.

(i) Tell me the Truth about Love (January 1938)

'Tell me the Truth about Love' has some of Auden's most amusing lyrics, but the poem reflects the poet's absorption during this period in attempting seriously to define love. It begins with the spoken words 'Liebe, l'amour, amor, amoris'; the last two words (the nominative and genitive of the third-declension Latin noun for love) are indicative of the poet's public-school education. I am old enough to find it rather alarming that few young artists today recognise these as Latin, let alone understand their grammatical significance. The opening lines – 'Some say that love's a little boy, and some say it's a bird' – is a typically sophisticated Audenian reference to love's ambiguous role as the classical Cupid or Eros as well as the Holy Spirit. Britten's vamping accompaniment and attractive, chromatically inflected melody seem influenced by Cole Porter; but Auden's lyrics ('His wife was very cross indeed' for example) seem rather to have taken the clipped diction of Noel Coward as their model.

(ii) Funeral Blues (revised solo version, June 1937)

This is the only piece from Britten's incidental music for *The Ascent of F6* that has survived on the concert platform of today. In the original show (Act II, Scene 5) the music is sung by Stagmantle and Isabel following the death of James Ransom. In the context of the play this is much more ironic (and amusing) than the solo version of the piece, which expresses the bereavement of a lover (a performance of which can be genuinely sad and touching). This accounts for the relish with which the piece was performed at Group Theatre cast parties of the time without in the least depressing the participants. The piano writing has a third stave given over to the 'muffled drum' effect deep in the bass; in the right hand the vocal line is shadowed by chords in dotted rhythms (the aeroplanes 'moaning overhead' are perfectly illustrated in droning triplets) while glittering sextuplets add an element of virtuosity to the downbeat mood. This piano writing, as well as a sudden heightening of the vocal tessitura, gives the last page of the piece a real sense of tragic grandeur. Britten's lazy triplets and slinky harmonies approximate to the American blues without being truly related to the American musical model. Britten's music is nowhere near 'black' enough for a real blues, but to be fair to him this is also the fault of Auden whose words have nothing to do with the authentic form either. The poet was nevertheless fond of using the term 'blues' for various poetic laments with a popular slant (for example, 'Roman Wall Blues', which was written a few years later).

In the film *Four Weddings and A Funeral*, the recitation of this poem by the Scottish actor John Hannah (at the funeral of his screen lover, the character played by Simon Callow) brought about an amazing boost in the sales of Auden's poetry throughout the world. The bookshops of New York and London were suddenly flooded by requests for the poem of 'Stop all the clocks' – and it must have been marvellous unexpectedly to discover such a poem in a comedy film, and out of the blue. There is evidence of the fact that this piece retained a place in the affection of Britten and Pears, even in the years when Auden was officially 'in exile' as far as Aldeburgh was concerned. John Culshaw tells the story how, in letting their hair down after a recording session for Decca in the late 1950s or early 60s, Pears and Britten launched into spontaneous performances of 'Tell me the Truth about Love' and 'Funeral Blues' – by memory, and long before the scores had been retrieved from the archives. The engineers secretly recorded this; when one listens to these extraordinary minutes[15] there is no doubt about how deeply (and affectionately) this music seems to have been ingrained in the heads and hearts of the two performers.

(iii) Johnny (5 May 1937)

'Johnny' is a hybrid work, a set of different scenes in different styles, which owes as much to German (and French) models as to American. The very title suggests a link with the 'Surabaya Johnny' from the Weill–Brecht collaboration *Happy End*. Britten has taken the opportunity to make of this song a suite of character pieces, each of which is deflated by the sadness of the refrain where Johnny, the object of the singer's affections, frowns like thunder and goes away. The opening verse ('O the valley in the summer') has the simplicity of cod folksong. With 'O the evening near Christmas' the charity ball is depicted with a polka that has something of the American square-dance about it. At the same time it prophesies some of the dance music in *Peter Grimes*. In the third verse ('Shall I ever forget at the Grand Opera') the composer parodies the inanities of Italian opera. It would have given a chance to Hedli Anderson (who was by no means an accomplished classical singer) to exercise her gifts as a comedienne and to make wicked fun of the genre and its practitioners There is a drawback when concert singers attack this repertory: when they come to this section it is as if they have at last found something to show off their voices. The disadvantage of

15. The British Library has a copy of this spontaneous performance in the National Sound Archives.

170

this passage being sung too well and too seriously is that it is no longer funny.

With 'O, he was as fair as a garden in flower/As slender and tall as the great Eiffel Tower' the marking changes to *Tempo di valse*. Mention of a Parisian landmark encourages Britten to write a French waltz – the model here is clearly Ravel in *noble et sentimental* mode. The song's last verse reverts to the blues style of the preceding song in the set. Hedli Anderson must have had a remarkable chest register – the sudden depth of this writing gives many singers a problem – specifically those easily capable of coloratura glitter in the opera episode. The piece was conceived by both poet and composer for an artist highly experienced in revue and light music, mistress no doubt of different types of parody: Anderson's talents were perhaps nearer to those of Hermione Gingold than Elisabeth Schwarzkopf. Most concert singers of today make of 'Johnny' a rather mawkish, deeply felt piece; the succession of heartbroken refrains dampen the potential comedy, and the amusing episodes which punctuate the tragedy lighten the pathos to the point that we are no longer engaged with her eventual suicide. What is our attitude to the narrator – are we to laugh at her, or pity her? One suspects that its original performer was able to make of the song a more believable whole.

☉ (iv) Calypso (May 1939 or later) ☉ CD2, track 11

'Calypso' was the last of the four poems to be written, and thus the last of these songs to be composed; Auden's lyric dates from May 1939. It is a virtuoso piece of verbal pastiche, aping the unique genre of the guitar-accompanied Afro-Caribbean topical song. Its rhymes and verbal emphases ('For he is the one that I love to look *on*/The acme of kindness and perfec-ti-*on*' and also 'For love's more important and powerful *than*/E'en a priest or politic*ian*') attempt to incorporate West-Indian accent and diction into the poem. These four cabaret poems were originally published in Auden's *Another Time* (1940). In later editions of his *Collected Poems* Auden decided that the words should be printed with the verbal stresses marked throughout, a unique case of this in his output.

Britten's music takes its cue from the sound of a steam train; this inspires the accompaniment, which chugs racily between the pianist's hands. *Molto moderato* is Britten's direction. The song often starts far too fast: if performers want help in determining the speed of this piece they should look at 'Midnight on the Great Western' (or 'The Journeying Boy') from the *Winter Words* cycle, which has a similar train-inspired accompaniment, and the same tempo. (Great song composers are often consistent in their

171

response to specific verbal imagery when it occurs in more than one song, even separated by a large number of years.) As speed gathers on this express (in response to the singer's perpetual commands to 'Drive faster') the accompaniment rises in pitch, the composer's scientifically accurate response to a phenomenon of physics. The song works itself up into a whirling fever pitch. At the end the singer abandons words for abandoned 'la la las'; at the end the singer is also required to whistle as if a train were letting of steam (another of Hedli Anderson's skills no doubt). Very few concert singers number power-whistling among their skills: Sarah Walker opted for the sound of an ambulance siren, Doppler effect and all; one ingenious solution is to use a whistle, which is concealed in the piano until the appropriate moment (as Katie Van Kooten does on the recording issued with this publication).

At the time of writing this poem Auden had already settled down in America. It is thus the only one of the *Cabaret Songs* with an American background. The poet was teaching at St Mark's School, Southborough, Massachusetts. His reason for hurrying up to Grand Central Station, New York, was to meet his new lover, Chester Kallman (1921–75). He had met this man, fourteen years his junior and also a writer, at a poetry reading, and it very soon became obvious that love was in the air. It so happened (pure coincidence?) that Auden established his relationship with Kallman at almost exactly the same time that Britten and Pears crossed the Atlantic to come to the New World.

Thus it was that Auden discovered his collaborator. There were to be many problems in the future with this friendship, much pain, and, on the poet's part, enormous determination to hang on to the dream of someone with whom he could work. Kallman's own poetry was to be indifferently received by the critics, but at least there were the libretti for operas by Stravinsky, Henze and Nabokov on which they were to work together. And it is perhaps appropriate that this set should end with 'Calypso', which was addressed to the person for whom he had waited so long. In writing of a non-productive relationship in 1936 Auden had referred to the sadness of those who could never have 'children', those who could never share a project: 'Their secretive children walk/Through your vigilance of breath/To unpardonable death'. Auden found it 'unpardonable' that two intelligent and articulate people who were lovers should not also devise a means to work together.

Work meant everything to Britten too. He came to America partly as a result of Auden giving him the intellectual freedom to do so. He spent three years away from home, and during this time continued his collaboration

172

with Auden – notably on the operetta *Paul Bunyan*, which was a critical failure at the time, but which is now valued as a fresh and lively work, a touching collaboration by two of England's greatest geniuses. All the time he was
working on *Paul Bunyan*, and notwithstanding Kallman's presence in his
life, Auden could not have failed to be aware that Britten, still young and
attractive, was easily the most talented collaborator he had ever met, or was
likely to meet. The composer had now grown up, was much more at ease
with his sexuality, and no longer needed an intellectual mentor. Instead of
Auden as a lover Britten had chosen a singer, Peter Pears, after a close relationship with a composer, Lennox Berkeley, that had failed to blossom –
collaborators both. It was with Pears that Britten drafted the first scenario
for *Peter Grimes*. Both Berkeley and Pears adored and 'looked after' Britten
and it is clear that the poet thought such cosy idolisation was bad for his
younger friend. Auden, Britten and Pears (as well as a number of other
bohemians, including Gypsy Rose Lee) had all lived together under the
same roof in a big house in Middagh Street, Brooklyn Heights, for a while
in late 1940. When the composer decided to return to Britain in 1942
Auden wrote a letter to Britten. It was to be a major reason for the rift that
quickly opened up between them:

Dearest Ben,

Very guilty about not having written. Perhaps I can't make myself
believe that you are really leaving us. I need scarcely say, my dear, how
much I shall miss you and Peter, or how much I love you both.

There is a lot I want to talk to you about, but I must try and say a
little of it by letter. I have been thinking a great deal about you and
your work during the past year. As you know I think you the white
hope of music; for this very reason I am more critical of you than of
anybody else, and I think I know something about the dangers that
beset you as a man and as an artist because they are my own.

Goodness and [Beauty] are the results of a perfect balance between
Order and Chaos, Bohemianism and Bourgeois Convention.

Bohemian chaos alone ends in a mad jumble of beautiful scraps;
Bourgeois convention alone ends in large unfeeling corpses.

Every artist except the supreme masters has a bias one way or the
other. The best pair of opposites I can think of in music are Wagner
and Strauss. (Technical skill always comes from the bourgeois side of
one's nature.)

For middle-class Englishmen like you and me, the danger is of
course the second. Your attraction to thin-as-a-board juveniles, ie to

173

the sexless and innocent, is a symptom of this. And I am certain too that it is your denial and evasion of the demands of disorder that is responsible for your attacks of ill-health, ie sickness is your substitute for the Bohemian.

Wherever you go you are and probably always will be surrounded by people who adore you, nurse you, and praise everything you do, eg Elisabeth,[16] Peter (Please show this to P to whom all this is also addressed). Up to a certain point this is fine for you, but beware. You see, Bengy dear, you are always tempted to make things too easy for yourself in this way, ie to build yourself a warm nest of love (of course when you get it, you find it a little stifling) by playing the lovable talented little boy.

If you are really to develop to your full stature, you will have, I think, to suffer, and make others suffer, in ways which are totally strange to you at present, and against every conscious value that you have; ie you will have to be able to say what you never have had the right to say – God, I'm a shit.

This is all expressed very muddle-headedly, but try and not misunderstand it, and believe that it is only my love and admiration for you that makes me say it.

Here are one and a half more movements. The second half of the fourth movement will be about the Taxing of the People.

All my love to you both, and God bless you
Wystan

This is of course a remarkable document, perspicacious and affectionate, and, as it happens, it deals with one of the major themes of *Death in Venice* – the opposition of Apollo and Dionysus. But it seems clear to me that there was a background to the Auden–Britten relationship whereby Britten was unable to accept this advice in the spirit that it seems to have been written. This was surely the build-up of seven years of tension whereby Britten was aware that he was unable to provide Auden with something he needed from him, something in return for the great amount he had received from the poet. Britten must have thought that the letter was a covert punishment for failing to participate in Auden's dream, which did not refer to him at all, and which had never really referred to him. The criticism of Pears was surely taken to mean 'I could have been a better partner for you; my type of bohemianism would be better for your development as an artist than the bourgeois nest which Peter will provide for you'.

Of course there were other reasons for the break-up: Auden's poetic style was changing and Britten now found it less amenable to word-setting. The end of the letter mentions a project that never came to fruition – a 'Christmas Oratorio' where the poet wrote words for something he designated a 'fugal subject': if that had ever been composed it would have been the longest fugal subject ever written. As he got older the poet was getting more set in his ways and dogmatic, more of a bully. Even Chester Kallman would find the poet increasingly difficult to live with, and spent less and less time with him as the years went on.

In 1964 Auden wrote the following words, which are at the heart of this whole question: 'Between two collaborators, whatever their sex, age or appearance, there is always an erotic bond … Queers to whom normal marriage and parenthood are forbidden, are fools if they do not deliberately look for tasks which require collaboration, and the right person with whom to collaborate – again, the sex does not matter. In my own case, collaboration has brought me greater erotic joy – as distinct from sexual pleasure – than any sexual relations I have had.'[17]

We can take it that Auden here admits to the 'erotic joy' of working with Britten, despite the lack of sex. Much could be forgiven to a poet of Auden's decency and goodness, despite his shambolic exterior, and however unattractive the determination of a giant intellect to have its own way. Was it Auden's essential kindness that Britten remembered towards the end of his life when news of the poet's death resulted in that 'storm of tears'? He would at least have reflected on the passing of someone who had played a crucial, and major, part in his life, someone who had loved him dearly and whom he had initially hero-worshipped, later admired, but was never able to love in return.

17. Davenport-Hines, *Auden*, p.137.

The programme at the 2001 Britten festival was comprised of:
Third Suite for Cello Op. 87; **The Poet's Echo Op. 76** *(Pushkin): 'Echo', 'My Heart', 'Angel', 'The Nightingale and the Rose', 'Epigram', 'Lines Written During a Sleepless Night';* **Sonata in C for Cello and Piano Op. 65**

Lecture 7

Britten and Russia

Britten's earliest known link with Russia was a piece for brass ensemble and percussion that he wrote in early 1936. This work, Britten's only opus for brass ensemble, was entitled *Russian Funeral*, and its first performance was on 8 March 1936 at the Westminster Theatre in London. It is based on proletarian songs played at the funeral of the demonstrators massacred outside the Winter Palace on 'Bloody Sunday', January 1905. Shostakovich was later to quote the same songs in his Eleventh Symphony (1955–57). Shostakovich was also the composer that Britten most admired among his contemporaries. He told me just this during a conversation in 1971 in which he also acknowledged Stravinsky, then still alive, as a great spinner of notes, 'but to what purpose? … what does he actually *say* with his recent music?'

Britten also mentioned to me how much he had always admired Stravinsky's *The Firebird*, another very Russian resonance that almost certainly went back to his teenage years. But feelings of resentment, and even intimidation, ran deep; in the early 1960s Stravinsky and Robert Craft published stinging criticisms of Britten, which were suppressed in the English editions of the *Conversations*. In the Moscow diary of Christmas 1966 Pears describes a meeting with Shostakovich where Stravinsky comes up for discussion between the two disenchanted composers: 'Ben tells his recent dream of Stravinsky as a monumental hunchback pointing with a quivering finger at a passage in the *Cello Symphony* 'How dare you write that bar?'[1]

A performance of Shostakovich's ill-fated opera *Lady Macbeth of Mtsensk* (conducted by Albert Coates in 1936) had been Britten's first experience of a large-scale work by this composer. The young Britten noted in his diary that the Russian was a 'real inspired genius'. He continued: 'The "eminent English Renaissance" composers sniggering in the stalls was

1. Peter Pears, *Travel Diaries 1936–1978*, ed. Philip Reed (The Boydell Press, 1995), p.139.

Opposite: Peter Pears, Galina Vishnevskaya, Benjamin Britten, Mistislav Rostropovich and Marion Thorpe, Moscow, 1963

177

2. Donald Mitchell and Philip Reed (eds), *Letters from a Life: Selected Letters and Diaries of Benjamin Britten. Volume 1, 1923–1939* (Faber and Faber, 1991), p.409.

typical. There is more music in a page of MacBeth [sic] than in the whole of their "elegant" output.[2] One notes the disapproval of his bourgeois elders in Britten's disparaging use of the word 'elegant'. It is clear that at this time his political leanings, like Auden's, inclined to the communist sympathies felt by many members of the British intelligentsia. These included many in the homosexual community who imagined, mistakenly, that the Soviet system was more sympathetic to their way of life than the British.

The conductor of *Russian Funeral* had been the distinguished English composer Alan Bush (1900–95), who was my composition professor at the Royal Academy of Music in the late 1960s and early 70s. Bush remained a committed member of the Communist Party to the end of his life; this was at great cost to his career and hopes of getting his works performed, particularly during the Cold War period. But the old-time affection felt for him by Britten and Pears was evident from the alacrity with which the great tenor responded to my request to take part in Bush's 70th birthday concert at the RAM in 1970. Accompanied by the composer, still a dab hand at the keyboard, Pears performed songs from *Voices of the Prophets*, which he had commissioned in 1952: a large cycle with some visionary texts (the Book of Isaiah, Milton and Blake among them) that seemed attuned to more modern left-wing sympathies. This birthday concert, which I organised, was also a turning point in my studentship. I had already met Britten in Aldeburgh in 1969, but it was this concert for Alan Bush (in which I also participated as a chamber-music pianist, a performance that turned out to have been my audition as far as Pears was concerned) which began my real association with Aldeburgh.

Pears's willingness to give his services to celebrate the birthday of a colleague was typical of his generosity. During my years of friendship with him I noticed countless acts of kindness to colleagues, both young and old. His was the exquisite tact born of a feeling of *noblesse oblige* as a leading member of the profession. (His fee was legendarily low; he believed it immoral to be paid too much as a performer – *autre temps, autre moeurs*!) His affection and admiration for a man of such unbending principle as Alan Bush was part of that side of the Aldeburgh philosophy which was instinctively sympathetic to the left whilst shying away from labels and party allegiances of all kinds (there were various futile attempts by those in the nascent gay liberation movement to involve Britten and Pears with their cause). I was brought up in the right-wing atmosphere of Ian Smith's Rhodesia, and I remember thinking that the political atmosphere at the Red House was strangely elusive by comparison. In Africa I had become accustomed to strong forthright expressions of political expression, both

178

left and right – albeit of rather extreme kinds. In Aldeburgh there was a complicated balance between a certain rural conservatism (not including much sympathy for the Tory party nor, of course, hunting, but encompassing friends of Tory sympathies and a fondness for the Queen Mother) and an old-fashioned, almost boyish, 'bolshiness'. As I have already written, the anti-establishment side of Britten's nature was rarely confrontational; instead he seemed to have delighted in changing the intellectual and moral landscape from within – a kind of subtly subversive Fifth Column within the otherwise ultra-respectable ranks of Aldeburgh society.

The period of my links with Britten was at the height of his friendship with the Rostropovich family, with Shostakovich and also Richter. These links engendered at the Red House a pro-Russian sympathy, which had profound musical and personal reasons as far as Britten was concerned, but which was still characteristic of many British left-wing sympathisers in the 1960s, and well into the 1970s. During this period there was also a strong sense of engagement with Russia at a cultural and official level. The sporting, balletic and musical achievements of the Soviet system were still of the highest order (although it is true that the large-voiced singers who were exported were more suitable for opera than song). During the incumbency of that famed Labour minister for the arts Jenny Lee, British composers and performers were made to feel that they could effectively contribute towards *détente*. In his personal links with people of Russia, Britten seems to have tapped into an old and residual sympathy for the principles of Marxism without being fooled by the heartless *apparachiks* who administered the Soviet state. In the early 1970s, for example, Pears commissioned the Scottish composer Ronald Stevenson, an ardent Marxist, to write a song-cycle, *Border Boyhood*, to the words of the famed Scottish communist poet Hugh MacDiarmid. And few people remember today that Montagu Slater, librettist of *Peter Grimes*, was a member of the Communist Party.

In retrospect, part of the romance of Russia in the composer's mind seems to have been the result of an emotional attachment to an idealised Russia that went back to the Audenesque period in which *Russian Funeral* was composed. Of course Britten had more than enough experience with the cruelties and irrationalities of the Soviet machine (the preventing of Vishnevskaya from participating in the première of the *War Requiem* in 1962 is one example) to be acutely aware of the oppressive nature of the communist regime. But another side of him was happy to be an honoured guest in a country where he seems to have felt more at home than anywhere else in the world, apart from England. Even that exception was not completely true: one feels that in some ways the composer felt more able to be

179

himself in a land free of potentially judgmental English-speakers. In August 1965 composer and singer visited Armenia for a month's holiday. Despite the grisly aspects of Soviet repression – which had, on and off, beset creative artists like Shostakovich – Britten and Pears experienced the legendary hospitality of a Soviet republic (not Russia itself as we understand it today of course) and were beguiled by the scenery, the people, the history, the food and the drink. The personal warmth of Rostropovich and his wife, Galina Vishnevskaya, was of course an important factor in the happiness of three Russian holidays (the other two were in Moscow in 1966 and 1971), but topography and historical myth (including Britten's own history of the 1930s) played a large part in the excitement felt by both Britten and Pears in spending time in a country that was, for them at least, literally a land of milk and honey (these foods were actually praised by Pears in his travel diary, *Armenian Holiday*). Thanks to the hugely privileged status of the Rostropoviches (whatever the question marks hanging over their status with the government of the day they were still treated as artistic royalty at this time), composer and singer were able to experience a part of the country that was hospitable and hugely colourful, intellectual company and earthy surroundings – in short something near to the bountiful Mother Russia of which so many left-wing intellectuals in the 1930s dreamed but which they never experienced. All this is in great contrast to the disillusionment with the Soviet way of life that followed visits to the Soviet Union by various English writers and intellectuals who had previously been enthused by communism.

It cost the Rostropoviches, Britten's beloved 'Slava' and 'Galinka', a great deal of time, energy and money to provide this sort of cosseting for their English friends. But apart from all their personal care the very surroundings in which he found himself on the holidays spent in Russia seem to have relaxed Britten in a way that was almost unique in his life. Apart from Shostakovich, always a special case, he met a large number of Soviet musicians of different kinds – some of them more talented than others – and Britten listened patiently to many a presentation of their music, either in live performances or, more usually, recordings. Here were composers who did not come from the Royal College or Royal Academy, who were not part of the British establishment, who were neither pro-Howells nor pro-Vaughan Williams, much less pro-Boulez or pro-Stockhausen. These were not the 'eminent English Renaissance composers sniggering in the stalls' that he had resented in 1936; in Russia he felt safe from the old wounds inflicted by his countrymen in his earlier career. In Russia he encountered open-hearted admirers, both composers and virtuoso performers, who

were able to inspire him to a new and special 'Russian' chapter in his compositional life. In Russia Benjamin Britten seems to have become much more relaxed, a person given to laughing with, and hugging, his colleagues if the evidence of the pictures is anything to go by. He seems like a spirit released. There is certainly little documented evidence of this kind of unbuttoned behaviour with his English colleagues. Perhaps he found a liberating influence in conversing in another language – 'Aldeburgh Deutsch', that strange language (German in English word-order) with which he was able to communicate with the Rostropoviches. (In a similar way Fischer-Dieskau seems much less formal and straight-jacketed when he speaks English than when he expresses himself in his own language.)

Opposite: Mistislav Rostropovich, Benjamin Britten, Galina Vishnevskaya and Peter Pears, Moscow, 1960

The following is a chronological list of the works by Britten that were inspired by his connections with Russia and Russian artists. Also noted here are other important dates in Britten's adoption of the Russian 'cause', and the dates of the composer's own visits to the Soviet Union with Peter Pears:

In September 1960, Britten was introduced to the cellist Mstislav Rostropovich by Dmitri Shostakovich following the first British performance of Shostakovich's Cello Concerto No. 1 at the Festival Hall. The cellist was thirty-three at the time, and Britten had already been fascinated by his playing a few days earlier on a broadcast. Rostropovich immediately begged Britten to write him something. The next morning at a meeting at the cellist's hotel Britten agreed to do so (he already had a cello and piano sonata in mind) on condition that Rostropovich would appear at the Aldeburgh Festival the following year.

In January 1961, Sonata in C for Cello and Piano, Op. 65 was composed. The first performance was given by Rostropovich and the composer at the Jubilee Hall, Aldeburgh, on 7 July 1961. At the same festival Vishnevskaya and Rostropovich gave their first recital in Aldeburgh with Rostropovich accompanying at the piano. George Odam was a student at the time: 'No one knew who she was except that she was Rostropovich's wife. I had heard him play the Bach Cello Suites in Aldeburgh Church that day. We attended Vishnevskaya's recital from a sense of curiosity and as a tribute to him. What we got was like a Force 9 gale from the North Sea! Mussorgsky *Songs and Dances of Death* full frontal! For an encore Ben (piano) and Peter (tenor) joined with both Rostros (soprano and cello) for a Bach cantata. Stunning!' It was also at this magical festival that Pears and Britten performed their first *Winterreise* at the Jubilee Hall.

In January 1962 the *War Requiem* Op. 66 was completed. The first performance was on 30 May 1962 in Coventry Cathedral. The soprano part had been conceived for Vishnevskaya who, at the last minute, was not permitted to leave Russia to take part in the performance. Heather Harper sang instead. It is clear that a major inspiration behind this great work was that it should be sung by soloists from three participant powers of World War Two: England (Pears), Germany (Fischer-Dieskau) and Russia (Vishnevskaya).

In March 1963 Britten and Pears made their first visit to the Soviet Union for a Festival of British Music. The following year, at this same festival, the Symphony for Cello and Orchestra Op. 68 was given its first performance by Rostropovich and the Moscow Philharmonic Orchestra, conducted by the composer (12 March 1964).

In June 1964, Britten provided Rostropovich with cadenzas to Haydn's Cello Concerto in C. This version of Haydn's work was given its first performance by Rostropovich and the ECO, conducted by Britten, in Blythburgh Church on 18 June 1964.

In December 1964 Britten's Suite for Cello Op. 72 was completed. It was given its first performance by Rostropovich in Aldeburgh Parish Church on 27 June 1965.

Between 3 August and 4 September 1965, Britten and Pears spent a holiday in Armenia (with days in Moscow at the beginning and the end of the visit) as guests of Rostropovich and Vishnevskaya, as well as of the Armenian Composers' Union. During this period the song-cycle *The Poet's Echo* Op. 76 to poems of Pushkin was written. Apart from an informal initial run-through with Pears and the composer, its first complete performance with Galina Vishnevskaya (soprano) and Mstislav Rostropovich (piano) was at the Conservatoire of Music, Moscow, on 2 December 1965.[3]

3. Rostropovich and Vishnevskaya performed Nos 2 and 5 on 29 August 1965 at the Philharmonic Concert Hall, Yerevan, Armenia.

In June 1966 cadenzas for Mozart's Piano Concerto in E flat (K.482) were composed for Sviatoslav Richter. They were first performed in July 1966 in Tours, France.

Between 25 December 1966 and 2 January 1967 Britten and Pears spent their Christmas and New Year in Moscow with the Rostropoviches.

In August 1967 the Second Suite for Cello Op. 80 was completed. Its first performance was by Rostropovich at The Maltings, Snape on 17 June, 1968.

Between February and March 1971 Britten composed his Third Suite for Cello Op. 87.

Between 16 April and 25 April 1971, Britten and Pears took part in the 'Days of British Music Festival' in Moscow and Leningrad. On 24 April they gave a recital at the British Embassy for an audience of important Russian guests (including Shostakovich). This was their last visit to the USSR.

On 21 December 1974 Rostropovich gave the first performance of the Third Suite for Cello at the Maltings, Snape. This had been postponed from its original date in the Aldeburgh Festival in June 1972.

In this lecture (which, as usual, follows the shape of our concert), I will discuss three of Britten's 'Russian' works, beginning with the last and ending with the first.

⊙ Third Suite for Cello Op. 87 (1971 revised 1974)

⊙ CD2, track 12

This is the last of the great works Britten wrote for Mstislav Rostropovich. It was composed in 1971 and the manuscript was handed over to the cellist by the composer in April of that year when Britten and Pears visited Moscow, as it happened for the last time. During that week in Moscow

Britten gave a performance of the piece (on the piano!) to a small invited audience that included Shostakovich and his wife, Sue Phipps (Pears's niece, at that time a concert agent), and Elizabeth Wilson, a cellist who was the daughter of Britain's Russian ambassador, and who acted as chauffeur and interpreter during this visit. The first performance of the work had to be held back a number of years because this was the period when the great cellist was finding it difficult to gain permission to travel to the West, partly because of his determination to champion the cause of the novelist Alexander Solzhenitsyn.

This is the single work among all the music written by Britten for the Russians that contains openly Russian influences. On one occasion when Britten visited Moscow he had admired the works of Tchaikovsky and expressed regret that he possessed so few of the composer's rarer scores. Imagine Britten's embarrassment when a packing case full of the complete edition of Tchaikovsky was presented him at the airport as a gift from Rostropovich – something like ninety volumes. (Another, possibly more accurate, version of this story was that Britten paid for the Tchaikovsky edition himself from the rouble account that he held in the Soviet Union because he was unable to bring currency earned in Russia to the West.) Volume 61 of this formidable set bound in green rexine is devoted to Tchaikovsky's folksong arrangements. In looking at these Britten found three that actually made their way into this third suite for unaccompanied cello. He also uses the *Kontakion* – that old Russian Orthodox hymn for the dead. The composer weaves his own ideas with this age-old Russian material to make a huge musical canvas.

This suite has ten sections played as a continuous piece. There is a lento introduction based on the *Kontakion* (there is a possible reference to Shostakovich in the DSCH theme: the *Kontakion* melody – C, H (= B natural), C, S (= E flat), D – is more or less a retrograde version of the Russian composer's musical signature). An allegro March is based on two of the Tchaikovsky folksongs; a Canto is based on the third Tchaikovsky folksong, entitled 'Little Apple Tree'; Barcarole recalls the water motif that occurs in the 'overture' to *Death in Venice* as Aschenbach is rowed across the lagoon; Dialogo echoes the idea that initiates the *Cello Sonata* from the 1960s; then comes a Fugue in which Britten as an ardent student of Bach shows his ability to suggest part writing in a single-line instrument. This is followed by a Fantastico recitativo section before a Presto; then a solemn Lento Passacaglia based on the *Kontakion* (the chromatic phrase always dropping to the bottom C – a mighty movement this). After this the composer reveals at long last the source of all these variations – the unadorned Tchaikovsky folksongs. The work ends with a 'plain' statement of the *Kontakion*, the hymn for the dead. In this way Britten writes a set of variations in reverse – revealing only at the end the unadorned source of his ideas. This is a process that he had already used to marvellous effect in two earlier works: the ⊙ *Lachrymae* for viola and piano and the *Nocturnal* for solo guitar.

⊙ **CD2, track 1**

This is perhaps the most ambitious and the most far-reaching of all the works written for Rostropovich, including the more elaborate Cello Symphony; since the composition of that work in 1968 (the year of the Soviet invasion of Czechoslovakia) Russia had taken an increasingly hard line with the outside world. The Third Suite is certainly animated by an extraordinary depth of feeling, which is witness to a unique musical friendship. Here the composer seems to mourn the plight of his friend Slava caught in the toils of an extraordinarily bitter political situation; but this is also obviously a lament for the whole Russian people. In this slender single cello line, and with magisterial art, Britten says all the things that were difficult to say in words at that time: his heartfelt sympathy with the dying Shostakovich as a composer, and the plight of all artists in Russia. By the time the work came to be performed in 1974, Britten was a man prematurely aged by illness. He had more or less come full circle, as he approached his own death, back to that 'Russian Funeral' of 1936. This highly concentrated cello suite is an epic portrait of a tormented, mighty country showing the darkness of the soul and a certain wild savagery despite its singular instrumental resources. As such it is surely Britten's most successful Russian stylisation.

The song cycle *The Poet's Echo* was written during a long holiday (long by the standards of the workaholic Britten) that the composer and Pears undertook in the summer of 1965, surely the most idyllic period away from home that either of them had ever experienced (in 1955–56 there had been an even longer holiday in the Far East). Extracts from Peter Pears's diary *Armenian Holiday* appeared in the Aldeburgh Festival programme book for 1966, but the whole diary appeared in *The Travel Diaries of Peter Pears 1936–1978*, the second volume in *Aldeburgh Studies in Music* edited by Philip Reed.

The following is a brief outline, my own synopsis sifted from Pears's diary, of the extraordinarily happy period which gave birth to the song-cycle *The Poet's Echo*.

Sunday 1 August 1965

The month began with a performance by the London Symphony Orchestra at the Royal Festival Hall at which Rostropovich had performed the last movement (the Passacaglia) of the Cello Symphony, with Britten conducting.

Monday 2 August

In London with a party for the Faber Music team in the St John's Wood flat (59c Marlborough Place, NW8) that Britten and Pears rented from the late Anne Wood and Johanna Peters, who lived in the main house. (Johanna Peters, who died in 2000, had been both Head of Opera and Head of Vocal Studies at the Guildhall School; Britten was a composer whom she knew so well, and her absence at the festival on which this book is based was a great sadness). Dinner was with the Russian guests at Prunier's restaurant.

Tuesday 3 August

Britten and Pears took a three-and-a-half hour Aeroflot flight to Moscow accompanied by the Rostropoviches, who were weighed down by their celebrated luxury goods purchases from Harrods – in this case eight parcels, which travelled on the English guests' first-class tickets. On arrival in Moscow VIP treatment at the airport, and then on to the Rostropovich flat. The evening was spent in a Georgian restaurant – 'caviar (vodka of course) and delicious mess of liver and nuts, and ham, beetroot, and cabbage salad, superb cucumbers and tomatoes and onion, an excellent bortsch soup, and a small crushed grilled whole chicken (a little too lifelike!), grilled rather peppery, to be torn apart and eaten with fingers, very good ice-cream (Russian possibly world's best) and Turkish coffee.'[4] (Pears's detailed culinary descriptions are among the delights of his diary.)

4. Pears, *Travel Diaries*, p.101. Henceforth in this section, page numbers for quotations from the *Travel Diaries* are given in parentheses in the text.

Wednesday 4 August

A visit to a Russian bank where composer and singer withdrew several hundred roubles from the bank account they had opened in Moscow on an earlier visit. In the afternoon they were taken on the fifty-mile drive to the Tchaikovsky museum in Klin. This is where the Russian composer had spent the last years of his life: 'Lots of photos and documents, his copy of the Mozart Gesamtausgabe, his piano, his narrow high bed, the desk where he wrote the 6th symphony … Modeste's room with Greek statues and a signed photo of Nijinsky' (102). The evening was spent at the Rostropovich *Datchya* with musical entertainment provided by the couple's talented young daughters, Olga and Helene.

Thursday 5 August

Another three-and-a-half hour flight (in a four-engined plane), this time from Moscow to Yerevan, capital of Armenia. Here there was a a welcoming dinner party of fourteen musicians including Eduard Mik'aeli

Mirzoyan (b. 1921), head of the Armenian Composers' Union, and Vladislav Alexandrovich Uspensky (b. 1937), pupil of Shostakovich.

Friday 6 August

The long drive to Dilidjan, a small town some three to four hours away from Yerevan. It is near here that the Armenian Composers had built in 1963 a summer colony of about a dozen houses some 5,000 feet up in a circle of wooded mountains. Britten and Pears took up residence in a bungalow that was about 20 yards along the lane from the bungalow inhabited by their friends Slava and Galya. One of the best chefs in Russia ('a charming character called Hachik') had been seconded to the task of providing a succession of amazing meals, which were produced under rather primitive circumstances. The two English guests settled down, in Britten's words, to 'three weeks reading, sunbathing, swimming and picking mushrooms'.[5]

5. Benjamin Britten, 'A Composer in Russia', *Sunday Telegraph* (24 October 1965).

Saturday 7 August

A wash-out of a day with the clouds closing around the new guests with torrents of rain. Pears noted that this time indoors on 'the south-eastern most limit of our journey' was 'a perfect moment to begin a Diary' (100). At another point in the diary Pears notes that 'we are very near here to Mt. Ararat and Noye's Fludde … The Armenians are Christians … The Azerbaidjanians to the north-east, the Turks south and west, and the Persians south-east are all Muslim … Religion may not be encouraged in the U.S.S.R., but religious differences are also not encouraged' (112).

Sunday 8 August to Monday 9 August

The weather settles down and Britten and Pears began a long series of walks of increasing adventurousness. After one walk Pears returned with a posy of flowers: 'it ranged from enormous viper's bugloss, great yellow headed thistles on top of round brown heads (no prickles), scotch thistles red and white, large minty herbs with strong smelling leaves, scabious white and mauve (huge), great canterbury bells blue and white, great wild hollyhocks pink and yellow, large-scale thyme (I think), wild pinks, some leguminacae, little, white pink and yellow, and large red, near orchid-like flowers on non-orchid stems with non-orchid leaves, vast marigolds, wild sunflowers, daisies, dandelions of every sort, yellow daisyish floribundas (?), heavily armoured thistles with silver leaves, down to coltsfoot and our old friend, bindweed, some rock roses and large crane's-bill' (105). I find it very moving to read this list some fourteen years after Pears's death; it seems so typical of his love of nature, and his broadness and gentleness of culture, that was not, dare one say, typical of a tenor.

Tuesday 10 August to Wednesday 11 August

Pears noted 'a long, memorable excursion … up on to the grassy downs high above our local woods'. With the help of a various buses, and in various stages, the English visitors reached a 'staggering view: all round green-topped hills with wooded valleys rich in trees and not a conifer among them' (106). After a marvellous feast that was laid on almost as if by magic Pears and Britten climbed even higher to contemplate the scenery '… somehow the whole world was explainable, so dizzy and beautiful it was.' The return journey lasted three hours. The next day was one of recuperation: Britten's toe was 'raw and in Elastoplast' (106); Pears himself was having problems with his knee.

Thursday 12 August

An excursion to Dilidjan, itself an ex-Turkish spa. Pears and Britten had begun to regret the lack of a camera; when such a thought was voiced it became Rostropovich's command. A selection of cameras was sent for from Yerevan. The selected model had already been paid for by Rostropovich – 'one can do nothing against his over-affectionate lavish kindness' (107). There is more contact with the three Armenian composers Mirzoian ('handsome, charming, a fair composer'), Babadjanian and Arutunjan. Of this composers' fraternity Peter Pears notes: 'Can one imagine Arthur Bliss, William Walton and Ben and lots more taking their holidays together on Windermere and entertaining Fischer-Dieskau and [Hans Werner] Henze for a month? Not quite' (107).

Friday 13, Saturday 14, Sunday 15 August

Three further days of low-key relaxation. Whenever Britten was confined to bed with illness the days following were always rich in compositional energy. In a similar way these days of non-eventful unwinding were also to bear musical fruit. On the Sunday afternoon Pears had the time to watch a blond Russian slowly scything the flower fields.

Monday 16 August

Adik Khudojan (b. 1921) presented Britten with his Solo Cello Sonata. The fact that Britten immediately spotted misprints in the score earned that composer's unconditional adoration. In the Pears diary this is the first day that we hear of Britten's new Pushkin settings. The composer had bought a book of poems at London airport. The fact that he is working on a Pushkin cycle soon became local knowledge in the composers' colony. By 16 August Britten was on his fourth song and Pears was already preparing the English singing translations. On this day the singer revealed his partiality to the old Russian custom of mushroom-gathering: 'A particularly unattractive dirty grey sponge-like growth, which is greeted with triumphant cries and is considered No. 1' (111). This search for *greebwee* was anathema to Britten, who did not care for mushrooms in any shape or form. But Pears was enormously touched by the industriousness with which Vishnevskaya and Aza Amintayeva (the pianist and coach who worked with the Russian couple) sat at the table, their heads done up in squares, cleaning mushrooms. He found it 'very dear and very Russian'.

In the afternoon of the same day the English pair drove off on a hectic and fast visit to a Pushkin monument. This turned out to be 'a fountain of beautiful water with a bronze relief of a scene in Pushkin's life, which in spite of many explanations in Armenian, Russian and Aldeburgh-Deutsch I could not fathom' (113). Britten was ill after the bumpy drive, and the return journey was more sedate. The diary notes the beauty of the scenery and of the villages, which 'might have been here since Noah bumped into Ararat' (113).

Tuesday 17 August – Wednesday 18 August

Britten had a stomach upset perhaps caused by the cold mineral waters of Lermontov drunk the day before. This was righted, with many remedies both ancient and modern, within 48 hours. He spent one day in bed, and the next recuperating on the sofa. The result of this was intense creative energy and more work on the Pushkin cycle, now completed up to the fifth song. Vishnevskaya heard them for the first time that afternoon 'and wants to get at them at once'. On this evening the English visitors were played a recording of Eduard Mirzoyan's Symphony for string orchestra and timpani (115).

Thursday 19 August

The composer Babadjanian visited the English guests to play his Six Pieces for Piano with 'tremendous gusto and agility'. His style was 'post-Bartók folk-based Armenian' (115).

Friday 20 August

Instead of a projected unofficial trip to Georgia (which apparently would have caused something of a diplomatic incident between Soviet republics and their rival composers) there was an excursion to the south-east of Armenia. First a car journey to Yerevan (where preparations for the Britten Festival were in progress) then a flight to the town of Goris. Here, in the woods above the town, a particularly lavish picnic was laid with increasingly extravagant toasts; Pears got a thick head from too much mulberry vodka, which he likened to that dangerous drink, slivovitz.

Saturday 21 August

In the morning another picnic; Pears waxed lyrical about the butter (the best he had ever tasted) and also the cream and honey. After an uncomfortable three-hour drive to Djermuk in the extreme heat there was a late-afternoon picnic lunch followed by a short flight back to Yerevan. There was then another three-hour drive back to Dilidjan taking the British visitors out of the heat of the plain into the cooler mountains.

Britten attending a reception during the Festival of English Music, Moscow, 1963

Sunday 22 August

A reception given for the visitors by the Mayor of Dilidjan on the annual Flowerday. The floral exhibition included 'a special flower piece with in the middle a plaque with Ben's name picked out in mauve phlox petals. It was absurd and very sweet' (118). At this reception the Museum Curator presented Britten and Pears with a real treasure – an amphora almost five thousand years old that had been dug up at an excavation in Dilidjan. This artefact was later carefully packed so as to arrive in England in one piece. It is still to be seen in the Red House Library. Pears noted: 'they were giving us one of their most priceless possessions as a gesture of friendship to two English musicians. It was an act of spontaneous natural hospitality which

190

one had really never met before' (119). It seems not to have occurred to the English pair that such an extravagant gesture with a treasure belonging to the people must have been sanctioned, if not suggested, at the highest level.

Monday 23 August

'A day of calm routine with a very long walk in the afternoon up and down the woods and hills looking for mushrooms' (119). This was also the day that Britten finished composing his Pushkin cycle. In the evening the composer Babadjanian came to supper to talk music. Pears notes that 'Webern and his followers' have passed these composers by; their main influences are 'Mussorgsky, Shostakovich, Bartók and perhaps Mahler, as well as folk music' (119–20).

Tuesday 24 August

Another picnic, this time given by the composers and musicians resident in Dilidjan. This was a merry occasion marked by 'Slava's determined and wholly successful campaign to quieten an over-talkative if sweetly-silly lady musicologist by insisting on drinking "Bruderschaft", with arms entwined, in large mugs of vodka.' In the evening Britten played through his six Pushkin settings to 'a handful, Slava-picked, of composers'. The cellist read the texts aloud and explained the plan of the cycle. Then Pears vocalised the music 'with an occasional Russian word'. After a round of brandies the piece was heard again to universal approbation, including 'astonishment at the feeling Ben shows for the language and Pushkin, not a foot wrong anywhere ...' (120).

Wednesday 25 August

A quieter day with 'a drive in the evening to re-find the charms of Lermontovo and the other villages of the Makhanite Russians, 'with their pretty painted houses, neat enclosed gardens full of sunflowers and holly-hocks, and their dazzling blond inhabitants and bearded old men' (121). In the evening the composer Alexan came to play his Symphony – 'a highly national affair ... using some very beautiful Armenian tunes ... This is the sort of music which has never been written in our country, I think, though Elgar's symphonies occasionally vibrate to the same feeling' (121–2).

Thursday 26 August

A relaxing day with an evening drive to the village of Gosh where both Pears and Vishnevskaya sang in the medieval church with its superb acoustic. Pears sang the Pérotin Hymn ('Beata viscera Maraie virginis' composed circa 1190), which, as he noted in the diary, was contemporary with the church. This particular diary entry is perhaps the singer's most eloquent piece of writing; it shows his acute powers of observation and memory when describing flowers, trees and landscapes. In this respect his was a painter's eye, and it is no surprise that the singer was a great connoisseur and collector of pictures.

Friday 27 August

Pears notes a happy domestic event: the dog Gilbars has given birth to 'five enormous black, white and brown puppies' (123). In the afternoon there was an idyllic picnic at Lake Sevan, 'forty miles long and 5–10 miles wide' which is considered the heart of the country by Armenians. Here there was the last of the many wonderful picnics which were such a splendid part of this visit, followed by a journey over the lake in a hydrofoil. Pears notes 'As always in Russia, time limps and totters, and the clock races'. Back at the composers' village the English pair were late for a coaching session with 'a very mixed bag' (124) of six singers and their accompanists (singing Britten and Purcell), as well as a solo pianist, who had been brought to Dilidjan by bus. This was in preparation for the Britten Festival at Yerevan which was to take place in the following days.

Saturday 28 August

The three-week holiday was coming to an end. On the morning of the last day Britten and Pears were obliged to listen to a tape of the music of Edgar Oganesjan (b. 1930), which gives them very little pleasure. They consoled themselves at lunch with 'Moscow-mineral-water, i.e. vodka (water in Russian is voda, without the k.)' (124). Fond farewells to all the people who had looked after them were followed by the drive to the much hotter and less comfortable Yerevan for the 'Britten Week'. The first evening's concert (in an unsympathetic hall with a bad acoustic) included Britten's First String Quartet (played by a string quartet from Moscow), various Britten songs, and movements from the Cello Sonata (played by Rostropovich and the ever-faithful Aza). The hit of the evening was a young soprano who had been intensively coached by Pears and had much improved in the process; she produced touching performances of some of Britten's Purcell realisations (was this the awakening of Pears's ambitions as a teacher?). It is notable that the Soviet authorities did not regard this as a provincial event: the second-in-command from the Ministry of Culture in Moscow was present, as was the conductor Djemel Dalgat (1920–92), who was a major proponent of Britten's music in Russia, including many performances of *Peter Grimes*.

192

Sunday 29 August

During the morning of a very hot day (Pears noted 90 degrees) the English visitors visited the Composers' House to hear tapes of Armenian music by such composers as Hovhannes Gurgeni Ter-Tatevosian (b. 1926) and Avet Terterian (b. 1929). Pears notes that 'Rhapsodical nationalist symphonies are hard to make and hard to take' (126). In the evening Vishnevskaya and Rostropovich gave a recital of Mussorgsky and Tchaikovsky songs (the latter received particular approbation from Pears, who resolved to learn some Tchaikovsky himself). In this stifling heat the Russian pair performed two songs from Britten's new Pushkin's cycle (No. 2 'My Heart' and No. 5 'Epigram') as encores. These were 'repeated and hugely applauded' (127).

Monday 30 August

This day was even hotter – 95 degrees. An excursion was arranged to Echmiadzin, half an hour away, which is the holy city of Armenia where the Catholikos, the supreme head of the Armenia world church, has his palace. The great man gave the visitors a delicious peach from his garden. The English visitors admired the well-housed collection of ancient manuscripts in a museum reflecting great pride in Armenia's history and national culture. Even this town had an opera house which was big enough to mount a Britten opera the following year.

In the afternoon, back in Yerevan, Pears gave an hour-long lecture concerning English musical life and his career. In the evening Britten and Pears visited two painters' studios, the second of which belonged to the famous Martiros Sergeevich Sar'yan (1880–1972), who was noted for his Armenian landscapes. In the evening Rostropovich and Aza Amintayeva gave a recital of Schumann, Tchaikovsky and Britten. Pears notes 'marvellous playing, overwhelming reception' but he also writes 'all feeling the heat and the strain!' (128).

Tuesday 31 August

A note of artistic discord for the first time. A young conductor from Moscow had underestimated the difficulties of the Cello Symphony and Britten was forced to forbid its performance in the evening concert, much to Rostropovich's embarrassment. To replace this large work Britten and Pears offered a programme of English songs (including folksongs and Purcell). They were then 'beflowered and speechified and toasted in the aid of the Young Pioneers (the Russian boy scout-girl guide movement – white shirt or blouses, and scarlet ties or scarves)'. After the performance they were presented with a picture by the famous painter Sar'yan (see above).

193

There was a closing gathering from the Armenian Minister of Culture, after which Pears notes 'Their goodwill is boundless' (130).

Wednesday 1 September

The two-and-a-half hour flight back to Moscow was uneventful. The change of temperature was from 90 degrees Fahrenheit down to 60. After a quick lunch at the Rostropoviches' Moscow flat the party was in the car by 3.30 for another very long drive – 'This time we were to drive across Russia – 'the real heart of Russia' – 'to Pushkin's birthplace' – 'not far from Pskov' (130). Pushkin was actually born in Moscow; the Pushkin house that was their destination was near Pskov, which was the estate which belonged to the poet's mother – hence Pears's confusion. Pushkin was banished to the country on a number of occasions in his life; his exile in disgrace at Mikhaylovskoye followed on from his period in Odessa where he had bedded the wife of his superior (see song 5 in the cycle).

The travellers allowed themselves a picnic dinner at 7.30 by the roadside. After eight hours driving the party reached Novgorod where, at 11.15 pm, they took refuge in a fully booked hotel, which would never have made room for them without Slava's strong-armed cajoling and charm.

Thursday 2 September

The next morning there was time for a short sight-seeing tour of Novgorod with its fascinating Kremlin and churches. By 11.15 the party was on the way to Leningrad (the shorter route to Pskov was waterlogged). They arrived eventually at Pushkin's house at 8 pm – exactly twenty-four hours after they had been expected. Their hosts (who had waited up all night in vain – Rostropovich had not thought to phone) were the custodians of the Pushkin museum, who lived nearby in a house that had been constructed by Pushkin's son – 'one tap in the middle hall, and lavs. in the garden.' Pears reserves some of his most poetical writing for this episode: 'The quiet was extraordinary; there were lilac bushes brushing the gutters, the beds of white phlox along the garden paths filled the Library with scent where we slept deep in books' (132). Before dinner the guests were taken on a candle-lit tour of the Pushkin museum, a simple six-roomed one-floored house full of pictures and old furniture. Between 1824 and 1826 the poet was forced by Imperial edict to live quietly in this house; here he wrote *Boris Godunov*, parts of *Yevgeny Onegin*, and much else besides. Outside the front door of this house was a little clock-tower with a cracked clock, still somehow in working order, that was contemporary with Pushkin's stay. What happened next inside the custodians' house (not in the Pushkin museum itself) is worth quoting in full for the student of Britten's music, not least because of the evocative quality of Pears's prose:

> After a meal of soup and excellent cold leg of lamb, and a sort of barley with meat balls (so good), marvellous coffee and plum syrup, our host begged to hear the Pushkin songs. We moved into the lamp-lit sitting-room with an upright piano in the corner, and started on the songs (after an introduction by Slava). Galya sang her two, and I hummed the others. The last song of the set is the marvellous poem of insomnia, the ticking clock, persistent night-noises and the poet's cry for a meaning in them. Ben has started this with repeated staccato notes high-low, high-low on the piano. Hardly had the little piano begun its dry tick tock tick tock, than clear and silvery outside the window, a yard from our heads, came ding, ding, ding, not loud but clear, Pushkin's clock joining in his song. It seemed to strike far more than midnight, to go on all through the song, and afterwards we sat spell-bound. It was the most natural thing to have happened, and yet unique, astonishing, wonderful. In the morning from our windows we could see the still silver pond beyond the field, with clumps of silver birches far away, and the great forest of enormously tall, enormously thin fir-trees. (132–3)

Friday 3 September

Near the Pushkin Museum is the country church where Pushkin was made to worship punctually each day at 1 pm during his exile, as well as the poet's tomb ('a curious, unbeautiful, masonic affair' (133)). Britten and Pears visited this before taking affectionate leave of their hosts and beginning the long trek back to Moscow – a drive of ten hours. This turned out to be another nightmare journey because of roadworks; the visitors had to walk part of the way so as to lighten the car's load in dangerously muddy conditions. They were due at Shostakovich's *Datchya* at 6 pm but arrived at 9.20. Shostakovich himself had just finished the composition of songs (*Five Romances on Texts from Krokodil Magazine* for bass and piano) but on hearing that Britten had set Pushkin he was immediately anxious to hear them. Pears notes that he was 'physically strung-up, but personally most welcoming and amiable' (133).

Saturday 4 September

The British visitors found themselves back at the Shostakovich table for breakfast. Conversation ranged from music to football. At the time the Russian composer expressed a desire to visit England for the World Cup of 1966. He also expressed an interest in coming to Aldeburgh Festival in 1967; in fact he never made it to the Festival, visiting Aldeburgh only once in July 1972, when Britten showed him what he had written of *Death in Venice*. After some shopping for presents in Gorky Street, the visitors' last Russian engagement was lunch with the valiant accompanist Aza Aminteyava. And thence to the airport and home.

Pears's diary ends with a paean of praise to Slava and Galya and those 'marvellous people', the Russians: 'Never could any two guests have been more royally treated; never can any country be more generous and hospitable to us than the Soviet Union was' (134).

At a distance of nearly forty years this holiday looks less spontaneous and improvised than it must have seemed to the enchanted guests. In her own highly dramatic memoirs Vishnevskaya describes the council-of-war that it was necessary to arrange in order to mend Britten's shoes in Armenia after he had damaged them on a jaunt (see the diary entry for 10 August – p.106). If this is the case for a broken shoe one realises that the seamless succession of excursions and extravagant meals (including the fleet of transportation involving a number of plane journeys, and even a hydrofoil) could never have been organised without the highest government collaboration. Rostropovich in effect delivered a coup to the Russian authorities (or he must have convinced them it was such) by bringing Britten to Armenia. His own motives were no doubt more complex than the mere dictates of friendship: it is clear that this 'Cerberus' (as Pears described him) regarded Britten as 'his' composer, and he always discouraged the idea that Britten should write music for anyone else but him. The cellist had a very clear idea of the musical history in the making that Britten's holiday represented, and despite his other achievements nothing in his later career as a conductor has matched his collaborations with the great contemporary Russian composers, and with Britten. It is thanks to his English friend that his name and that of his wife became household words in Britain, a fact which strengthened his hand immeasurably in his future confrontations with the Soviet government.

It seems to me that the feelings of Britten and Pears in their love affair with Russia were even more complex than Rostropovich's and Vishnevskaya's mix of impulsive affection and calculating self-interest in their love affair with their English colleagues. Here were composer and singer being welcomed like royalty in a land where political dissent was suppressed, and where less-exalted homosexuals were afraid to acknowledge, were even punished for, their relationships. By attributing the largesse of this hospitality to Slava and Galya personally, Britten and Pears could forget, despite all the evidence to the contrary at official events, that this visit was carefully orchestrated by Moscow. Madame Furtseva, whose deputy was so charming at the Yerevan Festival, was the same Minister of Culture who had prevented Vishnevskaya's participation in the *War Requiem* only three years previously. And yet much could be forgiven; they felt perhaps that they were greeted with a warmth by the Russian establishment that they had never quite experienced at home. Part of this was to do with the fact that great artists seem to have been taken more seriously in Russia than in England. But the final impression is that this holiday was a fantasy defection on the part of two left-winged children of the 1930s with more than a residue of feeling for the mythical 'Mother Russia' of their youth. Time and again one notices the same instinctive sympathy for 'the people' that was the viewpoint of the enlightened English middle-classes in the depression years, echoed in the early poetry of Auden and Cecil Day-Lewis. Theirs was a politically harmless defection, which lasted only a month, but during that period everything was done to ensure that the visitors experienced the idyllic Russia that most defectors might have wished to experience, but almost never did.

It is impossible not to notice that, apart from Shostakovich, all the composers Britten met in Russia were provincial celebrities, not particularly talented by world standards. Access to Britten had been vetted by Rostropovich, so he never met anyone who did not admire his music. Unthreatened by a Stravinsky or a Walton, or even a Peter Maxwell Davies, Britten was at his most warm and expansive. It is sad that he did not also contribute to the holiday diary. The tone of Pears's travel writing might be hard to admire for some; this can seem rather grandly Edwardian in manner, and one remembers that the singer's family had been in India. It is possible to hear in such words as 'dear' and 'touching' (often used by Pears in his diaries) the paternalistic voice of the Raj – the lofty English way of displaying an interest in the activities of foreigners as if they were children playing in a sweetly colourful third world. If it had the kindliness of the best British colonial attitudes, there were none of the demeaning prejudices (and I am certain of this from having known the man himself, and spoken to him at length on many issues). By today's politically correct standards Britten and Pears appeared to patronise foreign people, even while admiring them (in his recent article for the *New Grove Dictionary of Music and Musicians*, this was Philip Brett's opinion of Britten's attitude to the Japanese).[6] But it is also necessary to read this diary as a historical docu-

6. Philip Brett, 'Britten, Benjamin', *New Grove Dictionary of Music and Musicians* (Macmillan, 2001).

Britten and Rostropovich rehearsing at the Moscow Conservatoire, c. 1963

ment. Britten and Pears were no more, and no less, inclined to adopt a tone of this kind than most other liberal Englishmen of a generation for which Macmillan's 'Wind of Change' speech was a very recent pronouncement.

Harder to refute is the suspicion that in allowing himself to be fêted in Russia Britten was both having his cake and eating it – reserving the right to criticise the Soviet regime at the same time as enjoying the adulation (and VIP status) that Rostropovich could never have arranged without the full co-operation of the authorities. But then this dual approach was almost certainly the result of 'needs must'. Rostropovich had learned to 'play the system' in an extremely canny way. And why not? As he moved Britten and Pears around Russia, as if they were knights on a gigantic chess board of his own devising, he was thinking many moves ahead. Much was at stake: his political survival and an important thread in his own musical immortality.

The Poet's Echo Op. 76 (Alexander Pushkin) (1965)

Together with the *Songs and Proverbs of William Blake*, written for Fischer-Dieskau, *The Poet's Echo* was one of the two song cycles that Britten com-

198

posed in the musical wake of the first of his church parables, *Curlew River*. This Japanese-inspired opera of a new kind was written for the roomy acoustics of Suffolk churches; in the Blake cycle (first performed in Aldeburgh in June 1965, a short while before the Armenian holiday) the composer uses the Curlew sign of his own invention (where one performer waits for the other to re-align after a passage where they had been allowed a certain rhythmic freedom). In the Pushkin songs, particularly the opening number, the same feeling of acoustical space is built into the music (though without Curlew signs). This music seems made to resound over the vast emptiness of the Russian steppe, and the word 'echo' is at the very centre of the songs' meaning and effectiveness. They have a quality both passionate and desolate. It is the last of Britten's many foreign stylisations and a masterful compendium of everything he knew about Russian vocal music. We hear the brooding, pessimistic shadows of Mussorgsky, the ghostly shadows of the lyrical melodic expansiveness of Tchaikovsky, and the spare textures, and economy of diction, of Shostakovich.

Also an intrinsic part of this music is the blood-red colour of Vishnevskaya's voice; it can seem guttural at times, even curdled, but it is this which seems to embody the heartbreaking sufferings of a tragic people. Few will forget her recording of the *War Requiem* when she sings the imperious 'Rex tremendae majestatis' with a throbbing, almost violent quality of voice that was so full-hearted and dangerously impassioned that it exactly fitted the listeners' conception of how a Russian soprano should sound (this was of course Britten the glove-maker at his most empathetic and fitting). Those who heard Vishnevskaya in recital performance will remember how, on occasion, she would stamp her foot or strike the piano lid with the flat of her hand in an overflow of emotion. This feeling of pressure – as if built up in a story too terrible to be told, or too dangerous to express openly, and which suddenly needs to let off steam – is built into the music written for her (the very first words of the Pushkin cycle speak of 'a savage howl'). Certainly one is aware that no English soprano of the time could have inspired lyrical outpouring of quite this tightly wound kind. Not until *Phaedra*, written for Janet Baker in 1975, would Britten return to the challenge of writing for a starry female voice.

I Echo
This is music where overlapping layers of sound are at the core of the music's effectiveness. The piece is an exercise in canonic fragments: the figuration announced in the vocal line is shadowed by the pianist's left hand, which sets off in turn a similar melodic shape in the right. This echoing, as

if fragments of the strident semibreve chords were rebounding off every surface of the stave, both lines and spaces, takes us up into reaches of the keyboard, which are seldom heard in other Britten songs (and then we remember that this is, in fact, the only cycle of Britten's maturity conceived for soprano voice and piano, and that the tenor sounds an octave lower and needs a different kind of pianistic support). An exceptional aspect of the writing is that in performance these interweaving strands of melody sound free and improvised; in fact they are extremely carefully calculated and notated, locking together with a clock-maker's precision. This image is an appropriate one considering the way in which the cycle comes full circle (the only one of Britten's song cycles to do so) with the re-appearance of the opening music in the closing pages where it melds with the sound of a ticking clock. Pushkin's remarkable poem (a more savage Russian equivalent of Eichendorff poems set in Schumann's *Liederkreis* Op. 39 – 'Im Walde' for instance) asks what a poet (or, by implication, a composer or a performer) receives back from the society for which he or she strives to write. The answer is 'nothing'. Britten, who had proved himself capable of musical subversion on behalf of the Soviet cause (in *Russian Funeral* for instance), here shows himself capable of turning his guns on the Soviets in an equally subversive manner, using images from their own culture to reproach the cruelty of artistic suppression.

II My Heart

This song has a terse eloquence out of all proportion to its means. The accompaniment, with its little motif of two semiquavers falling to a staccatissimo quaver in the bass, is like the fall of a withered leaf. Above this slow heartbeat the voice spins a lyrical line, with note values carefully calculated to reflect the stresses of the Russian language. Slowly the music, climbing imperceptibly in tessitura, seems to judder into life: this heart has sworn to feel no more but, despite itself, is called into artistic service by the power of beauty and responds almost involuntarily. The song runs the gamut from Russian depressive apathy to a sudden outburst of inflamed colour at the end. The *crescendo ed animando* of the last lines is unique in Britten's songs; its volatility reflects an aspect of impassioned Russian performing style (where a crescendo almost always betokens a simultaneous accelerando, and a diminuendo a rallentando) to perfection. In this music we hear the heart surge into new life before our very ears.

III Angel

If there are echoes of Tchaikovsky in the preceding song, here the influence

200

seems to be Shostakovich. We hear this in the onrush of octaves and the eloquent use of impervious semibreves in the icier regions of the treble clef. The poem suggests a counterpoint between two forces, good and evil, represented by the opposition of the two ideas. Satan flies over hell's abysses 'sullen and rebellious'; he is represented by gloomy and turbulent semi-quavers, which marvellously convey grumbling dissatisfaction. The angel, shining bright with lowered head, is untouched by this; he inhabits quite another part of the keyboard, the higher reaches of the treble clef. His enig-matically pure semibreve chords suggest unsullied innocence. The con-frontation between these two forces of good and evil is a drama played out in the accompaniment while the voice narrates the story with little attempt at melody, concentrating instead on an eloquently gestural arioso which shows the hand of the practised opera composer.

The truly masterful aspect to this song is the way in which Britten makes these two ideas seem briefly to conjoin as the devil is influenced and soft-ened by the heavenly presence, if only momentarily. This section (the song's third and fourth pages) is marked *tranquillo*. The chords descend into the middle regions of the stave as if looking down with kindness from the untouchable heights; the querulous grumbling of Satan moves upwards as if attempting to understand this new source of wonder and inspiration. In so doing, his strident octaves yield to single notes. The extended grumbling of the opening has now been reduced to a shadow of its former malevo-lence, a mere nervous tic. The postlude allows an epigrammatic appearance of both characters; the rumbustious opening has been softened to a whis-per; Satan has not been converted but he has been touched in passing by the force of goodness. The power of beauty to silence and neutralise dissent is at the heart of Britten's Hölderlin setting 'Sokrates und Alcibiades', a song that is a close relation of this Pushkin song. The confrontation of goodness and innocence is a famous Brittennian preoccupation, and this song belongs to that genre. Satan is a more mercurial presence than Claggart in *Billy Budd*, but the angel's seraphic semibreves and minims, denoting goodness and simplicity, bring to mind the extraordinary orchestral interlude preceding Billy's great aria 'in the Darbies' towards the end of that opera. Needless to say, the declamation has a grandeur appropriate to the subject, and a turn of phrase marvellously suited to Vishnevskaya's voice.

IV The Nightingale and the Rose

At the heart of the cycle there is a poem that to the English reader stirs memories of Oscar Wilde's story of the same name where the nightingale presses its heart to the thorn of the rose, draining its life blood to allow the flower to bloom. Pushkin's poem describes no such suicidal aspiration, but one feels that the nightingale is so hopelessly in love that he may be driven to do the same. The lack of answer, or reciprocation, of any reward for so much melody (for the nightingale is the unheeded musician whose true creative nature is a matter of indifference to the flower of society) has a similar tragic pathos. It seems to me that Britten has here evoked a more eastern aspect of Russian music, as if memories of Borodin, Balakirev and Rimsky-Korsakov were stirring in his memory, and under his fingers. In Armenia he had found himself near the Muslim borders of the Soviet Union, and strange darkly exotic melismas of this music may seem to evoke the mosque's minaret more than the onion-domed church. Of course the music of Armenia might also have played a part in the atmosphere of this piece. What we hear here is truly sumptuous; the garden where this scene takes place might be found in a seraglio, just as the poem might be the opening of a tale from *The 1001 Nights*.

Britten composed music for many an English bird, but this nightingale owes no such national allegiance. If a bird could sing in Russian this is how it might warble – throatily and passionately. The melismatic nature of this music, punctuated by rests, and where vocal semiquavers interlock (and do not quite align) with the piano's throbbing triplets, does not relate to Purcell. Rather it seems to be an exotic combination of animal rapture, human sorrow and religious incantation. The closing section of the piece (with a new E major key signature) is as magical a postlude as Britten ever wrote for a song – the piano continuing the birdsong as the voice reflects, first in a mutter and then tracing a mournful trajectory, as if rising in hope and falling away in melancholy disappointment. Another aspect of the success of the poem in this context is the relation of its subject matter ('there's no answer') to that of the first song. This considerably strengthens the cycle's sense of unity, particularly as Britten chooses to recapitulate material from the opening in the final song.

V Epigram

This is what Poulenc used to call a *mélodie tremplin*: a short song whose main purpose is to provide a contrast between two more serious ones, allowing the singer to be propelled, as if on a trampoline, between the two pieces. Britten's angry trills and snatched vocal phrases catch Pushkin's vehement dislike for his superior Count Vorontsov, governor-general of the province of Odessa. Pushkin had cuckolded him and Vorontsov asked for the poet's transfer to Odessa. It was because of this that Pushkin began his lonely, if fruitful, exile in Mikhaylovskoye, near Pskov, on his mother's estate. This is one of those pieces that sounds incomparably better in Russian than English. The style was later to bear fruit in the cycle *Who are these Children?* where Britten handled William Soutar's pithy verses in Scots dialect with a similarly epigrammatic virtuosity.

VI Lines Written During a Sleepless Night

Pears's own description of this song has already been given above. For the pianist this is an *étude* in different touches for each hand: in the left an ebbing and flowing of smooth quavers (and subsequently triplets) and in the right the gentle, but relentless, tick-tocking of the clock. Instructing the left hand Britten writes *con Ped*; for the right *senza Ped*. This is of course a pianistic impossibility, but a good pianist can achieve the correct effect with control of touch and a judicious use of the pedal (enough to help link those undulating left-hand quavers, but not enough to over-oil the clock mechanism). It is of course not only the sound of the clock that the tormented poet hears; he is also confronted by the *Nachtgespenster* – those ghosts of regret-by-night that torment so many artists, including the poet Mörike in Hugo Wolf's 'In der Frühe'. Those roving bass-clef quavers now spread upwards to the treble clef and take on a new and more sinister life. They erupt into the constituent parts of those wild diminished chords with which the cycle had begun. Once more the poetical tone is rhetorical and bewildered. What more can anyone expect from a poet than that he obeys his dictates as an artist, honestly baring his mind and heart? This is not what Stalin expected of artists (including Shostakovich) and not what the Czar of Russia had wanted from the politically embarrassing Pushkin. A bridge passage (*agitato ed animando*) leads to a *largamente*, where Britten steers the music into a transposed recapitulation of the first song's opening bars. But as in some of the greatest Schubertian recapitulations there is a remaining tremor, something that has happened in the development that the return of the original material cannot shift from our minds. In this case it is the tick-tocking of the clock, which dies in the distance in a way that enables us exactly to re-experience the sense of awe felt by the handful of listeners during that late night recital at Mikhaylovskoye in 1965. And it also reminds us that across the mighty Russian steppes, seemingly so impervious to the poet's call, the march of time will bring change, come what may. Indeed, the process of change began only a few years after Britten's death.

Sonata in C for Cello and Piano Op. 65 (1960–61)

This lecture ends with the first of Britten's 'Russian' works – in fact a piece that is not at all Russian in the same way as the Pushkin cycle or the last of the Suites for unaccompanied cello. It was written at the height of his career, those fertile years between the composition of *A Midsummer Night's Dream* and the *War Requiem* – a period in Britten's late forties when he seemed able to conjure musical magic at will. This is the first fruit of his link with Rostropovich, whose playing had impressed him, both on the radio and at the Festival Hall in Shostakovich's Cello Concerto No. 1 in September 1960. In this work the veiled homage to a great contemporary is to be heard in the experimental nature of the instrumental writing (the roguish Scherzo-pizzi-cato) as well as in the rather grotesque and ghostly Marcia (not that Britten himself had not already explored this mood in such works as the *Serenade* and *The Holy Sonnets of John Donne*). The heavily mournful and majestic third movement – Elegia – seems reminiscent of 'O might those sighes and teares returne againe', the third of the John Donne Sonnets.

When Britten played the Cello Sonata with Rostropovich at the Royal Academy of Music, he was asked to say something about it. The audience was expecting a fascinating lecture but all they received was 'Sonata in C, by me'. But even that phrase contained significant information. The compos-er had not attached a tonality to a work since the String Quartet No. 2 of 1945 (also in C major) and it was the last work that would have such a label. The word 'Sonata' is quite different from 'Suite', the title Britten used for his work for violin and piano composed in 1935. Indeed this is the adult Britten's only *Sonata* of any kind by that name, and the reason why this work merits the label is to do with the perfection of its first movement, the Dialogo, which is written in the most lucid sonata form, including a mirac-ulous coda on a tonic pedal. Whilst obeying these classic rules of form (exposition, development, recapitulation), the piece superbly suggests all nuances of conversation between two instruments, or two people. This is of course a piece without words; but its efficacy stems from the words that are implied in the discourse – everything ranging from gentle murmurs of approbation and concern to much more passionate engagement, and even momentary heated confrontation. Like so much of Britten's best instru-mental music this could only have been written by a great composer of vocal music and operas. In knowing that he could not speak Rostropovich's language (and before the solution of 'Aldeburgh Deutsch' had been prac-tised to perfection) it is as if the composer is determined to have a conver-sation with his cellist, come what may, in purely musical terms.

I have already mentioned the three next movements, which are charac-ter pieces: the second taking the place of the typical scherzo to be found in classical sonatas; the third is, of course, the work's slow movement. But it is in the final Moto Perpetuo that Britten recaptures all the *joie de vivre* of a real sonata. This is one of his most exciting chamber-music movements, requiring virtuosity from both players, but never for its own sake. If there is a touch of the same brilliance that we encounter in the Piano Concerto and other works for piano from the 1930s, this is of a different, more concentrated, kind where ebullience does not exceed the work's formal content. The movement is an exhilarating exercise in chromaticism; the only real chord in C major is the peremptory flourish that ends the whole piece. It is as if the composer were quietly laughing at the whole concept of tonality, and cocking a snook at those composers who would have been horrified by anything 'in C' (actually the title of Stravinsky's Symphony in C of 1938 was probably similarly confrontational).

The abiding impression made by this sonata is that Britten is celebrating, and cementing, a new friendship. We hear how he was *energised* by Rostropovich's playing and his company. We regret that there were so few of his British contemporaries who were able to inspire him in this way. But this is probably not their fault, however superiorly gifted the Russian cellist seemed to be. Britten's struggle in England was not that he was unrecognised, but rather that he was recognised too well, and sometimes for the wrong things. This brought untold envy and jibes into his life, and he was painfully susceptible to criticism. One forgets that he and Pears were the regular butt of innumerable jokes and snide references to their lifestyle (see 'Guide to Britten' by Flanders and Swann). The *Gloriana* débâcle was still a painful memory. In the shires there were still people who puffed and grunted about the composer's war record, or lack of it. Musicians from a foreign nation, and a musically powerful one, came to him with open arms, free of all this British baggage from the past. He could speak to them in a *dialogo* where words were less important than the sheer musical impulse; he felt they were listening to his music, with a clean slate, for its own sake (as they no doubt were). It is little wonder that he embraced a chance to begin a new chapter in his composing life in the company of such warmth and (in the case of the Rostropoviches at least) such world-class talent.

The programme at the 2001 Britten festival was comprised of: ***Songs and Proverbs of William Blake* Op. 74**: 'Proverb I' and 'London', 'Proverb II' and 'The Chimney-Sweeper', 'Proverb III' and 'A Poison Tree', 'Proverb IV' and 'The Tyger', 'Proverb V' and 'The Fly', 'Proverb VI' and 'Ah! Sun-flower', 'Proverb VII' and 'Every Night and Every Morn'; ***Canticle III - Still Falls The Rain (The Raids, 1940. Night and Dawn)* Op. 55** (Sitwell); ***Winter Words* Op. 53** (Hardy): 'Winter Words', 'Midnight on the Great Western', 'Wagtail and Baby', 'The Little Old Table', 'The Choirmaster's Burial', 'Proud Songsters', 'At the Railway Station, Upway', 'Before Life and After'; ***Canticle II - Abraham and Isaac* Op. 51** (Anon.)

Lecture 8

Britten and the English landscape

Previous lectures have included surveys of Britten's Russian-inspired works, and his evocations of the musical styles of past centuries. He inhabited different topographical and historical landscapes with such ease that one can almost forget that he was a great 'English song' composer in the more conventional sense of the term. We began with a survey that included Britten's youthful settings of, among others, William Blake and Walter de la Mare where both of those poets employed an authentically English tone of voice (as opposed to one with a foreign accent) as the composer's starting point. In this lecture we come full circle as we encounter Britten's later version of the same Blake lyric, 'A Poison Tree', in the company of music that includes settings of English poets of the nineteenth and twentieth centuries. This music was composed when Britten was at the height of his powers.

Our final lecture in this book thus returns to the composer's roots – not to Suffolk (his songs do not include a cycle based in that county) but to England in general, and to London in particular – that city about which Britten had such equivocal feelings. William Blake and Edith Sitwell follow each other in works that, among other themes, provide an outline of the capital city in some of its horror, danger and pathos. There is also an element of time-travel as we visit these two different Londons – first during the Industrial Revolution, and then in the darkest days of World War Two. In terms of their metropolitan backgrounds *Songs and Proverbs of William Blake* and *Canticle III – Still Falls the Rain* are strangely related: in the first work, Regency London where poverty and injustice and arrogant prosperity live starved cheek by bloated jowl; in the second, a chastened city brought to its knees during the Blitz of 1940. It comes to mind that one of the so-called advances pursued so ruthlessly by the money-makers of

Opposite: Britten and Pears, Snape, Suffolk, 1974

207

Blake's time (and ever since) has been the ability to wage war with ever greater sophistication. In the second half of the lecture we move into the West Country, although the dangers of taking a train to London are also implicit in the second song of *Winter Words*. Britten's incomparable contribution to the catalogue of Thomas Hardy song settings is followed in this discussion by *Canticle II – Abraham and Isaac*, a setting of a medieval miracle play from Chester where the music, for all its biblical background, seems firmly set in an English landscape.

Songs and Proverbs of William Blake Op. 74 (1965)

This is Britten's only song cycle specifically written for the baritone voice (the revised juvenilia of *Tit for Tat* are designated for medium voice, but are usually sung by male singers). Shortly after the Blake cycle was written it was John Shirley-Quirk who became the composer's baritone of choice, culminating in that singer's appearances as the manifold figure of death in the opera *Death in Venice*. But the Blake cycle was written for Dietrich Fischer-Dieskau, a singer with whom Britten was not in regular contact (in comparison with Shirley-Quirk for example), and with whom, it seems, he had much less in common. Nevertheless, Britten must have enjoyed creating such a substantial piece for an uncontested master of his craft; there is scarcely a composer in the world who would not have been similarly tempted. At the time Dietrich Fischer-Dieskau was the world's most famous lieder singer; an association between him and Aldeburgh added greatly to the festival's lustre, and to the roll-call of great artists it was able to offer its audiences. As for Fischer-Dieskau himself, he seems always to have been pleased to work with contemporary composers (Schoeck, Blacher, Lutosławski, Henze, Stravinsky, Messiaen and Reimann come to mind, among others). In 1962 the singer's nationality had exactly suited the masterstroke whereby Britten had cast the *War Requiem* with a German baritone, a British tenor (Pears), and a Russian soprano (Vishnevskaya) as a symbol of reconciliation between former combatant nations. Fischer-Dieskau recorded this work for Decca under Britten's baton in January 1963. In December of the same year, and for the same label, he recorded the *Cantata Misericordium*, the baritone part of which was also conceived for him (he had already performed the first performance of the work under Ansermet in the previous September). Fischer-Dieskau went on to perform the *War Requiem* under many other conductors (Kubelik, Haitink, Sawallisch, Davis, Karajan). Of Britten's other works he later performed the *Hölderlin Fragmente* (originally a tenor cycle) with Aribert Reimann in 1986 – a transposition that it seems might not have received Britten's endorsement when he was alive.

Songs and Proverbs of William Blake was the only one of the works written with Fischer-Dieskau's voice in mind that was also dedicated to the singer. The cycle is prefaced with the words 'To Dieter, the past and the future' – an aphoristic phrase, almost worthy of Blake, in which a sad acknowledgement of the death of Irmgard Poppen Fischer-Dieskau in childbirth in 1963 is combined with the hope that new paths would bring new happiness. The poetry of Blake was also a part of the composer's past: 'The Sick Rose' ('Oh rose, thou art sick!') is one of the most telling movements of Britten's *Serenade* for tenor, horn and strings (1944); the first of the *Charm of Lullabies* for mezzo soprano is Blake's 'A Cradle Song'; and 'Spring' ('Sound the Flute!') is from the poet's *Songs of Innocence* and is one of the most energetic choral sections of the *Spring Symphony* (1949).[1]

Songs and Proverbs of William Blake were given their first performance in Aldeburgh by Fischer-Dieskau and the composer on 24 June 1965; in this concert he also sang Purcell's cantata *When Night her Purple Veil* with the Alberni String Quartet and Britten (who had made a realisation of the Purcell for the occasion) at the piano. The Blake cycle was recorded in London for Decca in December 1965. By all accounts this was not a happy experience for the composer, who was made very nervous by Fischer-Dieskau's meticulously planned recording schedule (he had allotted no more than four hours to the task) whereby the piece was committed to tape in sections according to the demands of its tessitura on the singer's voice (in these days of digital editing this is a fairly normal way of working, but it was unusual at the time). Britten had arrived at the studio expecting to play the piece through; instead – much to his chagrin – he had to perform it in fragments, and in an entirely different sequence. A few days after this experience the London première of the work was given in the Fairfield Hall in Croydon and the composer seems to have been very nervous. The singer noted in his autobiography 'Ben touchingly apologised for his bad playing, and I admitted his errors in precision. But we were nevertheless happy about the outcome …'[2]

How 'happy' Britten really was is not certain. The cycle was performed once again with the same duo at the Edinburgh Festival in August 1968. The last time that Britten and Fischer-Dieskau worked together was in June 1972 (the year when a wonderfully memorable recording of Schumann's *Szenen aus Goethes Faust* was also made at the Maltings) when their recital included the Blake cycle as well as a group of ten Schubert songs. The preparation of these songs was recalled by Fischer-Dieskau in his autobiography: 'Over and over, when Ben would interrupt himself during rehearsals at his old piano in the wonderful large studio of Red House to

1. In celebration of the bicentenary of William Blake, the Aldeburgh Festival in 1957 held a competition for the best setting of one of his poems by a composer under the age of thirty. Four were selected for the concert: 'Why cannot the ear be closed to its own destruction' set by Cornelius Cardew (aged 21), 'A Cradle Song' set by Michael Nuttall (aged 20), 'Narration' from *The Marriage of Heaven and Hell* set by Alexander Goehr (aged 25), and 'The Fly' set by Malcolm Williamson (aged 26).

2. Dietrich Fischer-Dieskau, *Reverberations*, trans. Ruth Hein (Fromm International Publishing Corporation, 1989), p. 262.

209

think out loud about tempi and techniques, I needed only to keep my ears open to profit from his ideas'.[3]

3. Fischer-Dieskau, *Reverberations*, p.272.

This Schubert group is among the most vivid of all Britten's song recordings, as well as Fischer-Dieskau's as a matter of fact. Both artists were on the most extraordinary, if rather tense, form. When the famous singer came to rehearse this programme it must have been novel for him to be challenged about tempo and phrasing (for this was what Britten was doing 'over and over' in his most tactful manner, not 'interrupting himself … to think out loud'). There was no other pianist alive, including Gerald Moore, who would have dared to question Fischer-Dieskau's interpretations in this way. On the other hand, such was Britten's reputation as an accompanist that it was unheard of that he should be instructed (as was Fischer-Dieskau's custom) in the playing of Schubert's accompaniments by a singer. There was no British artist who would have dreamed of going to the Mecca that was Aldeburgh and asking the composer to vary or adapt his tempi and phrasing – these things were treated as sacred givens, and perhaps too much so. On this occasion we can be sure that this was a meeting of the Titans – not a *War Requiem* (where Fischer-Dieskau would have reckoned that Britten, as the composer, had a right to lead), but something of a battle nevertheless (Fischer-Dieskau noted that 'although [Britten] hated quarrels, he had no trouble asserting himself against opposition'[4]). If Britten was entitled to ask for what he wanted in his own piece, Fischer-Dieskau would have been confident of his own ascendancy in Schubert lieder. On the other hand Britten was also a great Schubertian and he too would have been absolutely certain about how he wanted these songs to be performed.

4. Fischer-Dieskau, *Reverberations*, p.262.

Much of the electricity of this encounter, the wordless bartering for control, and the consensus hammered out on the spot, lives on in the superbly riveting live recording, now available on BBC records.[5] This is a performance that bristles with drama and the deepest concentration. For Fischer-Dieskau this was an accompanist impossible to hector; and Britten must have been all too aware that to drop (or attempt to replace) Fischer-Dieskau at this point (surely the fate of a lesser singer) would be deeply embarrassing for the Aldeburgh Festival. All this produced a tension that must have been rather like the famous meeting between Goethe and Beethoven where mutual irritation was concealed, but only barely. In this Schubert recording the artists, both on their respective mettles, seem to listen to each other with an acuity that reminds one of gladiators sizing up their opponents in case they will have to fight to the death (the stormy anger of Britten's opening to *Prometheus* seems to reflect this). What is wonderful is that such a clash of two different temperaments (and nation-

5. *Britten the Performer* BBCB 8011-2.

210

al types) is not permitted to ruin the music – in fact the opposite happens. Because singer and composer were both great artists they obeyed Schubert's demands for unification, and it is he who is the winner of a confrontation that never really was. Much of the problem was sheerly temperamental: Britten told me he found the great baritone very difficult to accompany because he could not seem to get on his musical wave-length – something of a strange indictment from one of the century's most musical people concerning another. A written remark where he equated the singer to a schoolyard bully is also documented.

One must admit that some of this inherent unease between the two artists is to be heard in these Blake settings: it is built into the music in the same way that Britten's love for, and veneration of, Peter Pears steals into the very fabric of the tenor songs without any conscious effort on the composer's part. As with the hard-won success of the Schubert recital described above it does not mean that the result is not convincing and impressive. If the Blake cycle is self-consciously intellectual (in a letter to the singer Britten promised a cycle that was 'Very serious!'[6]) it has a rigour that some of Britten's critics find lacking in some of the more easily approachable works. If the cycle is rather forbidding and lacking in that charm which can make much of Britten's music instantly loveable, the settings are always a match for Blake's searing imagery. Britten has clearly created the cycle for a performer who is aloof and magisterial; nevertheless, the elevated tone of the work is surely a compliment to Fischer-Dieskau's musical stature – its diction is that of a prophetic visionary, and this fits the singer's enormous stage personality like a glove. Of course Blake was as famous as an illustrative artist as a poet, and the composer seems to have taken into account Fischer-Dieskau's own fascination with painting – the singer's autobiography tells us that visits to the Tate Gallery turned him into a Blake enthusiast.[7] (Peter Pears owned a large Blake watercolour, *St Paul and the Viper* (ca. 1803–05), which is one of the great glories of the Red House Library. He was offered two of them but at the time only had enough in the bank for one; he used to say that he spent the rest of his life regretting not having bought that second Blake.)

The contribution of Peter Pears to this cycle was crucial: he had already constructed a libretto with a masterful cutting-down of Shakespeare's *A Midsummer's Night's Dream*. Here he provides a cunning combination of prose proverbs (taken from the 'Proverbs of Hell' section of *The Marriage of Heaven and Hell*) and lyrics drawn, with one exception, from *Songs of Experience* (both of these are among Blake's illuminated books). Pears interleaves these two different aspects of Blake's writings so that the songs

6. Fischer-Dieskau, *Reverberations*, p.261.

6. Fischer-Dieskau, *Reverberations*, p.261.

are made to seem to spring from ideas already cryptically fore-shadowed in the proverbs.

(i) 'Proverb I' and 'London'

From the outset it is clear that this is a work in the new Britten style that followed the innovations of *Curlew River*, the first parable for church performance. The twelve-tone element in this music looks back to *The Turn of the Screw*, and forward to *Owen Wingrave* and *Death in Venice*. Although by no means rigorously applied, the ascetic discipline of serialism, even if there is only a whiff of it by Webern's standards, seems somehow appropriate to a work written for a twentieth-century German singer. To that extent these Blake songs are also stylisations. But the Curlew signs that are to be found in this score come from music designed to be heard in an English church. Pianist and singer in their respective flourishes and declamatory phrases must listen to each other carefully to allow a quasi-free interaction between voice and piano that is untrammelled by the exactitude of barlines. This freedom suggests the echo of church acoustics and gives an expansive resonance to the music from the outset – an 'English' freedom moreover, which modifies any suggestion of 'Germanic' rigidity in the work's tonal organisation.

In the opening proverb (lines 22–25 of the 'Proverbs of Hell') the 'nakedness of woman' introduces an unremittingly bleak picture of London and its benighted inhabitants, which eventually culminates in that powerful phrase about the 'youthful Harlot's curse'. This is, incidentally, the only sung reference I know to the ravages of syphilis (which 'blights with plagues the marriage hearse') in a repertoire that has had more than its fair share of great composers who were victims of this disease. The accompaniment is an uncomfortable swirling mist of right-hand quavers (a veritable pea-souper of notes), while left-hand triplets suggest the restlessness of the poet's survey of the sinister city. (Blake's own illustration for this poem depicts the trudge of a stooping bearded ancient who bears a resemblance to Brahms!) In this music of uphill struggle the singer seems to be somehow pushing himself through swathes of heaving humanity; the uneasy clash of conflicting rhythms in the piano suggests wading against the tide. The vocal line remains somehow above the fray and always contemplative; each phrase ends with a pianissimo semibreve (or minim) as if the singer-poet were pausing for thought while the harmonic fog momentarily clears, allowing him at last to glimpse a clear perspective. These prolonged notes, each of which is harmonised by one of twelve different chords, come to rest in the *passaggio* of the baritone range, where Fischer-Dieskau had a unrivalled ability in *mezza voce*. This command of the heights was put fully to the test to haunting musical effect. Here and elsewhere in the cycle, the music has been exactly tailored to a baritone voice of superior accomplishment.

It is impossible to imagine any composer remotely fond of London (John Ireland, say) writing a song such as this. Britten said to me once 'I associate London with visits to the dentist' and he seems to have increasingly associated the town with harrowing and unpleasant experiences: it was the site of nerve-wracking concerts, the centre of hostile critics, and in the later years it became associated with doctors, hospitals and mortality. In any event it was a noisy place with little peace (see also, for example, the London May-day commotion described in the Beaumont and Fletcher text that closes the *Spring Symphony*). Since composer and singer returned from America to England (when they were house-guests of Erwin and Sophie Stein in a flat in St John's Wood High Street) the composer and Peter Pears always kept a London pied-à-terre, changing addresses every five years or so. This included apartments in West London (Melbury Road W14), Regent's Park (Chester Gate NW1) and back to St John's Wood between 1958 and 1965, where they stayed in a flat owned by the singers Anne Wood and Johanna Peters in Marlborough Place NW8. After that they favoured Canonbury, a part of North London that was more convenient for the traveller driving from Suffolk. They had a flat in Offord Road N1, and then an attractive modern studio built adjoining the house in Halliford Street N1 that belonged to Sue and Jack Phipps (Sue was Peter Pears's niece). Britten himself was much less often there than Pears, who still had a very active concert schedule in the 1970s. It was in the Halliford Street studio that I worked with Pears when he was learning *Death in Venice*. The singer cared for the attractions of big cities (he loved New York) a great deal more than the composer.

(ii) 'Proverb II' and 'The Chimney-Sweeper'

In the short Proverb linking the first and second songs (No. 21 of the 'Proverbs of Hell'), the mention of prison and brothels looks back to the 'youthful harlot' of 'London'; brothels are built with 'bricks of Religion', and it is the hypocritical aspect of English religious life that is condemned in the second song. The chimney-sweep will allow his maltreated and terrified boys their Sunday rest, as prescribed by religion, even if it means turning them loose inadequately clothed in the freezing snow.

The music glints with crystalline coldness. Each of the staccato semi-quavers in the accompaniment seems to signify a granule of ice, the contrast between these and legato writing in the piano as stark as black soot on white snow. The character of the accompaniment (both hands are placed in the treble clef) also denotes littleness, timidity, and the youthfulness of an unbroken voice. The vocal line is separated with rests, a device that implies extreme diffidence – indeed, the singer (who takes over the role of the boy in the first person) and the accompaniment that depicts him are made to cringe with the servility of someone who expects a blow to rain down on him at any moment. We also hear the shy, uncertain smile of a child who has unexpectedly encountered someone kind and interested in his sad story. With these short and nervous little musical movements Britten, the great opera composer, has created a deft sketch of a victim of abuse and cruelty. He wrote a lot of music for happy children, but in this music we can hear a shivering waif taking shape before our ears. The syncopations between voice and piano (at 'And because I am happy and dance and sing') create a jerky little dance of the greatest pathos: the little sweep's appalling destiny cannot entirely extinguish the child's high-spirits. The realisation that the heaven of rich and powerful people is made out of the hellish misery of the oppressed is one of Blake's most powerful aperçus. In 1949 Britten had composed a children's opera (*The Little Sweep* from *Let's Make an Opera*), which drew the attention of a post-war generation to the cruelties of the past, when small boys had been made to claw their way up chimney flues several storeys high in order to dislodge soot, their bruised bodies acting as human brushes in conditions that threatened suffocation. It was only in the middle of the nineteenth century that legislation made it illegal to employ children in such work.

⊙ CD2, track 13

⊙ (iii) 'Proverb III' and 'A Poison Tree'

The short proverb (No. 31 in a sequence of proverbs printed – and illustrated by Blake – as if it were a single ongoing poem) aptly introduces the idea of friendship. Britten had set 'A Poison Tree' in 1935 (see p. 29) as a rather march-like, and acerbically dissonant, scherzo. Here his music is much more portentous and also more dangerously insidious. The murky bass-clef introduction (which also serves as a postlude) seeps into the ear like a gradually spreading bloodstain – this represents a new type of piano writing from a composer who had always favoured clearer and leaner textures. The rather abstract imitative writing at the heart of the song suggests to an uncanny degree the style of Paul Hindemith – a composer whose music Britten had known since his youth. Fischer-Dieskau recounts how Britten told him that he once asked Hindemith's advice when the older composer seemed delighted to be consulted by his 'young colleague'.[8] It so happened that Fischer-Dieskau was studying 8. Fischer-Dieskau, *Reverberations*, p.258. Hindemith's opera *Cardillac* for a production in Munich at exactly the same time as he was preparing Britten's cycle for its first performance in Aldeburgh. The increasingly complex fugato-like part-writing in this song provides a growing density of texture, which suggests the almost cancerous growth of the singer's hatred for his erstwhile friend. For the accompanist accustomed to Britten's piano writing this layered counterpoint, bristling with accidentals, feels strange under the fingers and untypical of this composer; it is certainly much less pianistic, and more awkward than most of Britten's music for this genre. As in certain other passages in this work one feels that one is playing a piano-score of an orchestral reduction – and it may have been at the back of the composer's mind to make an orchestral version of this cycle one day. Some of the effects are remarkable: luminous piano writing high in the keyboard makes Blake's bright apple glow in an almost supernaturally poisonous way, but all pianists find the enmeshing of fingers it requires extremely tricky. The cumulative effect of this long song is truly impressive: the peroration 'Glad I see/My foe outstretched beneath the tree' is as mighty a piece of singing as is required in any of the Britten cycles and, once again, one can imagine the sound of a large orchestra to back it up.

(iv) 'Proverb IV' and 'The Tyger'

The fourth proverb (No. 41 of the 'Proverbs of Hell'), one of the shortest in musical terms, introduces the idea of 'Sleep in the night'; with sleep comes dreams, and with them the exotic idea of the tiger (or 'tyger' as Blake chooses to spell it) – an idea that would have fascinated Freud. This is one of the most devilishly difficult and exciting of scherzi in any of the cycles – and an indispensable item in any recitalist's group of animal songs. The lyric is among the most famous of any that Blake ever wrote, and Britten rises to the challenge with a song boasting a terse little tune – breathless, nervously syncopated, and almost impossibly fast – which is instantly memorable. Once heard this tiger-chant is seldom forgotten, a sign that the poem had been waiting well over a century for its definitive setting. This is music where one can immediately detect the ripple of dangerous muscles under the striped skin of the eponymous beast, which moves with the greatest stealth (Britten requires the pianist to use *una corda*) as if ready to *pounce* at any moment. The accompanist's hands are made to stalk each other throughout – there is a rumble of tiny fragments of imitative canon (though these convulsions seldom have time truly to register with the listener's ear) as they pursue each other in the lower regions of the keyboard.

The build-up to the climactic moment of 'Dare its deadly terrors clasp?' is achieved with a masterful use of harmonic screw-turning. And then a whole bar of silence followed by another miracle. Hitherto all the pianistic activity has moved *up* the keyboard. With a change from a key-signature of B major to one of E-flat major this direction is reversed. On the words 'When the stars threw down their spears', such is Britten's uncanny ability to respond to Blake's imagery that we *hear* this raining down of these tiny spears of twinkling light. The accompaniment, which has momentarily moved to the higher reaches of the keyboard for the first time, falls earthward under the fingers of a pianist whose cascades of descending scales must be as light as stardust.

The placing of the two crucial enquiries 'Did he smile his work to see' and then 'Did he who made the Lamb make thee?' is also managed in masterful fashion. Just the right amount of rhetorical pause is built into the music after each of the questions, and the musical sequence, where the second of the questions is placed at a higher pitch than the first, engineers a recapitulation that is so perfectly set up that one simply smiles at Britten's sovereign – and unashamedly conventional – control of his resources. We have heard this music at the beginning of the song and, as Schubert also knew, there is nothing wrong with a repeat of effective music. After that, the twelve-bar postlude moves in impatient circles: the pacing of a big cat caged in a zoo. Is it only our imagination that we can hear the tiger's pleasure – or anger – in those rumbling triplets that set each other off as if they were catherine wheels igniting under the accompanist's fingers, and whirring in different directions? Or is a growl, or purr, concealed in those ominously rolled minim chords that punctuate the fervid movement of this tightly wound *moto perpetuo*, giving it momentary pause (or even paws) for thought?

(v) 'Proverb V' and 'The Fly'
The sequence of words (an arrangement by Pears that joins together Proverbs 44, 18 and 52) makes immediate mention of 'the tigers of wrath', which refers back to the previous song. Mention of 'the horses of instruction' makes it clear that this is a section of the work, a miniature bestiary where man is to be compared to nature. If 'The Fly' is less memorable melodically than 'The Tyger', it is no less remarkable an achievement in terms of its illustrative power. This is one of Britten's most ingenious piano parts: the fourth and fifth fingers of each of the pianist's hands trace the contours of a melody while juxtaposed thumbs, a semitone apart, pick out the movements of the insect in alternating semiquavers that hover and buzz

216

in a mixture of staccato and legato. As in many of Britten's inspirations the idea seems obvious enough when one hears it – it is just that no one else, apart from Bartók perhaps, would have thought of it. As in 'The Chimney-Sweeper', an unexpected little dance enlivens the middle section of the song, which suddenly gives the fly a jaunty – even reckless – personality. Apart from this, as in 'The Chimney-Sweeper', we have a portrait of little-ness in all its delicacy and vulnerability, a drama in exquisite miniature. For the central question 'Am I not/A fly like thee?/Or art not thou/A man like me?' the composer invents a haunting sequence of chords in smooth crotchets where the harmonies manage to suggest a fly-like drone.

(vi) 'Proverb VI' and 'Ah! Sun-flower'

Pears was especially ingenious in setting up the song of the sun-flower that is 'weary of time'. Proverbs 10, 11 and 12 are quoted in reverse order; this leaves the words 'Eternity is in love with the productions of time' as the cue for the song itself. In this proverb Britten suggests the passing of time with a tick-tock movement in deadpan crotchets in the pianist's left hand, while a tremolo in the right signifies sand running through an hourglass. This same effect was later used in one of Aschenbach's monologues in the Second Act of *Death in Venice* (at figure 260), where an hourglass is actual-ly mentioned. The idea of a ticking clock appears in the last of Britten's Pushkin songs, which were written in the same year as the Blake and also for a distinguished foreign singer.

As in 'A Poison Tree' the accompaniment (written out in three staves, as if it were a Debussy prelude) does not seem typical of Britten's other songs. The whole of this piece is an *étude* in the use of the tremolo – quick-ly oscillating chords in the piano requiring an accompanist with a flexible wrist – at all dynamics. This succession of pianistic *frissons* suggests both the glow of the sun and the head of a tall flower shivering on its stem as it turns toward its guiding light. At the other end of the keyboard, deep in the bass clef, a motif in semiquaver quintuplets shuffles lugubriously between the song's various harmonic pivotal points, the various fixed points of the sun's journey across the sky. These rumblings convey the lassitude of a giant who is 'weary of time' and able to move only in his imagination. The poem has something in common with Heine's 'Ein Fichtenbaum steht einsam', where a lonely fir tree dreams of a palm tree far away in the Holy Land. In Blake's poem the sun-flower's longing also extends to a 'sweet golden clime' that the sun is freely able to traverse, a freedom denied to a flower rooted in its native soil and 'doing time' as it were. This longed-for destination is the place

Where the Youth pined away with desire,
And the pale Virgin shrouded in snow,
Arise from their graves and aspire
Where my Sun-flower wishes to go.

What great words these are! And there is little in Britten's song catalogue which is as mournfully impressive as this music where the resources of the whole range of the keyboard are called upon to surround the sun-flower with a panoply of sumptuous, gently throbbing and shimmering harmony. The vocal line often moves in baleful descending thirds largely built on the diminished triad between D flat and the G below. That the composer sees the sun-flower's longed-for destination as somewhere exotic and perhaps eastern (apart from the religious implications of the text) is suggested by ⊙ CD2, track 9 comparison with a later work – ⊙ *Canticle IV*, Britten's setting of T.S. Eliot's 'The Journey of the Magi'. On their way to Bethlehem the three kings come across ' a temperate valley' –

Wet, below the snow line, smelling of vegetation,
With a running stream and a water-mill beating the darkness,
And three trees on the low sky.

The composer's use of a tremolando accompaniment here (a parallel passage encompassing travel and biblical topography) is reminiscent of that in 'Ah! Sun-flower' composed some years earlier. Only Schubert might similarly have had the courage to imagine the stationary sun-flower on the march, as if it were fulfilling its dreams to move on and accompany the sun on exotic journeys that could never flower into reality (compare this, for example, with the staccato-emphasised footsteps of the moon in 'An den Mond in einer Herbstnacht' D614). The feeling of unfulfilled longing that pervades Blake's melancholy invocation to a sun-flower is also reminiscent of Schubert's 'Atys' D585 (a Britten–Pears favourite), where the suicidal castrated boy longs to return home over the sea, yet is transfixed by his destiny. As we have noticed in connection with the Eliot canticle, Britten's music is tinged with a similarly eastern melancholy. Atys was an acolyte of the goddess Cybele in Asia Minor and we are reminded that the composer was soon to write *The Burning Fiery Furnace*, the most pagan of the church operas in terms of illustrative colour. Those double-bass-like quintuplets in 'Ah! Sun-flower', for example, prophesy passages in this very church parable.

Further Schubertian resonances in 'Ah! Sun-flower' occur to me: a march incorporating dried flowers brings to mind the powerful 'Trockne

218

Blumen' from *Die schöne Müllerin*. But if I were to think of a lied that might match 'Ah! Sun-flower' in terms of grandeur it would be 'Freiwilliges Versinken' D700 (Mayrhofer), where the sun god Helios describes his majestic descent over the horizon. It is perhaps no coincidence that this very song was given a matchless performance in the Schubert group performed by Fischer-Dieskau and Britten at Snape in 1972. It was certainly astute programme-planning to have included it in a recital that also included the Blake *Songs and Proverbs*.

(vii) 'Proverb VII' and 'Every Night and Every Morn'

These are the only texts that come neither from the *Proverbs of Hell* nor the *Songs of Experience*. The words of both the 'Proverb' (not really a proverb like the others, more of an aphorism) and the following song are taken from a long poem entitled *Auguries of Innocence*, which appears in the so-called Pickering Manuscript of Blake's works. The first four lines of this poem are set in the proverb style, though for once the piano takes a subsidiary role and the vocal line is entirely melodic, made up of all twelve tones in the scale.

Britten then cuts 114 lines of the poem; at line 119 we discover 'Every Night and every Morn' – a fourteen-line sequence: seven simple rhyming couplets as opposed to a sonnet. This is such a powerful part of the poem that one might imagine it were famous (as is the 'World in a Grain of Sand'), but it is not to be found among the celebrated Blake lines in the *Oxford Dictionary of Quotations* – in fact it is an inspired discovery for which Peter Pears was probably responsible. Britten's music sets the seal on a cycle that has already proved unremittingly serious. An implacable bass line of quavers in the left hand veers between 2/4 and 3/4 while mournfully dissonant right-hand chords in sticky *mezzo staccato* crotchets trudge through the mire and misery of life. The vocal line is almost a monotone with tiny, but telling, inflections. It is remarkable how the composer manages to convey such *darkness* in this music – the shadowed horrors of the worst slums, and the cowed hopelessness of those entrapped in them. The circular movement of these quavers in 3/4 somehow suggests the creaking of a giant treadmill to which prisoners condemned to hard labour are chained: for those 'born to endless night' life itself is a punishment of this unremitting kind. The subtly changing metre also avoids the banality of an over-symmetrical jingle – always a danger with rhyming couplets. Key words in the phrase are elongated into triple time, a sign of Britten's superb handling of words: for example, in the phrase 'sweet delight' the word 'sweet' is stretched into two lingering beats.

At 'We are led to Believe a Lie' the accompaniment turns into a heaving, stealthy mass of contrary-motion quavers in both hands. As this inventive two-part writing threads itself through both staves one cannot help but think of snakes writhing in a pit. In response to the words 'Beams of Light' the quavers rise into the right hand of the accompaniment, which is now *forte* and punctuated by heavy left-hand chords. At 'God appears and God is Light' the vocal line is also *forte*, and the effect is of a blazing day of judgement that blinds supplicant mortals; the clashing and grinding discords of this passage leave no doubt that this is a time of condemnation and retribution rather than of release and forgiveness. It is 'those poor Souls who dwell in Night' who do not doubt that 'God is Light'; religion has long been the means by which the rich and powerful have controlled the subservient poor, and a belief in the after-life is their only comfort. It is remarkable how Britten builds to the grandeur of this climactic point, all the more so because there has been nothing else in a cycle full of impressive moments that has been as imposing as this. The climax is a short one; the music begins to die down as soon as it has reached its most vehement point. Blake's final haunting question – 'But does a Human Form Display/To those who Dwell in Realms of day' is left without a question-mark by the poet. Instead the composer provides one in the music itself. The way that the turbulence of this cycle dissolves hauntingly into a gentle major-key triad in the final bar of the postlude is extremely moving; it seems to look back to that final, haunting and inconclusive 'Amen' in the *War Requiem*. It is little wonder that this cycle has long been considered one of Britten's most disturbing and uncomfortable works.

⊙ CD2, track 14

⊙ *Canticle III – Still Falls the Rain* (*The Raids, 1940. Night and Dawn*) Op. 55 (1954)

I had the good fortune to perform this work with Peter Pears and Alan Civil in 1978 for a concert in Aldeburgh that was recorded for the BBC. Something I wrote nearer that time still seems apposite to any discussion of Britten's music in relation to its first interpreter:

> It is given to very few singers to forget themselves so entirely, to immerse themselves with such selflessness, that they make us believe they stand for an entire faith, that they mourn on behalf of an entire generation. Yet this was Pears's achievement in the *War Requiem*, as the Evangelist in the Bach Passions, as Elgar's Gerontius, and in *Still falls the rain*.[9]

9. *The Britten Companion* ed. C. Palmer (Faber, 1984), p. 298.

When Britten composed *My Beloved is Mine* (*Canticle I*) in 1947 it was surely the inspiration behind Francis Quarles's seventeenth-century reli-

220

gious meditation that suggested the word 'Canticle' as a title for this music (Quarles uses 'Canticles' as an abbreviation for Solomon's *Canticum canticorum* or *Song of songs*). In his setting of the Chester miracle play, *Abraham and Isaac* (discussed later in this lecture) Britten re-employed the word in designating that work as *Canticle II*. When he came to look for another text along these lines he must have been influenced by the title of a volume of poetry (published in 1950) that Edith Sitwell had named *The Canticle of the Rose*, a copy of which was in his library. Perhaps a volume with such a promising title might contain the text of another canticle? And sure enough, on page 164 of this book the composer found the poem 'Still Falls the Rain', destined to be his third Canticle.

This work was dedicated to the memory of the Australian pianist Noel Mewton-Wood who, distraught at the death of his older lover, had committed suicide in a flat in Wigmore Street at the age of 31. The horn part was conceived for the incomparable Dennis Brain who, soon after this work was performed, died in a tragic accident. These mournful circumstances seem both reflected and prefigured in this music. In setting Edith Sitwell, Britten would have been very aware that her name was closely linked with William Walton and the brilliantly light-hearted *Façade*. It is not by chance that this Sitwell setting shows a completely different aspect of the poet's work – visionary, almost surrealist, searingly religious – a side of her verse that Walton had not set to music. In this poem we sense that violence breeds violence, that war goes on and on and that mankind will never learn its lesson: 'Still falls the rain' – as it has fallen since the beginning of time – and each time an act of war occurs it is a fresh wound in the side of the crucified Christ. Sitwell also explores images of 'The wounds of the baited bear' and 'the tears of the hunted hare'. Not for the first time in Britten's output we hear the hunting horn in its braying arrogance and, with it, the composer's distaste for bloodsports and cruelty to animals first encountered in *Tit for Tat* and *Our Hunting Fathers*. When that Auden cantata was written in 1936, cruelty to animals was equated with the rise of fascism and anti-Semitism. When Sitwell wrote this poem 'the helpless flesh' of beaten and murdered Nazi victims was a contemporary horror. When Britten wrote the music it was less than a decade since the liberation of Belsen and the discovery of a tale of inhumanity to haunt the world.

The work was completed a few months after the first performance of the opera *The Turn of the Screw* and owes something to Britten's fascination with twelve-tone composition, which is also at the heart of that opera. Both canticle and opera are also cast as themes and variations, albeit in very different ways. The poem of *Still Falls the Rain* is divided into six sections, each beginning with the refrain of the title, and concludes with a short four-line epilogue. Britten follows this by numbering each of these six verses and interpolating instrumental variations between them. The work opens with the 'Theme', where heavy chords cast the harmonic outline in the piano-writing while the horn provides fragments of melody. The use of all twelve tones in this music is obvious to a musical ear of any sophistication. This single page is followed by the entry of the tenor ('Still falls the rain') – the sparsely accompanied bleak incantations of Verse 1, which mention the 'nineteen hundred and forty nails/Upon the Cross' (this year, 1940, was one that Britten spent in America, away from his beloved homeland, and this must have occurred to him). This is followed by Variation I, where the movement quickens into duplets for the horn against staccato triplets in the piano.

The piece continues to unfold in this manner – the voice hauntingly continuing to interrupt what is effectively a set of variations for horn and piano. 'Verse II' is enlivened by mention of the 'the pulse of the heart' and 'the hammer-beat/In the Potter's Field' and 'Variation II', reflecting this increased agitation, is a tiny *étude* in chromatic scales for the horn. The burrowing worm 'with the brow of Cain' (Verse III) engenders Variation III, which is a staccatissimo three-part invention (this recalls the 'Nor time, nor place, nor chance nor death' section of *Canticle I*). In 'Verse IV' the extreme economy that has characterised the vocal line so far yields to something less stringent and minimalist; there is an expansive melisma on 'have *mercy* on us' and an archaic chant-like cadence at 'On Dives and on Lazarus' (the apposition and opposition of these two symbolic characters are a recurring theme in Sitwell's work). In Variation IV the horn is *cuivré* or 'brassed' with stopped notes, which shudder in quintuplets with pungent effect. This is part of a gradual increase in musical tension that has been skilfully planned from the beginning.

Verse V is longer than the others, and the piano takes a more active part in mirroring the increasingly distressing words. The following Variation V is a march that would be thrillingly stirring, were it not for the uncomfortable conjunction of the words; in the context of the tortured bear and the hunted hare its rhythms seem merciless, its intention bellicose and persecutory. Muted echoes of this music pervade and punctuate the spare piano writing in Verse VI. The familiar swivel of adjacent semitones (between E flat and D) that is the basis of this vocal plaint is suddenly interrupted by a strange outburst:

O Ile leape up to my God: who pulls me doune –
See, see where Christ's blood streames in the firmament:

Britten sets this passage as *Sprechgesang* – words spoken, or rather half-sung, at pitch. This device, untypical of the composer, separates these two lines from the rest of the poem which is no doubt the intended effect. Neither the score nor the printed poem makes clear (beyond a use of Elizabethan spelling) that Sitwell has taken these lines directly from Christopher Marlowe's *Doctor Faustus*. They occur towards the end of that play, where Faustus, condemned to hell like Don Giovanni, continues with words that show his longing to procure Christ's blood – 'One drop would save my soul, half a drop'. Incidentally, in order to make Marlowe's meaning clearer, there should be a question-mark after 'who pulls me doune?'. I have heard performances where the second part of this line is made to sound like a relative clause – as if it were 'God ... who pulls me down'.

It is fitting therefore that Britten should have set this interpolation differently from Sitwell's own words. And the point in not continuing with Marlowe's merciless denouement (whereby the sinful voluptuary Faustus is taken off to hell by the devils of Mephistopheles) is that salvation is possible because of the redeeming powers of the Passion. The strongest illustration of this appears in the quiet radiance of the work's concluding page, the passage that announces the arrival of 'Dawn' after the nightmare of the raids. The surprise of this 'Variation VI' is that voice and horn sing together for the first time. It is a moment worth waiting for. As in *Canticle II*, Britten suggests the voice of God (or in this case the crucified Christ) by the combination of two of the performers – here the voice and horn. The piano only re-emerges for the last five bars of the piece. The words 'Still do I love, still shed my innocent light, my Blood, for thee' are sung on a monotone B flat (the horn also remains on this same note) while the piano restates the crucial chords on which the theme has been based.

The surprising thing about this canticle is how moving it is despite its rather abstract form, where a sense of mourning and ritual pervade the music at the expense of greater narrative immediacy. Narration is hardly the point; here man's sin and agony remain constant. All those repetitions of 'Still falls the rain' after the various instrumental interludes give the music a feeling of timeless threnody. Its response to, and illustration of, verbal detail is perhaps less than any other piece of Britten's vocal music with piano. This is also because Sitwell's is the sort of poetry and imagery that this composer normally avoids. In this respect its parallel is probably *Canticle V – The Death of Saint Narcissus* where once again Britten is willing to set verbal imagery that is less than crystal clear to the first-time reader, or listener.

There is a final point. The canticle paints the agony of London in the Blitz – the rain of bombs ever falling to bring agony and death to a civilian

223

population. As such this work has every right to be regarded as one of the pieces that leads to the definitive pacifist utterance of the *War Requiem* in Britten's output. But just as *Canticle I* had both a religious and a personal agenda (in that case the composer's solemn declaration of devotion to Peter Pears) the mourning of *Canticle III* bemoans one single death – a London suicide – as much as the many. The demise of the gifted young pianist Mewton-Wood, a man with a Mephistophelean keyboard gift (one hears this as he accompanies Pears in the Tippett cycles) coincided with a particularly nasty phase in British post-war history regarding the prosecution (and persecution) of homosexuals. One could easily see a reference to this in the lines about 'the baited bear,/The blind and weeping bear whom the keepers beat/On his helpless flesh', and one cannot forget that the quoted poet Marlowe was homosexual and possibly died as a result of his proclivities. The hostility, prejudice and legal prosecution faced by gay men has engendered, either directly or indirectly, countless tragedies in the private lives of those susceptible to instability or self-torturing guilt. Perhaps they would have been comforted by Sitwell's words:

> He bears in His Heart all wounds, – those of the light that died,
> The last faint spark
> In the self-murdered heart, the wounds of the sad uncomprehending dark,

When heard in the context of the sad story of the 'self-murdered' Mewton-Wood, a great artist who had felt tormented by 'the sad uncomprehending dark', this canticle takes its place among the many Britten works that have seem designed to function on more than one level: the all-inclusive ritual embracing London's fate as a whole contains within it a much more private grief about a single tragedy in Wigmore Street. This is emblematic of the ongoing suffering of those who have the courage to say, come what may, 'Still do I love', and once again the soft-spoken Britten is their secret spokesman.

Winter Words Op. 53 (1953)

The one famous poet of English song that Britten never set was A.E. Housman. It is a paradox that this most angrily subversive of gay poets should have been the special province of a phalanx of heterosexual British composers, some of then completely unaware of the bitter emotions that fuelled the texts, and often lay cunningly hidden in them. Perhaps Britten thought that Housman had been set for all time by George Butterworth – his performances with Pears of that composer's *A Shropshire Lad* were particularly masterly. If Housman 'belonged' to Butterworth (and Vaughan

Williams, among many others) then Hardy had long seemed the special territory of Gerald Finzi; many people must have been rather surprised that Britten decided to compose a cycle of Hardy poems.

Neither Britten nor Pears was a fan of Finzi (nor he of them, an awkward position for the publisher they had in common, Boosey and Hawkes), and that must have played its part in Britten's determination to set these poems. Another factor was that in the 1890s Thomas Hardy had visited Aldeburgh on several occasions, although it was very far from his own part of the country. In the Suffolk seaside town he was a guest of the eccentric Rationalist, and Omar Khayyám enthusiast, Edward Clodd, who lived at Stafford House on Crag Path (there is a picture, taken in the 1950s, of Britten talking to a fisherman on Crag Path with the white balconies of Stafford House in the background). Hardy enjoyed his time in Aldeburgh, particularly valuing 'the sensation of having nothing but sea between you and the North Pole'. If he had liked Britten's part of the country, so different from his own, then it was perhaps up to the composer to return the compliment in the direction of Wessex.

Thomas Hardy.

Of course a comparison with Finzi's music is inescapable, although there is only one of the poems of *Winter Words* – 'Proud Songsters' – that was set by both composers. Gerald Finzi's centenary year was in 2001, and there has been ample opportunity to hear most of the Finzi songs in performance; the difference between the two composers' approaches is enormous. Finzi is a *petit maître* who loves and understands the poetry like few others; his songs are suffused with the gentlemanly melancholy of English forbearance. If this sometimes fails to encompass the larger aspects of Hardy's nature, Finzi's reflectiveness in both joy and regret (as in the incomparable *Lizbie Brown*) perfectly suits much of the poet and his landscape, both topographical and emotional. One would not be without this special voice in English song. Britten, on the other hand, declines to tussle with the longer discursive poems that Finzi sets with varying degrees of success. In Britten's songs we are reminded that Thomas Hardy was a great novelist and story-teller. Britten, as an opera composer, a man of musical action, chooses to present his Hardy on this semi-dramatic basis; there is always something *happening* in these songs until the last, 'Before Life and After', which is suddenly deeply mystical and contemplative, and something of a surprise as a result.

The choice of title for the cycle, *Winter Words*, is also the title of Hardy's last collection of poems. There were eight volumes of poetry, all published in green cloth bindings with the poet's monogram on the cover. The first two were issued under the imprint of Harper and Bros in slighter larger format, and the rest by Macmillan and Co. The first was *Wessex Poems*, which appeared in 1898 with the poet's own illustrations. (Hardy's drawing for the frontispiece of this collection also appears on the cover of the song cycle as printed by Boosey and Hawkes.) As it happens, Britten selected nothing from this first collection, nor the second, *Poems Past and Present* (1902). 'Wagtail and Baby' and 'Before Life and After' are from *Time's Laughingstocks* (1909); 'At Day-Close in November' is from *Satires of Circumstance* (1914); 'Midnight on the Great Western' and 'The Choirmaster's Burial' are both from *Moments of Vision* (1917); 'The Little Old Table' and 'At the Railway Station, Upway' are from *Late Lyrics and Earlier* (1922); there was nothing selected from *Human Shows, Far Phantasies* (1925), and 'Proud Songsters' comes from *Winter Words* (1928).

From this it is clear that Britten trawled through the *Collected Poems* for his Hardy cycle, but that he was taken with *Winter Words* as a title for the whole of his own collection. The reason why is not hard to fathom: any musician could not fail to connect a title containing the word 'Winter' with Schubert's great song cycle of 1827, *Winterreise*, which Britten and Pears were beginning to perform together at this time. Was it a symbolic gesture that Britten began his cycle in the D minor tonality in which Schubert makes the traveller embark on his winter journey? And is the melting change to the major key for the song's last strophe another hidden homage to the same work? Is 'Midnight on the Great-Western' not an *Erlkönig* for modern times where the steam train has replaced the galloping horse, and where the child is equally threatened by dark forces? And is the accompaniment of 'Wagtail and Baby' not a loving reminiscence of 'Auf dem Wasser zu singen'? Does the bleak scenario of 'Before Life and After' owe something to 'Der Leiermann'? Schubert's influence is to be heard mightily in this cycle, in the economical but supremely telling piano writing, and in the way that the Biedermeier parochialism (or its English equivalent) of the songs' geography does not deny them a depth of utterance which seems universal. Britten was a man who loved the *local* aspects of life, Hardy was the same way in a different part of England, and Schubert savoured the here-and-now with such keen observation, and with such pleasure, that poems about the banal rituals of everyday life ('Der Einsame', with its chirping cricket on the hearth, is just one example) take on, in his hands, an aspect of the sublime. As we shall see, Britten's cycle is packed full of musical snapshots of shifting scenarios, and that too is something we find in Schubert's *Winterreise*.

(i) At Day-Close in November

The ten hours' light is abating,
   And a late bird wings across,
Where the pines, like waltzers waiting,
   Give their black heads a toss.

Beech leaves, that yellow the noon-time,
   Float past like specks in the eye;
I set ev'ry tree in my June time,
   And now they obscure the sky.

And the children who ramble through here
   Conceive that there never has been
A time when no trees, no tall trees grew here,
   That none will in time be seen.

This is an 'autumn', rather than a 'winter' word. The biting winds of November were marvellously characterised by Schubert in his Rellstab setting 'Herbst'; Britten achieves a similar impetus here as left-hand duplets vie with right-hand triplets in interlocking arpeggios that blow upwards through the stave. A fascinating succession of descending chords in dotted minims are enlivened by a sufficient number of crotchets to establish what turns out to be an urgent waltz rhythm. The composer has looked forward to the end of the first strophe, where Hardy refers to 'the pines, like waltzers waiting'; the trees toss their hair as petulantly as belles of the ball ignored by their beaux, the whole of this piece of countryside suddenly turned into a gigantic, windswept dance-floor. The extraordinary trajectory of the vocal line as it zigzags its way down the stave seems to trace the flight path of the 'late bird' as it 'wings across' the horizon.

We have begun this piece with a *forte* introduction; for the second strophe the same piano figurations appear in a delicate *pianissimo* to suit the sight of beech leaves floating down 'like specks in the eye'. This observation ages the narrator in that it tells us that his sight is not what it once was; he too is in the November of his life, though still fit and robust due to a life of fresh air and exercise. Britten is uncannily able to create this lean, ruddy creature before our eyes using only sound and rhythm as his paint and canvas. If Hardy meant this to be a self-portrait at the age of seventy-four this music does not fit our picture of a sedentary poet. Instead we see a farmer, a man who has always worked on the land, and who tells us that he has planted (or 'set') these trees when he was much younger – in his 'June time' in fact – and now they have come to dominate the skyline. The robust way in which he sings these lines denotes pride in his contribution to something which will last – or will it?; the end of the phrase 'obscure the sky' ushers in his own intimations of mortality.

Suddenly the winds, and all indications of physical activity, are stilled; there is a different kind of chill in the music. The accompaniment gently rocks between minims and crotchets, denoting introspection that wanders back into memory, and also worries about the future. This change has been brought about by the word 'children', and we sense his realisation that the future belongs to the next generation. A straightforward reading of the poem could easily depict these children 'who ramble through here' as being a nuisance with scant awareness of the achievements of their elders. There is nothing in Hardy's poem that implies tenderness towards these representatives of the next generation. But this is exactly how Britten's music (marked *pianissimo* and *sweetly*) fills in the gaps in an amplification of verbal meaning that is only available to the great song composer.

Britten's protagonist had begun in a tone that is gruff, even vehement to match the mood of the weather. But he softens when he thinks of love (just as Schubert's winter traveller eventually softens from anger into affection in the opening song of *Winterreise*). There is something about the shape of the phrase at 'And the children' which instantly suggests the tender concern of a normally down-to-earth man who is moved to tender lyricism by the beauty of his own grandchildren – one would expect nothing less from the countryman who has shown us his handiwork with such pride. An F sharp has already insinuated itself into the D minor tonality. At 'When *no* trees' (Britten alters Hardy here in missing out the word 'tall' until a repetition of the phrase) we hear for the first time a pure D major chord; this moment (which parallels a similar key-change in 'Gute Nacht', the Schubert song mentioned above) seems to be accompanied by a gentle smile as he thinks of trying to explain to the little ones how bare this copse was years ago when he himself was a young man.

But what use to talk to them about the past! They are firmly rooted in the present and unable to imagine life differently from present reality. He has the benefit of experience; his long life as a countryman has taught him that landscapes, like lives, are in a constant state of change. He has now reached his autumn years and his trees will last for a long time after he dies; but he knows that they will not last into eternity. 'A time …That none will in time be seen' is one of those closing thoughts in Hardy's poems which seems to launch a rocket into the night sky. It conjures a moonscape of another era unimaginable by man (if man is indeed still part of the picture), an acceptance that we can have no control of the future after our deaths.

The postlude continues with a brief continuation of the rocking *berceuse* motif, a short recapitulation of the windswept arpeggios, a crystalline spread chord (two tied bars of dotted minims) and a sudden resolution in short and dry unison octaves on a single D. At that moment we realise how man and his achievements are doomed to vanish suddenly from the earth's surface, their absence scarcely noticed.

(ii) 'Midnight on the Great Western' (or 'The Journeying Boy')

In the third-class seat sat the journeying boy,
 And the roof-lamp's oily flame
Play'd down on his listless form and face,
Bewrapt past knowing to what he was going,
  Or whence he came.

In the band of his hat the journeying boy
 Had a ticket stuck; and a string
Around his neck bore the key of his box,
That twinkled gleams of the lamp's sad beams
  Like a living thing.

What past can be yours, O journeying boy
 Towards a world unknown,
Who calmly, as if incurious quite
On all at stake, can undertake
  This plunge alone?

Knows your soul a sphere, O journeying boy,
 Our rude realms far above,
Whence with spacious vision you mark and mete
This region of sin that you find you in,
  But are not of?

The *Great Western* (the train service that took its name from the famous transatlantic steamer service between Britain and America) made its way, then as now, between London's Paddington Station and the West Country – Hardy country in fact. It is clear from the poem that the journeying boy is making his way alone *to* London with the poet as a fellow-passenger – thus ominous mention of 'a world unknown', and of a dangerous 'plunge'. That such a journey should be taking place at midnight is an indication of busier timetables than those advertised by train companies in modern times. The mention of 'third class' also seems archaic – a train version of steerage on the *Titanic*, and a stratum of social and monetary differentiation unknown in these days where two classes suffice. The sight of the solitary child has touched Hardy who muses, with typical English reserve, about the story behind the journey of this enigmatic little traveller. One can scarcely imagine an American, or a European, refraining from interrogating the child, and expressing direct concern for his plight, but this is one of those poems where Hardy appears more of a Victorian than someone writing in the middle of World War One. The whole song is *thought* rather than voiced. At no point do we imagine that the poet addresses the boy face to face; this is one of those mute fantasies, resulting from a mixture of curiosity and compassion, which are familiar to all users of public transport who, in thinking whatever they may imagine, must always mind their own business. The detachment shown by the poet as he analyses the possible fate of the boy (while simultaneously being concerned for his welfare up to a point) confers on this music an emotional reserve that strikes the foreign observer as utterly English.

The song opens with one of Britten's more spectacular effects – a Doppler effect in fact. The mournful whine of a train whistle as it changes pitch in motion is not the easiest thing to imitate on the piano – but the composer manages it with an elaborate use of the pedal and keys depressed without actually re-striking the opening C minor chord. After this extraordinary piece of sonic conjuring we have spiky staccato passages that suggest the chugging of a nineteenth-century train; the hemiolas in this accompaniment suggest the lurching of the carriages as they move between points and from one piece of track to another. Above this churning accompaniment (in which we sense that some distance is being covered as we move progressively through various keys) there is a vocal line of some legato and some elegance, not precluding the occasional use of melisma. The word 'journeying' is a particularly happy instance of English word-setting by Purcell's twentieth-century successor: the word lives up to its meaning in its extended expedition across the bar-lines. This succession of triplets when sung against the piano's quavers and semiquavers adds to the feeling that both the narrator and the boy are lurching and rolling to their terrible destination – a journey to Hades such as we encounter in Schubert's 'Fahrt zum Hades'. The boy and the narrator are locked into their mutual journey, and the implacable train rhythms in the piano writing further imprison them. But it is uncanny how many illustrative details are allowed to emerge between the railway tracks to enrich the picture: the flickering of the roof lamp's oily flame, the listlessness of the boy's form, the 'twinkled gleams of the lamp's sad beams' – all these things are reflected in twists and turns of the vocal line and the accompaniment.

The third verse contains a rare instance of questionable word-setting on the composer's part. This is because of Hardy's highly unusual grammatical construction where the adjective 'journeying' also functions as a verb. The poet's phrase 'O journeying boy/Towards a world unknown' actually means 'O boy *journeying towards* (who journeys towards) a world unknown'. Because of the way the music is laid out, the words 'O journeying boy' seem attached to the previous phrase 'What past can be yours' with an implied question mark to close the sentence. An unhelpful change of tempo ('Slow') is marked in the music before 'Towards a world unknown' so that this phrase often seems to be the beginning of a new thought instead of being connected to the previous words; this means that the next phrase 'Who calmly, as if incurious quite' can easily sound as if it refers back to 'world' (as if the world were incurious, rather than the boy). The secret of making sense of this passage is for the singer to connect 'O journeying boy' with 'Towards a world unknown' (they are linked by enjambement in the poem) without allowing the intervening bar of piano writing to suggest a real caesura between the two phrases. The whole of the page encompasses a single question, but it will not sound as such unless the singer makes every effort to convey the unity of Hardy's complex strophe which is (admittedly awkwardly) constructed as one long sentence.

This passage of musing speculation has been cast in semi-recitative form where a certain freedom in the vocal line suggests the narrator's puzzlement and concern. It might have been easier simply to ask the boy questions about his life, but the poet prefers to speculate (one cannot help but think of Aschenbach's monologues about Tadzio in *Death in Venice* where not a single word is exchanged between these two characters). The words 'undertake/This plunge alone?' lead to an interlude (a touch of that Doppler effect again); after this, two bars of tremolos elaborately decorate a somewhat triumphant perfect (dominant to tonic) cadence, as if the train had turned a corner and were moving into the home stretch. But there is also a revelation implied in this key change where, in true Schubertian manner, C minor yields to C major. This is music of transfiguration, and how well Britten has understood the poet's sudden vision of the boy as an angel in disguise (Aschenbach's Tadzio is also a disguised angel, but the angel of death). A victim of adults' indifference and neglect is now made to shine and gleam in music in the major key; as an avenging judge of mankind's sins, perhaps he will 'mark and mete' the sinful regions of London, but will be untouched by them. Britten responds to this image with a musical grandeur implied by the tenor's more heroic tessitura. Such is the power of the observer's thought and fantasy that an object of pity now engenders awestruck, even reverent, feelings. It is as if poet has seen the image of the Christ child in this neglected waif, and the composer's fervid response is worthy of this epiphany.[9] A train journey has turned into a mystical experience and a revelation. An echo of the opening train brings this extraordinary song to a close, incorporating a questioning final cadence: perhaps the little traveller is only a poor, vulnerable boy after all.

9. One must point out, however, that Hardy was not religious in any conventional way.

(iii) Wagtail and Baby (A Satire)
A baby watch'd a ford, whereto
    A wagtail came for drinking;
A blaring bull went wading through,
    The wagtail showed no shrinking.

A stallion splash'd his way across,
    The birdie nearly sinking;
He gave his plumes a twitch and toss,
    And held his own unblinking.

Next saw the baby round the spot
    A mongrel slowly slinking;
The wagtail gazed, but faltered not
    In dip and sip and prinking.

A perfect gentleman then neared;
    The wagtail, in a winking,
With terror rose and disappeared;
    The baby fell a-thinking.

232

The words 'A Satire' following this title are not in Hardy's original edition, nor in the latest and most scholarly edition of *The Complete Poems*; they may have come from a later edition of the *Collected Poems*, or the words may be the composer's own gloss on a little fable which is indeed a satire on man as an enemy of nature. This is a poem that is anti-bloodsports at one remove; it shows how different members of the animal kingdom distrust mankind much more than they fear each other.

Once again we hear how the clarity and elegance of Schubert's piano writing with voice (especially in music the composer has played himself) has influenced Britten. Like many of Schubert's accompaniments this is derived from a single pianistic motif. Any lieder pianist will feel that 'Wagtail and Baby' is somehow related to Schubert's 'Auf dem Wasser zu singen'. There is a similarly chugging succession of quaver chords in the left hand (in barcarolle rhythm) and a similar cascade of semiquavers, which require the pianist to change fingers on repeated notes with nimble dexterity; water is also of the essence in the little series of cameos observed by the baby.

Within this formula a story unfolds where all the various events watched by this perceptive baby are illustrated in different ways. So mercurial is this music in its ability to mirror the movements of birds and animals that we are reminded of Britten's experience as a composer of film music; this style would certainly suit a nature documentary perfectly. There is something essentially wagtail-like about the twitching movements that flutter cheekily up and down the piano. The same figurations, played in lower regions of the keyboard, do service for the wading of the 'blaring bull' and the splashing stallion; the treble clef is reserved for the 'twitch and toss' of the bird. At 'held his own unblinking', Britten's music is deliciously illustrative: the equilibrium of the accompaniment is shaken and momentarily totters, slipping into G minor before settling back on its heels in F major. The 'slinking' mongrel really does slink as the pianist's right hand crosses the left in a rather abject manner. In contrast to this skulking menace the sheer wit of 'dip and sip and prinking' appropriately illustrates the wagtail's insouciance in most circumstances.

But not quite all. The appearance and approach of a member of the human race – 'a perfect gentleman' is ushered in with what seems like a courtly bow in music – how does Britten manage to make the word 'perfect', set as a rising fourth in this tessitura, seem so humorously … perfect? This is not someone dangerous or malevolent – in fact an over-fastidious clergyman comes to mind (see the next song). No matter; from the wagtail's point of view this is mankind, the enemy. The bird, who has proved impervious to all other distractions, disappears in a flurry of flashy octaves, part of an inspired passage of recitative that seems to grow completely naturally out of what has gone before. What moral is to be drawn from this? We are told that 'The baby fell a-thinking'. The postlude in Peter Evans' estimation is 'grotesque'.[11] It is certainly odd; that is, until we imagine a film of a baby's face with its various changing expressions reflecting those unfathomable dramas which seem too deep for the words that, in any case, are not yet at its disposal. The postlude to this song shows us an infant's mind searching about in several unlikely keys before coming to its inscrutable conclusion – something along the lines of 'Our kind is not well thought-of … I wonder why?' In the song repertory, only Satie in the final 'Ah' of his song 'Daphéneo' has got anywhere near depicting a similar vein of comedy, inherent in the thought-processes of small children.

11. Peter Evans, *The Music of Benjamin Britten* (JM Dent, 1979), p.359.

⊙ CD2, track 15

⊙ (iv) The Little Old Table

Creak, little wood thing, creak,
When I touch you with elbow or knee;
That is the way you speak
Of one who gave you to me!

You, little table, she brought –
Brought me with her own hand,
As she look'd at me with a thought
That I did not understand.

– Whoever owns it anon,
And hears it, will never know
What a history hangs upon
This creak from long ago.

Much of Hardy's greatest poetry is about looking back into the past, regretting events that cannot be changed, and minutely re-examining incidents he feels he should have better understood, or better managed, at the time. Here we have a love story told through an inanimate object, a table, to which both poet and composer give life, as if it were the key witness to an incident of great emotional import. The table was brought to the narrator by a woman who looks at him with a look he fails to understand (Hardy frequently berates himself for misreading the signs of love, and for not being sensitive enough at the time to guess the complexities of a woman's mind). The table's female owner seems, nevertheless, to have successfully

234

initiated a relationship. We infer this from her look, and the thought behind it; the singer refers to a 'history', which hangs on 'this creak from long ago'.

The song is masterfully constructed along the Schubertian lines that govern so much of this cycle. A smooth right-hand figuration in oscillating quavers propels the music forward while the table's 'speech' is illustrated by staccato major seconds that echo the voice's exclamations of 'Creak' as they cross hands into the treble clef. (The Schubert song 'Der Einsame' comes to mind; this depicts the song of the cricket and the curling flame of contentment in the hearth with a similar combination of contrasting motifs in the piano while aspiring to a similar domestic cosiness.) The composer constructs a colloquy between the vocal line and the left hand of the accompaniment – as if the poet were speaking to the table and it was holding a conversation in return. It is clear that this table is all that remains of this relationship from long ago; for this reason the narrator speaks to it with affection, an eccentricity that adds a delightful edge to Britten's music.

And yet, of all this composer's songs it is perhaps this one which is most open to unkind comment, and it is one that some singers find embarrassingly precious. As a small boy at St George's School at Ascot, Winston Churchill was brusquely instructed about first declension nouns in Latin, and told to learn the declensions for 'mensa', the Latin word for 'table'. Churchill did not understand the vocative case, and the teacher informed him he would use it when addressing a table. 'But I never do', replied Churchill cheekily, and that remains the problem in the believability of this song. Those staccato quavers ('Creak! Creak!') followed by the potentially precious 'little wood thing' (here repeated in a manner that might encourage parody) seem hilariously mannered to those unimpressed by Britten in winsome mood.

This is a pity because the song is remarkably well written, and its daintiness is well within Hardy's own stylistic parameters. The dialogue between the singer and the cello-like semiquavers of the left hand are superbly economical – the line of this table, a simple piece of furniture, are somehow delineated in the music's essential plainness. This does not preclude a generous use of vocal melisma at the end of each of the three strophes; this heightens the mystery as to the depth of the relationship between the narrator and the mysterious woman. These decorative phrases conceal much detail – 'if only you knew the whole of the story!' is the singer's subtext, and this will never be shared with us: despite his ability to address a table, we sense that the narrator is a man of few words. The final vocal phrase 'from long ago' captures to perfection the melancholy of attempting to turn the clock back – as we hear the song's closing page we have the impression of retreating down a corridor of time becoming ever smaller and quieter as we do so. One is reminded here of Gerald Finzi's dramatic, though not entirely successful, Hardy setting 'The Clock of the Years'.

(v) The Choirmaster's Burial (or The Tenor Man's Story)

He often would ask us
That, when he died,
After playing so many
To their last rest,
If out of us any
Should here abide,
And it would not task us,
We would with our lutes
Play over him
By his grave-brim
The psalm he liked best –
The one whose sense suits
'Mount Ephraim' –
And perhaps we should seem
To him, in Death's dream,
Like the seraphim.

As soon as I knew
That his spirit was gone
I thought this his due,
And spoke thereupon.

'I think,' said the vicar,
'A read service quicker
Than viols out-of-doors
In these frosts and hoars.
That old-fashioned way
Requires a fine day,
And it seems to me
It had better not be.'

Hence, that afternoon,
Though never knew he
That his wish could not be,

236

To get through it faster
They buried the master
Without any tune.

But 'twas said that, when
At the dead of next night
The vicar looked out,
There struck on his ken
Thronged roundabout,
Where the frost was graying
The headstone grass,
A band all in white
Like the saints in church-glass,
Singing and playing
The ancient stave
By the choirmaster's grave.

Such the tenor man told
When he had grown old.

This is the uncontested masterpiece of the set, and the one that is most often sung out of its context in the cycle. Here the influence is not Schubert, but rather the music of the English Hymnal. Even on the page the song looks almost as archaic as something to be found in a Psalter. And yet, it could only have been written by a master of opera. The narrator of the poem is one of the deceased choirmaster's singers who both introduces the song, and provides its epilogue in unaccompanied simplicity. This reminds us of *Billy Budd*, and the way in which Captain Vere, an old man searching for some answer to the conundrums of his life, both introduces and closes the opera that unfolds on the vast stage of his memory.

To understand this poem one has to know that Hardy grew up on stories about an old and defunct tradition of Anglican church music which had more or less died out in England by the time of the poet's adolescence. His father, Thomas senior, was an amateur musician, and Hardy was raised on nostalgic parental memories of 'Gallery Music' (so called because the band was normally situated in a gallery at the west end of the church), which accompanied church services before the edicts of the Oxford Movement strongly discouraged all recent and secular music in places of worship. The establishment of the organ-dominated disciplines of *Hymns Ancient and Modern* (1861) took place gradually, but the church-going of Hardy senior had been enlivened by his involvement in this merry gallery fraternity. A group of enthusiastic village musicians (bassoons, cellos, clarinets, flutes and violins, old-fashioned viols – or whatever else was available) doubled the choral contribution (where the tenor voice was usually prominent) with instrumental elaborations that were sometimes complex, often idiosyncratic, but always performed with energy and affection. Sometimes there was music without voices. Much of this was cheerily tuneful, but some of it derived from the archaic musical practices of the Renaissance with open fifths and false relations. What shocked the purists was that these church musicians were often the same local men who played for local dances and festivities. In 'The Choirmaster's Burial' we shall hear how this spurned 'ancient stave' is heard in the rhapsodic improvisations played by the ghost musicians at the choirmaster's graveside.

For longer than any other part of England the West Country resisted innovations that were seen by many a Wessex worshipper as sanctimonious interference from Canterbury. Hardy bemoaned the loss of the old music on many occasions in his writings, and it plays a major part in his nostalgic evocations of the past. In this poem the tenor (the lead singer of many of these old ensembles) remembers how the choirmaster often expressed the wish that a group of his younger colleagues should play around his graveside (this of course was only possible with a selection of portable instruments). The vicar (probably a stranger to Dorset, and no doubt a servile admirer of the Proudies from Trollope's *Barchester Towers*) will not permit the revival of these yokel shenanigans.

The poem mentions the 'psalm' 'Mount Ephraim' – actually a hymn tune by B. Milgrove (1731–1810). Of course Britten uses this melody in the accompaniment, a chorale of minims under the words 'After playing so many to their last rest'. This first section of the song is a gently urbane portrait of the choirmaster himself and his gentle tone of voice; the wafting triplet melisma to which the word 'seraphim' is set is the first indication of how these gallery musicians decorated and enlivened the contours of a hymn melody with spontaneous elaborations – not at all, in this case, to the vicar's taste. The portrait of this desiccated cleric that now follows is one of Britten's finest pieces of satire: finicky, unimaginative, emotionally inhibited – these traits are conveyed by a piano figuration (a heavy dotted crotchet followed by a penny-pinching shudder of semiquavers) which suggests laying down the law with a rigidity that will not brook dissent. This music of coming to a decision is prefigured in a much more gentle manner in Britten's Auden setting 'What's in Your Mind', first published 1997. The restricted movement of the vocal line at 'I think, said the vicar,/A read service quicker' manages to suggest the bleat of rehearsed dogma; this awful man then blames the weather for his decision, thus claiming to have everybody's well-being at heart – a particularly English type of cant.

The choirmaster is duly buried 'without any tune' – that is, without the heartfelt melodies that would have accompanied a burial in the older dispensation. Once again Britten's mastery of the dramatic situation is dazzling: impatient quavers in the left hand depict the dry, uninvolved haste of the vicar. The singer's triplets at 'To get through it faster/They buried the master' are on a single repeated tone; this cunningly depicts the deliberately impersonal austerity of intoned prayers, the re-establishment of which was favoured by the new wave of Anglo-Catholic reformers. (Pianists should take special care that the rhythms of this section are tightly held; there is no change of tempo or pulse beyond the indicated quickening of note values. The vicar is punctilious, if heartless, in his attention to duty.)

And then the miracle occurs. Just as the G sharp of the tiny piano interlude after the burial meets the unaccompanied enharmonic A flat of 'But 'twas said that, when' there is a moment of transfiguration. The vicar looks out of the window 'at the dead of next night' and sees a convocation of ghosts, 'singing and playing' (and how marvellously, and with what relish, Britten repeats these words to music which soars ever more recklessly upwards in rapturous twos against threes). These white-robed musicians are both ethereal and vigorous: there is an other-worldly tinge to their spaced-out harmonies, while the gleeful embellishment of 'Mount Ephraim', bowed in expansive triplets and duplets, becomes increasingly wide-ranging and daring. Thus a group of angel musicians shows the vicar that he has defied local tradition at his peril, and the ascendancy of 'the ancient stave' is triumphantly asserted. Such a mixture of the religious and the supernatural is worthy of the great German poet Mörike, and the lieder of Hugo Wolf ('Die Geister am Mummelsee', for example). The long melisma on this very phrase reminds us that the suppression of Purcellian melisma was also effected by Victorian killjoys. In this case Britten is on the side of the angels.

The return to unaccompanied recitative with the words 'Such the tenor man told/When he had grown old' adds a further twist of time-travel. These are the only words the persona of Hardy himself in 1917 (aged seventy-seven) contributes to a poem that has been in inverted commas from the beginning – the story of the tenor. We realise that the poet was still a young man when the old singer (one of his father's colleagues perhaps) told his stories about a long time ago. Thus the corridors of time connecting that time with ours are twice as long as we have first thought: Hardy places this legend in his mind's eye (it is almost certainly a fiction of course) in the 1840s, shortly after his own birth.

(vi) Proud Songsters (Thrushes, Finches and Nightingales)

The thrushes sing as the sun is going,
And the finches whistle in ones and pairs,
And as it gets dark loud nightingales
    In bushes
Pipe, as they can when April wears,
  As if all Time were theirs.
These are brand-new birds of twelve-months' growing,
Which a year ago, or less than twain,
No finches were, nor nightingales,
    Nor thrushes,
But only particles of grain,
  And earth, and air, and rain.

'Proud Songsters' is the only poem in Britten's cycle that was also set by Gerald Finzi in 1932, as part of his cycle *Earth, and Air and Rain*. Both are fine and typical examples of the two composers' work, so nothing could better illustrate the difference between the two men's songs. The Finzi unfolds as a gentle meditation on the great themes of nature and the time, as well as the mysteries of birth and creation. The poem is from the last of the poet's eight great collections; these are the reflections of an old man in his late eighties as he marvels at the young songsters who sing their hearts out, though they did not even exist a year earlier. Hardy knows that he has come to the end of his own time of singing, and he prepares to yield his craft to the new-born who will take his place. Finzi understands this mood exactly, and his song is cast as a gently paced observation, as if through the eyes of the aged poet, tinged with melancholy and a gentle smile of acceptance.

Britten is much less aware, it seems, of the poem's place in the poet's canon. He could not claim to be the Hardy expert that Finzi was. Instead his music is written as if he were flying high *with* the birds, as if he *were* the birds, sharing their visceral joy in being alive. His 'Proud Songsters' is full of a kind of kinetic energy that is beyond Finzi – and to which Finzi would have claimed he never aspired – the explosion of creation before our very ears. These fervid trills and mad triplets in octaves between the hands are as near as Britten got to Messiaen's *Catalogue d'oiseaux* and the music, though on a small scale by comparison, engenders a similar mad ecstasy as if the birds were singing their hearts out with reckless abandon: here is all the cacophony of nature. (Incidentally Britten has a fine flight-record when it comes to his music for birds – from his early Belloc setting 'The Birds' to the memorably evocative birdsong to be heard in the *Spring Symphony*, and the haunting calls of *Curlew River* – to name but a few.)

Virtuosity is demanded from both singer and pianist. The 5/4 time-signature, ideal for a song about the creation of new life where everything is 'work in progress', puts both performers on their counting mettle; a scherzo at this point is just what is needed to keep the cycle varied in tempo and tone (in Schubert's *Winterreise* the same function is fulfilled by 'Der stürmische Morgen' and 'Mut'). It is as if Britten has thrown a handful of dust up into the air and conjured the fluttering of nascent wings with a flurry of pianist's flaying arms, fingers and pumping feet. The middle section of the song ('these are brand new birds of twelve-month growing') strikes a new note of gentle delight; even with birds Britten cannot resist a smile of tenderness when he deals with the young, but in terms of the song's overall shape this is *reculer pour mieux sauter* – everything moves with an inevitable impetus towards those great lines 'particles of grain/And earth, and air, and rain', and we can really hear those dispersed particles in Britten's clearly articulated piano writing. These closing words are set high in the stave and poised between E-flat minor and major with a thrilling melisma on the word 'air'. The vocal cadence on the word 'rain' (the triumph of an exuberant E-flat major) sets the piano off on a recklessly hectic postlude. This final splurge of triplets and trills ends with a hammered E flat in double octaves, a big bang, nuclear fission. This is as elemental a moment as exists in any of Britten's songs – the collision and coalescence of all those particles has resulted in a sudden explosion of new life and energy. One cannot help but think back to the comparatively modest ecstasy in '*Tu creasti, domine*' from Britten's Belloc setting 'The Birds' (see p. 21). Next to this it is inevitable that the Finzi setting should seem careful and leaden; but if a song aims to evoke the poet's own tone of voice, which accepts with quiet joy that there will always be new voices singing in the air, it is the lesser-known composer who comes nearer to the old sage of Dorchester.

(vii) At the Railway Station, Upway (or The Convict and Boy with the Violin)

'There is not much that I can do,
  For I've no money that's quite my own!'
  Spoke up the pitying child –
  A little boy with a violin
At the station before the train came in, –

'But I can play my fiddle to you,
And a nice one 'tis, and good in tone!'

 The man in the handcuffs smiled;
The constable looked, and he smiled, too,
 As the fiddle began to twang;
And the man in the handcuffs suddenly sang
  With grimful glee:
  'This life so free
  Is the thing for me!'
And the constable smiled, and said no word,
As if unconscious of what he heard;
And so they went on till the train came in –
The convict, and boy with the violin.

Once again it is the skills of the opera composer that astonish us. 'At The Railway Station, Upway' is an extraordinary little drama. It has always reminded me of how Oscar Wilde was spat on and vilified on a station plat-form as he was taken by train to Reading Gaol. One would like to think he encountered a fellow-traveller of a compassion similar to this little boy violinist. The convict in this story is no aesthete, but he does turn out to have a Wildeian sense of irony.

The ancient stave of 'The Choirmaster's Burial' has required the full resources of the keyboard, but here Britten becomes a minimalist. On the printed page the piano accompaniment (on one stave) is made to look like violin music – what else? – and proves, not for the first time, that *multum in parvo* is a speciality of this composer. The composer's marking 'Lightly and like an improvisation' belies the extraordinary organisation that has gone into making this piece a convincing whole. Many an aspect of violin playing is evoked here: open strings, double-stopping, *détaché* bowing, *spiccato* – and as if by chance the strumming sound of the third bar (and else-where) also evokes the chugging of a steam train puffing its way into a sta-tion. It is significant that these effects definitely require *both* of the pianist's hands in performance, and both are required to show extreme delicacy and subtlety of colour. The boy's passages of vocal recitative evoke the artless-ness that conceals high art. Perhaps only a composer who was already thinking hard about the character of Miles in *The Turn of the Screw* (also an instrumentalist incidentally, though a pianist) would have been capable of evoking this kind of child whose innocence is combined with a frank directness of expression beyond his years.

242

The weaving of the other characters into the story – the constable and the convict – seems simple enough, but any composer will tell you how hard it is to achieve what Britten does, seemingly without effort; here he is at his most enviable to his contemporaries, showing the lightest of touches, but the touch of genius nevertheless. To adapt a Hardy line from a previous song in the cycle, one might say that these little cameo appearances (the surprised delight of the convict, the embarrassed smile of the constable), flicker like living things. They are pictures of a passing moment, but they remain to haunt us. At same time we sense the boy's determination to play his violin; unconcerned by his lack of skill he is suddenly possessed of a demonic bravura such as overcomes children who are concerned with *fairness*, and who feel that something is unjust, yet beyond their control. Therein lies the spark of the future liberal reformer. Did Britten realise, I wonder, that when this poem was written in the early 1920s he himself was more or less the age of the violin-playing boy? The convict joins in with 'This life so free/Is the thing for me!', no doubt words from a well-known Victorian ballad. Perhaps this is the ditty that the boy has proffered in all innocence; the convict sings the refrain 'With grimful glee', perfectly aware of the chasm between art and life. We hear two repetitions of 'This life so free' within a plaintive diminuendo – it is the composer's privilege to repeat Hardy's words and thus allow this gruff man the chance to add a touch of regret, even desperation, to his ironic outburst.

The constable may even silently sympathise. He sits on the fence in the best English manner; he does not attempt to stop the convict singing in a public place as he thinks a member of the German police force might have done. Instead he pretends not to have taken on board the subtle little comedy that is being played out in front of him. 'And so they went on till the train came in' (we hear this arrival in the chugging of the song's penultimate line); the postlude is a little miracle where the listener's attention is refocused on the sound of violin music. The composer has another string effect up his sleeve and he reserves this for the very last note – a final aerial harmonic serves to bring the curtain down on this exquisite little *scena*.

(viii) Before Life and After

A time there was – as one may guess
And as, indeed, earth's testimonies tell –
  Before the birth of consciousness,
    When all went well.

None suffered sickness, love, or loss,
None knew regret, starved hope, or heart-burnings;
None cared whatever crash or cross
Brought wrack to things.

If something ceased, no tongue bewailed,
If something winced and waned, no heart was wrung;
If brightness dimmed, and dark prevailed,
No sense was stung.

But the disease of feeling germed,
And primal rightness took the tinct of wrong;
Ere nescience shall be reaffirmed
How long, how long?

Here we are suddenly confronted by a song with that has about it nothing deft nor theatrical. Unlike the other songs in the set there are no characters, and no events, that might be illustrated by an opera composer's craft and experience. Finzi was given to setting some of Hardy's philosophical ruminations, but he never attempted this poem – it was perhaps too bleak for him as it exists in a landscape, a moonscape rather, where no English flora or fauna are discernible. It seems to me that the title might encompass various meanings: does the poet mean 'before life existed *on earth*', or simply 'before life' as each of us experiences it individually? On one level the poet seems to be describing a Darwinian, prehistoric landscape before the arrival of man and the burgeoning of the feelings that come with the (partly regrettable) evolution of the species and the human condition. But the 'disease of feeling' also germinates with life itself *in utero*. When we are merely gleams in our parents' eyes, our souls and spirits are not as yet susceptible to emotional pain. Only death, the individual death of each one of us, will return the soul (if so it may be called) to this condition. In truth, this is the only 'nescience' that the poet can reasonably hope will be 'reaffirmed'. The things of which Hardy complains are quite simply the cost of being human. The poem therefore seems to me to long for death as a solution to life's pains and ills, for it is only in death that we can cease from 'regret, starved hope, or heart-burnings'. This is of course also the poet's negation of the concept of the Christian after-life. As for God, Hardy preferred to acknowledge the Immanent Will or the Prime Cause – incapable of attaching any meaning to the terms right or wrong, and indifferent to, because unaware of, the sufferings and happiness of the sentient beings it has indirectly created.

244

'Before Life and After' comes full circle with 'At Day-Close in November', the first song in the cycle, which had ended with words about the nature of time ('And none shall in time be seen'). 'Before Life and After' is also about a treeless landscape of a larger sort; both songs share the tonality of D, thus the minor key of the first song is complemented by the major key of the last. Schubert's bleak, snow-bound 'Der Leiermann' (the closing song of *Winterreise*) opens with a droning open fifth in the bass; in Britten we also have a fifth (D–A), albeit filled in with an F sharp, but this chord in this position on the keyboard suggests a similar barrenness. Britten here depicts the music of nescience: the piano seems stuck in the depths of something like a prehistoric swamp – it will emerge from this in the fullness of time, as will the human race. The eerily high vocal tessitura seems to indicate a void, the emptiness of a clean slate. This disembodied state of consonance depicts a time 'Before the birth of consciousness/When all went well'. The second of these lines occasions one of the three spacious cadences (at the end of each of the first three strophes) that punctuate this song before its overwhelming final peroration.

The second strophe introduces an increasingly chromatic element into the music. The twinges of 'sickness, love or loss', as well as 'regret, starved hope, or heart-burnings', are described in a vocal line that engages in an increasingly intense and gradually wider-ranging duo with the piano's right-hand octaves. The third verse is remarkable for the long diminuendo (in harmony as well as dynamics) of 'If brightness dimmed, and dark prevailed': the vocal line sinks in semitones as the chords of the left hand rise in semitones, an exercise in contrary motion that seems to squeeze the light and air out of the music with each successive progression. In the fourth verse 'the disease of feeling' takes hold: the music between the pianist's two hands now pushes outward (contrary motion in the opposite direction) as if this 'germ' were spreading insidiously into the world, filling every nook and cranny with emotion and, more specifically, hate and guilt (the thickening textures of 'A Poison Tree' come to mind!). The various strands of this music interact in fervent layers of counterpoint until the voice breaks its way free of this thicket of chromaticism and rises up to the higher regions of oblivion in which the song began ('Ere nescience shall be reaffirmed/How long, how long?'). In this tessitura the voice seems to teeter on a knife-edge of emotion, as if it were asking to be released from the sufferings of a lifetime

The key phrase for someone like Britten was surely 'And primal rightness took the tinct of wrong'. A person's sexuality always feels primally 'right' from their own point of view, but the 'disease of feeling', and senses stung into a reaction, make other people wish to judge and control, to regulate, compare and condemn. One may also equate this 'disease of feeling' with the rise of religious consciousness. Here is encapsulated the tragedy played out in many of Britten's dramatic works where characters suffer for what is perceived by others as 'the tint of wrong'. One feels that, in Britten's case at least, the cry for the reaffirmation of 'nescience' is not a death-wish, but a plea for the cleaning of the slate, a wiping away of the accrued layers of prejudice, hate and guilt that have poisoned the world as a result of 'feeling', doctrine and creed. In a similar way Schubert memorably set Schiller's 'Die Götter Griechenlands', which looked back with heartbreaking nostalgia to a time when the ancient Greek world was innocent of demagoguery and Christian prejudices. It would be better for everyone to be indifferent to the fate of others than to live in an interfering society that is tempted to 'mark and mete/This region of sin that you find you in' (that quotation is from 'Midnight on the Great Western' of course). Those familiar with Britten's Auden song 'Fish in the Unruffled Lakes' will recall how that poet envies the freedom of the animals who 'Act and are gone/Upon Time's toppling wave' and who are free of 'Duty's conscious wrong' (see p.157).

Hardy's impassioned closing question ('How long, how long?') opens up an enormous emotional vista. Once again we are reminded of the frozen wastes of Schubert's 'Der Leiermann'; the question that closes that composer's *Winterreise* is also to do with the mysteries of an unknown future, a threshold into a new life. It could well be about crossing the bar into another state of existence:

Wunderlicher Alter,	Strange old man,
Soll ich mit dir gehn?	Shall I go with you?
Willst zu meinen Liedern	Will you grind your hurdy-gurdy
Deine Leier drehn?	To my songs?

No one who ever heard Peter Pears sing the concluding song of either cycle will forget what he brought to this music. As a result of listening to a broadcast of *Winter Words* (where he himself was the pianist) Benjamin Britten (convalescing from heart surgery, and no longer able to play the piano) wrote Peter Pears a letter that defined the entire nature of their friendship. At the time the tenor, aged 64, was at the Metropolitan Opera in New York, singing the role of Aschenbach in *Death in Venice*:

Sunday, 17 November, 1974
My darling heart (perhaps an unfortunate phrase – but I can't use any

other) I feel I must write a squiggle which I couldn't say on the telephone without bursting into those silly tears – I do love you so terribly, not only glorious *you*, but your singing. I've just listened to a re-broadcast of Winter Words (something like Sept. '72) and honestly you are the greatest artist that ever was – every nuance, subtle & never over-done – those great words, so sad & wise, painted for one, that heavenly sound you make, full but always coloured for words & music. What *have* I done to deserve such an artist and *man* to write for? I had to switch off before the folk songs because I couldn't [take] anything after 'how long, how long'. How long? – only until Dec. 20th – I think I can *just* bear it.

But I love you,
I love you
I love you – -
B.[12]

12. Britten, *Letters from a Life*, p.60.

I remember working with Peter Pears very shortly after his return from America when he told me that he had received a letter from the composer that no human being had the right to hope for from another. He did not let me read it at the time of course, nor did I know about his immediate reply to Britten from New York; but it seems to me now that the composer's letter, and Pears's reply, are as much evidence as anyone may need as to the 'primal rightness' of a relationship which bore fruit as few others:

My dearest darling
No one has ever ever had a lovelier letter than the one which came from you today – You say things which turn my heart over with love and pride, I love you for every single word you write. But you know, Love is blind, and what your dear eyes do not see is that it is *you* who have given *me* everything, right from the beginning, from yourself in Grand Rapids! through Grimes & Serenade & Michelangelo and Canticles – one thing after another, right up to this great Aschenbach – I am here as your mouthpiece and I live in your music – And I can never be thankful enough to you and to Fate for all the heavenly joy we have had together for 35 years.

My darling, I love you –
P.[13]

13. Britten, *Letters from a Life*, pp.60–1.

⊙ CD2, track 16

⊙ *Canticle II – Abraham and Isaac* Op. 51 (1952)
This wonderful canticle is a piece of such unending felicity of expression

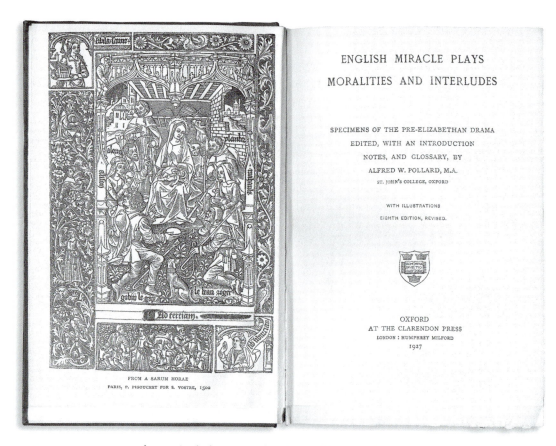

ENGLISH MIRACLE PLAYS

MORALITIES AND INTERLUDES

SPECIMENS OF THE PRE-ELIZABETHAN DRAMA
EDITED, WITH AN INTRODUCTION
NOTES, AND GLOSSARY, BY
ALFRED W. POLLARD, M.A.
ST. JOHN'S COLLEGE, OXFORD

WITH ILLUSTRATIONS
EIGHTH EDITION, REVISED.

OXFORD
AT THE CLARENDON PRESS
LONDON : HUMPHREY MILFORD
1927

FROM A SARUM HORAE
PARIS, P. PIGOUCHET FOR S. VOSTRE, 1502

The edition from which
Britten took the texts for
Abraham and Isaac *and*
Noyes Fludde

that a single hearing of it shows clearly and simply the nature of Britten's genius at its most direct and touching.

We recall that the first *Canticle* (1947) had been a piece for solo tenor and piano. Very shortly after that Britten had made a marvellous realisation of Purcell's *Saul and the Witch of Endor* for soprano, tenor, bass and piano. It was perhaps the example of this work – a *scena* with the vividness of opera but which somehow remains within the realms of concert piece – that suggested to him the possibility of composing a modern equivalent. Some years later, in the early years of the English Opera Group tours, it became desirable for Pears and other leading company members to give recitals between performances. *Canticle II* was written for the tenor along with the contralto Kathleen Ferrier, who had given the first performance of the title role in *The Rape of Lucretia*. The canticle was given its first performance in Nottingham on 21 January 1952.

The words are from the second of two medieval mystery plays from Chester, which were acted until the end of the sixteenth century, and last

248

copied in 1607. Both these Chester plays were printed in Britten's modern source, a book entitled *English Miracle Plays, Moralities and Interludes*.[14] The first of these plays was *Noah's Flood* to which the composer was to return in 1957, with immortal results. The second, an extract from the fifteenth-century *Histories of Lot and Abraham*, was *The Sacrifice of Isaac*. This was performed by the 'Barbers and the Wax Chaundlers' when these dramatic events were very much linked to the medieval guilds. The composer makes considerable cuts and certain adaptations to the original text.

14. Alfred Pollard (ed.), *English Miracle Plays, Moralities and Interludes – Specimens of the Pre-Elizabethan Drama* (Clarendon Press, 1927).

The first master-stroke is one of the better-known and most cited. The voice of God (which another composer might have assigned to a bass) is in fact the combination of the tenor and alto (the role of Isaac can also be performed by a boy alto or a counter-tenor). To the accompaniment of a repeating E-flat major arpeggio (compare the repetitive role of that chord in Wagner's *Das Rheingold*!) this unearthly timbred voice commands Abraham to sacrifice his son Isaac. At the end of this section the alto has a long E flat that fades away as the same note, softly sung by the tenor, takes over from it. The vowel brightens as the alto's 'befall' dovetails with the tenor's 'My ....'; imperceptibly the vocal timbre seems gradually to deepen and thicken, and the audience is never aware as to how this is achieved – it is a real piece of conjuring. Underneath this changeover the piano's striding quavers engineer a brusque modulation from F7 to D-flat major. With this new chord the tenor sings the word 'Lord'. This cunning bridge between divine utterance and human reality suggests that Abraham has re-emerged gradually from a trance during which God has been speaking through him. Abraham's real voice, after the transformation of an otherworldly voice to the sound of a manly tenor, signals the beginning of the human drama.

In an impassioned reply to this terrible command, Abraham signals his obedience to God. There follows a duet in 6/8 in A major ('Make thee ready, my dear darling') between father and son. The piano writing is mostly in duplets while Abraham and Isaac sing in lilting triplets and touching melodic sequences. One senses that the tuneful limpidity of this music, which paints a child who is totally relaxed (Isaac is as yet unaware of his fate) has been written with the abilities of a boy musician in mind. We know that it was conceived for Ferrier, but the composer made her voice remain within a boy's vocal possibilities. Indeed this is music designed to appeal to, and to be accessible for, a young musician. And it has remained so; as a result countless boy altos have been able to sing the role with success, and they always seem delighted to do so.

In another recitative ('O! My heart will break in three') accompanied by

piano tremolandi Abraham bemoans his plight, though he reaffirms his obedience to God. There are lightning exchanges between father and son as the dialogue becomes increasingly panic-stricken. Abraham draws his sword and, accompanied by heavy striding crotchets in the piano, confesses to his son that he has to kill him. This is followed by an agitated aria for Isaac ('Alas! Father, is that your will'), which turns into a duet of some contrapuntal sophistication. The key is D minor for music that sets the pulses racing. Most memorable are the tiny gasps of fear built into Isaac's 'For I … am but … a child' where the vocal line is broken up by rests. Abraham's counter-melody is in much longer note values; this signals his grim determination to do the deed, a tenaciousness to counter Isaac's terrified pleas.

Now there is an infinitely touching recitative: 'Is it God's will I shall be slain?' would break the heart of any parent, as would Abraham's crushed reply 'Yea, Son, it is not for to layn'. Now Isaac, in an unaccompanied passage that betokens the greatest humility and piety, begs for this father's blessing. Portentous chords in spread (or arpeggiated) semibreves accompany the beginning of this ceremony, perhaps suggested by Isaac's words

250

'Your blessing on me spread'. The actual blessing of the Trinity, when it comes, is a miracle in more ways than one – it is a rainbow of piano sound from one end of the keyboard to the other; it begins slowly in the bass clef in minims and crotchets, gradually accelerating until it explodes with a burst of colour in the highest regions of the treble clef. It then descends slowly as if fragments of stardust were scattered on the supplicant from above. One may imagine the bass chords symbolising the Father, the middle register of the piano the Son, and that descent of soft *mezzo staccato* quavers as the Holy Ghost. At moments as illustrative as these we detect the manner of the old-fashioned pageant or school play, and of course this is the composer's unashamed intention. But how Britten can make the music seem simultaneously home-spun and dazzlingly sophisticated remains his special secret. Abraham's line of recitative beginning 'Come hither my child' is of such a sad tenderness that the parting caress between father and son seems built into the very contours of the tenor line.

There does not seem much that can cap this, but Britten manages to do just that. The D-flat major duet beginning 'Father, do with me as you will' is, for me at least, the jewel in the canticle crown. Rocking between a tonic and dominant bass line, this piece, both chaste and sensuous (because so sweetly yielding) could only have been written by the composer of *Billy Budd*, and of the last act of that opera in particular where Billy sings his aria 'in the Darbies'. In both cases an innocent victim is about to be sacrificed. Throughout, simple sequences fall to simple cadences in the deepest obeisance – no great sophistication here – but there is truly something sublime about the ineffable sweetness of this music; this is a state of musical grace to be found in Schubert when he is at his most unreachable by other composers, and there, as here, the listener can only feel grateful.

This is followed by the music of execution, a tense and terrible march to the scaffold, although there is no actual march, only a ceremony where the boy is blindfolded. D-flat major has yielded to an ominous march ('Very slow and solemn') in C-sharp minor. The piano writing goes into three staves as both of the pianist's hands, an octave apart, depict shudders of fear held within the pitiless frame of gruesome ritual. Abraham screws up his courage to do the dreadful deed. A succession of dotted minim C sharps, deep in the bass clef, adds to the feeling of menace and imminent danger, and the tension becomes almost unbearable. The way Britten builds this cliff-hanging scene from muted beginnings to the pianistic cacophony, three pages later, which signifies God's last-minute intervention, is nothing less than awe-inspiring. That he should achieve this with piano writing that is much less than virtuosic (it sounds harder to play than it is) is another, generally unnoticed aspect of his mastery in matching almost a school-type play to almost school-type musical means.

A diaphanous E-flat major arpeggio is somehow made to emerge from the gigantic rumblings in the bass of the piano; the gauging of this to the best effect is one of the challenges facing the pianist. Suddenly God speaks again (the same combination of voices as before emerges as if by magic from the brouhaha). After He has announced His merciful reprieve, a brief and joyful scherzo announces the ram caught in a thicket by his horns. Abraham is overjoyed ('Sacrifice here sent me is') as he signs a paean of praise solidly supported by celebratory double octaves in the piano; this must surely be the only occasion in all of Britten's music when this composer sanctions the slaughter of a dumb animal! The closing 'Envoi' returns to the E-flat major of the opening, a moral played as if in front of the curtain, which is accompanied by gentle peals of bells. The entwining of the vocal lines in imitation and counterpoint imply a unanimity of faith and station between the two characters, now that the stage hierarchy between father and son has been dissolved (one is reminded here of the concluding pages of the church operas when the characters revert to their clerical garb). On the last page this music broadens into the manner of a closing hymn – here as in other places *Noyes Fludde* comes to mind. One realises that this canticle was of enormous importance to Britten as an upbeat to that work where simplicity, directness and everyday accessibility are even more evident.

And so it was that with the closing lines from *Canticle II: Abraham and Isaac*, 'for ever and ever, "Amen"', our Festival to commemorate the 25th anniversary of Britten's death came to an end. There was no need to expand any further on this composer, our affection for his music, and our ongoing gratitude. That I was privileged to know him personally, to have spoken with him and, up to a point, worked with him, remains an abiding joy in the memory. But I must confess that I think the luck of such personal contact conferred no special understanding on me. I was simply at the right place at the right time, and I have had to do all the really hard work since then. The wonderful thing is that the music of this composer is as accessible to our students at the Guildhall School (some of whom were not yet born when Britten died) as it is to me. And this fact was proved by the festival, and by seeing, and sharing, the joy of a new generation in discovering Britten's genius for the first time. These are indeed our very own proud songsters.

CD contents

CD 1

1. A Poison Tree (first version)   2.40
   John Evans *baritone*, Asako Ogawa *piano*

from *Tit for Tat*

2. A Song of Enchantment   2.03
   Michelle Jueno *mezzo-soprano*, Asako Ogawa *piano*

from *Friday Afternoons*

3. A New Year Carol   2.15
4. I Mun Be Married on Sunday   1.03
   Carl Ghazarossian *tenor*, Joana Thomé da Silva *mezzo-soprano*, Olivia Canolle *piano*

5. Lift-Boy   2.55
   Ruth Kerr *soprano*, Kate Warshaw *mezzo-soprano*, Paul Hopwood *tenor*, John Evans *baritone*, Olivia Canolle *piano*

from *Seven Sonnets of Michelangelo*

6. XVI Sì come nella penna   2.04
7. XXX Veggio co' bei   3.09
8. LV Tu sa' ch'io so   2.04
9. XXXVIII Rendete a gli occhi miei   2.03
10. XXIV Spirto ben nato   4.47
    Adrian Thompson *tenor*, Graham Johnson *piano*

11. *Introduction and Rondo alla burlesca*   9.03
    Ronan O'Hora and Jonathan Oshry *piano*

from Folksong arrangements, Volume I

12. The Bonny Earl o'Moray   2.09
13. O Can ye Sew Cushions?   2.17
14. Oliver Cromwell   00.39
    Giles Underwood *baritone*, Katie Van Kooten *soprano*, Iago Núñez *piano*

from Folksong arrangements, Volume III

15. The Miller of Dee   2.02
    Jonas Samuelsson *baritone*, Paul Cibis *piano*

from Folksong arrangements, Volume V

16. Ca' the Yowes   4.10
17. The Lincolnshire Poacher   1.54
    Douglas Bowen *baritone*, Ruby Hughes *soprano*, Marc Verter *piano*

from *Moore's Irish Melodies*

18. How Sweet the Answer   2.15
19. The Last Rose of Summer   3.43
    Claire Platt *soprano*, Lefki Karpodini *piano*

from Folksongs with guitar

20. Sailor-boy   1.32
21. The Soldier and the Sailor   2.15
22. The Shooting of His Dear   2.39
    Paul Hopwood and Adam Tunnicliffe *tenor*, Jørgen Skogmo *guitar*

from Folksongs posthumously published

23. Tom Bowling   3.04
24. Soldier, Won't you Marry Me?   2.04
    Claire Booth *soprano*, Adam Tunnicliffe *tenor*, Pamela Lidiard *piano*

254

CD 2

from *Lachrymae – Reflections on a song of John Dowland*
1. Lento, Allegretto molto comodo, 5.58
Animato, Tranquillo
   Tim Boulton *viola*, Asako Ogawa *piano*

from *Canticle 1 – My Beloved is Mine*
2. He is my altar... 3.04
   Adam Tunnicliffe *tenor*, Denis Frenkel *piano*

from *The Holy Sonnets of John Donne*
3. Oh My Blacke Soule' 3.01
4. Batter my heart 1.28
5. O Might those Sighes and Teares 2.53
   Adrian Dwyer *tenor*, Olivia Canolle *piano*

from *On This Island*
6. As It Is, Plenty 1.42
   Kate Royal *soprano*, Iago Núñez *piano*

7. To Lie Flat on the Back 2.57
8. When You're Feeling like Expressing your Affection 00.48
   Claire Platt *soprano*, Paul Cibis *piano*

9. Canticle IV – The Journey of the Magi 11.38
   David Clegg *counter-tenor*, Ben Hulett *tenor*, Douglas Bowen *baritone*, Paul Cibis *piano*

10. Underneath the Abject Willow 1.59
    Katie Van Kooten *soprano*, Joana Thomé da Silva *mezzo-soprano*, Paul Cibis *piano*

from *Cabaret Songs*
11. Calypso 2.17
    Katie Van Kooten *soprano*, Marc Verter *piano*

12. Third Suite for Cello
Fantastico (recitativo) 7.31
Presto (moto perpetuo)
Lento solenne (passacaglia)
   Marie Macleod *cello*

from *Songs and Proverbs of William Blake*
13. Proverb III – A Poison Tree 5.10
    Balcarras Crafoord, *baritone*
    Catherine Milledge, *piano*

from *Canticle III – Still Falls the Rain (The Raids, 1940. Night and Dawn)*
14. At the feet ... of the hunted hare 2.58
    Paul Hopwood *tenor*, Alison Butcher *horn*, Asako Ogawa *piano*

from *Winter Words*
15. The Little Old Table 1.24
    Adam Tunnicliffe *tenor*, Marc Verter *piano*

from *Canticle II – Abraham and Isaac*
16. Abraham ... I must thee kill! 5.12
    David Clegg *counter-tenor*, Paul Hopwood *tenor*, Eugene Asti *piano*

255

Index

Principal entries are in **bold** type.
Pages in *italic* type contain illustrations.
Britten's works are indexed under their titles.

263